W9-BGZ-064

Basic Skills in English

BOOK 1

Basic Skills in English

McDougal, Littell & Company
Evanston, Illinois

AUTHORS

The Editorial Staff of McDougal, Littell & Company,
with the assistance of Kraft and Kraft, Developers of Educational Materials.

Consultant: Hope Burke, Oliver Wendell Holmes Junior High School, Wheeling, Illinois

Editor-in-Chief: Joseph F. Littell
Editorial Director, English Programs: Joy Littell
Project Editor: Trisha Lorange Taylor
Director of Design: William A. Seabright
Editorial Coordinator: Kathleen Laya
Design Associate: Lucy Lesiak
Assistant Editor: Mary Schafer

Acknowledgments: See page 461.

ISBN: 0-88343-760-0

The Handbook section contains, in revised form, some materials that appeared originally in *The Macmillan English Series, Grade 5*, by Thomas Clark Pollock et al., © 1963 by Macmillan Company. Used by arrangement.

Composition

These eleven pages consist of additional writing assignments. There is an exercise for each Part in the eighteen Sections. Your teacher may choose to assign each of these exercises as additional practice after each part. The exercises will give you extra practice in improving your writing skills.

Handbook

Words: Building Your Vocabulary

It Grows on You

Learning About Language

Here's the Idea English is a living language. Like other living things, it is constantly changing. Some words outlive their usefulness and are dropped from our language. At the same time, new words are constantly being added. All of these changes occur in many ways.

Borrowed Words Many of our words are borrowed from other languages. English has borrowed words from the American Indian languages, from French, Spanish, German, and Dutch, among others. The words *squash, garage, cigar, noodle,* and *cookie,* for example, have been borrowed from these languages.

Compound Words Other new words come from combining two words, like *motor* and *cycle.* Each word is older than the new word *motorcycle.* Other examples of compound words include *halfback, downtown, outdoors,* and *birthday.*

Words from People's Names Sometimes a person's name becomes a word, like *sandwich,* named after the Earl of Sandwich. It is believed that he ate such a snack while he gambled so he wouldn't have to leave for meals. We have also added words to English from the names *Boycott, Diesel, Fahrenheit,* and *Pasteur.*

In these and other ways, words have been added to our language. Some words are so common today that it is hard to imagine that they have not always been in use. However, new ideas and new inventions need new words. English continually grows and changes.

Building a good vocabulary will help you to express ideas in a variety of ways. A good vocabulary will help you communicate clearly.

Check It Out   Read the following sentences. Notice the words that have been added to English.

1. Sometimes in class I *doodle* on my paper.
2. Hamburgers taste better with *ketchup*.
3. Do you remember the story in which a *tornado* picked up Dorothy's house?
4. Luis Tiant left the *dugout* to warm up in the *bullpen*.
5. Dad's blue *cardigan* is patched and worn, but it's still his favorite sweater.

- Do you see how English is enriched by new words?
- Do you see how new words can help to communicate ideas more clearly?

Try Your Skill   All of the following words have been added to our language. Some of the words have been borrowed from other languages. Others are compound words or words made from a name. Using a dictionary, try to find out how these words came into English.

tea	vampire	anteater	bloomer	zeppelin
pajamas	outfield	watchdog	watt	bookcase

Keep This in Mind

- English is a living language. It changes and grows.
- A good vocabulary will help you to express ideas in a variety of ways. It will help you communicate in a clear and lively way.

Now Write   Choose any five words that are mentioned but not explained in this lesson. On your paper, list the words. Using a dictionary, check the meanings of the words and their histories. Then write a sentence using each word. Keep your sentences in your writing folder.

Look Around

Learning Word Meaning from Context

Here's the Idea English has so many words that no one knows them all. Every reader comes across unfamiliar words from time to time. Sometimes you must look up a word in a dictionary. Sometimes you don't have to, because the context tells you the meaning.

Context means the words and sentences around a word. Context will often help you figure out what a word means. It may not tell you the exact meaning, but it can give you a general idea.

Look at the following example and try to figure out what the *italicized* word means.

> Australia has some strange native birds, like the *kookaburra*.

You couldn't draw a picture of a kookaburra from the information in this sentence. You do know, though, that it is a native Australian bird. The context has helped you determine the meaning of a new word.

However, you cannot always depend on the context to help you with new words. There are times when the context is no help. The example below gives no hints about the meaning of *kookaburra*.

> On the postcard was a picture of a *kookaburra*.

From the information in this sentence, a *kookaburra* could be a mountain, a native feast, a kind of house, or almost anything.

When you see a new word, look for context clues to its meaning. Sometimes they are in the same sentence as the new word. Other times you may have to read two or three sentences to find them. Here is a paragraph that provides context clues.

> You will rarely see pets on a farm. Every animal has a job to do. If a cat is not a good *mouser*, it has no place on a farm.

If you had read the word *mouser* in a list of words, you might not know what it meant. However, in the context above, you can tell it has something to do with a cat's working. From this you can guess that a *mouser* catches mice.

Check It Out Read the following sentences. Try to figure out what each italicized word means. Use context clues to help you.

1. Jill loves *marzipan*, which is a candy made of almond paste.
2. The *galleon*, like all large ships, had a crew of hundreds.
3. We heard the *oriole* sing and saw its nest in the tree.
4. Everyone else hurried out, but Elaine *lingered* after class.

  • What is the general meaning of each word in context?
  • What context clues helped you figure out the meaning?

Try Your Skill In each sentence, there is a word in italics. Use context clues to help you figure out what that word means. Write what you think the italicized words mean.

1. These streets *intersect*; that is, they cross one another.
2. Religious statues, or *icons*, filled the small room.
3. Some blood diseases, like *hemophilia*, are inherited.
4. *Nocturnal* creatures, such as bats, often sleep during the day.
5. The pony was not one color; instead, it was *piebald*.
6. If you don't obey the rule, you will be forced to *comply*.

Keep This in Mind

  • Context, the words surrounding a word, often gives clues to the meaning of that word.

Now Write On your paper, list four words you know. Write a sentence using each word. Make the sentence give context clues that would help a reader figure out what your word means. When you have finished writing, put the paper into your folder.

Spell It Out

Definition and Restatement

Here's the Idea There are several different kinds of context clues. The most direct clues to the meaning of a word are definition and restatement.

When **definition** is used, the meaning of a new word is stated directly.

> We sailed the boat near Longboat Key. A *key* is a low-lying island or reef.

When **restatement** is used, the meaning of a new word is usually restated with key words like *or, is called, that is, which is,* or *in other words.* Sometimes the meaning of the new word is indicated by a comma or a pair of commas.

> At the zoo we saw a *gnu,* which is a large African antelope.
>
> Carbon monoxide is a *noxious,* or poisonous, gas.

Writers use definition and restatement to make sure that readers understand uncommon words. If you stay alert for context clues, you will learn new words more easily.

Check It Out Read these sentences. Each uses definition or restatement as a clue to the meaning of the italicized word.

1. A mammal that carries its young in a pouch is called a *marsupial.*
2. The horse's coat had a healthy *gloss,* or shine.
3. We ate *scrapple,* which is a food made from cornmeal and scraps of pork.
4. Our garden has spiky, colorful flowers called *gladioli.*
5. Jill saw a colony of *gannets,* large white sea birds, on the beach.

- What is the meaning of each italicized word?
- What is the clue in each sentence that indicates a definition or restatement?

Try Your Skill   Each sentence has one word in italics. If you read carefully, you can tell what that word means from context clues. Write each word and its meaning.

1. A *cowlick* is a patch of hair that sticks up and won't lie down.
2. I bought a *yucca*, a plant with stiff, pointed leaves.
3. Jim is *indecisive;* that is, he has trouble making up his mind.
4. The *smelt*, a small, silvery fish, has a delicate taste.
5. At first, McCall Junior High seemed like a *labyrinth*, a maze, to me.
6. Our cycling club stayed in *youth hostels*, which are inexpensive places to stay for young people who are traveling.

Keep This in Mind

- The most direct context clues to the meaning of a word are definition and restatement.
- These kinds of context clues usually come after certain words or phrases, like *or, is called, that is, which is,* or *in other words.* A definition or restatement may be set off by commas.

Now Write   On your paper, list four unusual words that you can define. For example, the words might be special objects, tools, or foods that you know well.

Imagine that each word you chose is completely unfamiliar to your reader. Write a sentence for each word, using definition or restatement in the context. Use a key phrase or punctuation to alert the reader. Check your sentence by having a reader see if your meaning is clear to him or her. When you have written and checked your sentences, put the paper into your folder.

Look Again

Using Context Clues: Examples

Here's the Idea A context clue does not always tell you exactly what a new word means. Sometimes you may be able to understand the general meaning of a word through **examples.**

When you read, check to see if an unfamiliar word is followed by one or more examples. The examples may indicate the meaning of the word. Look at this example.

Quinces, like other hard fruits, are best when they are cooked.

The context tells you that a *quince* is a kind of hard fruit. The word *like* alerts you that one or more examples are used as context clues.

There are several key words and phrases that tell you to look for an example. These include *especially, like, other, this, these, for example, for instance,* and *such as.*

Read two more sentences in which the context gives you the meaning of the word *quince.*

Some hard fruits, *like* quinces, are good only in cooked dishes.
My parents make jelly from fruits *such* as apples and quinces.

None of these sentences tells you exactly what a quince is. However, they all use examples to make the general meaning of the word clear.

Check It Out Read the following four sentences. In each sentence the context clue is an example.

1. Some herbs, *basil* for instance, have a fragrant odor.
2. Many extinct birds, like the *dodo*, lived in only one small area of the world.
3. Wandering tribes used movable shelters such as *yurts*.

4. *Gliders* and other aircraft without engines are flown long distances in races.

- What is the meaning of each of the italicized words?
- Which words or phrases signal that an example is used as a context clue?

Try Your Skill In each sentence, use the context to help you get the meaning of the italicized word. Number your paper from 1 to 6. Then write a definition of each new word.

1. At camp, we were attacked by *midges* and other tiny bugs.
2. In early times, families often had only one large cooking pot, like a *caldron*.
3. Rosie Grier is well known for his *needlepoint* and other decorative needle work.
4. Stringed instruments, especially guitars and *zithers*, are fun to play.
5. We rode a *toboggan* and another snow sled last winter.
6. The *sari*, like other traditional clothing of India, is often very colorful.

Keep This in Mind

- Examples are sometimes used as context clues.
- Several key words and phrases will alert you to look for an example. These words include *especially, like, other, this, these, for example, for instance,* and *such as.*

Now Write Choose three of the following words to use in sentences: *baseball, fish, fudge, monkeys, measles,* and *carrots.* Write a sentence using one or more examples as a context clue to the meaning of each of the words you have chosen. Make sure your examples are clear.

Put your work into your folder.

Make It Clear

Learning About Synonyms and Antonyms

Here's the Idea   Many English words are close to each other in meaning. Such words are called **synonyms.** Synonyms do not mean exactly the same thing, however. One of them will have a meaning closer to the idea you are trying to express than another.

Here is a sentence that does not give much information.

I put the clothes into the suitcase.

You could use a synonym for *put* in this sentence. Below are three examples.

I *arranged* my clothes in the suitcase.
I *tossed* my clothes into the suitcase.
I *stuffed* my clothes into the suitcase.

Each synonym suggests something different. The word *arranged* suggests that care was taken. The word *tossed* implies a careless way of packing. The word *stuffed* suggests that the suitcase was being overloaded.

A knowledge of **antonyms** is also helpful. Antonyms are words with opposite meanings. The words *long* and *short* are antonyms. So are *stop* and *go*.

Antonyms are useful when you want to make a contrast in order to focus attention on a particular idea. For example, look at the following sentence: "Roberta was so *generous* that she made me feel *stingy*." In this sentence, the word *stingy* helps to emphasize the meaning of its antonym, *generous*.

When you write, think about exactly what it is you are trying to say. What idea or feeling are you trying to give the reader? When these ideas and feelings are clear in your mind, decide which words would best express them.

Check It Out   Read the following sentences.

1. Joan is a *fast* walker.
2. Dr. Brown was *quick* to take notice of Martha's symptoms.
3. The deer made a *swift* retreat when Jerry approached it.
4. We noticed a *rapid* change in temperature.
5. Don's remark was *hasty*, and he regretted making it.

- Notice how the word *fast* or its synonyms have their own special meanings. Can you explain each meaning?
- What is an antonym for the word *fast?*

Try Your Skill   Decide which synonym would best fit in each blank. Then write the complete sentence.

1. We are studying the art of _____ Rome.
   antique   ancient   old
2. What we need are _____ approaches to old problems.
   immature   young   fresh
3. Our Thanksgiving turkey was _____, not plump.
   slim   small   scrawny
4. The _____ sound of the big bell was soothing.
   loud   deep   thunderous
5. I heard Kim _____ when I made the same mistake again.
   talk   murmur   mutter

Keep This in Mind

- Synonyms are words that have similar meanings. Decide which synonym best expresses your idea.
- Antonyms are words that have opposite meanings.

Now Write   On your paper, list two synonyms for the word *small*. Write a sentence for each synonym so that it fits the special meaning of that synonym. Then write antonyms for the words you chose. You may use a dictionary or thesaurus to help you. Put your work into your folder.

Get Down to Bases

Learning Word Parts: Base Words

Here's the Idea One way the language grows is by adding parts to base words. A **base word** is a word on which other words are based. If you recognize a base word, you have a good idea what a larger word means.

Some base words have parts added in front of them. The word *untie*, for instance, is built on the base word *tie*. *Hopelessly* is built on the base word *hope*. A word part added at the end of the base word gives it a slightly different meaning. A base word may have a word part added at the beginning and at the end. The word *removable* is built on the base word *move*.

Recognizing base words is useful because it helps you to get the meanings of many unfamiliar words. You may see what at first appears to be a strange word. If you look again, you may recognize a base word. If you know the meaning of the base word, you can probably decode the meaning of the entire word. This becomes even easier when you learn the meanings of some parts that are added to the base words.

Some base words are easy to spot. In the word *joyful*, the base word *joy* is easy to see. In some words, the base word may be harder to recognize. One letter may be changed or dropped. The word *famous*, for example, is based on the word *fame*. The letter *e* from *fame* has been dropped from the longer word.

When you look for base words, remember that the final *e* or final *y* in base words is often changed or dropped in longer words. The word *persuasive* is based on *persuade*. *Beautiful* is based on *beauty*. A consonant may sometimes be doubled, as in *runner*.

12

Check It Out Read the three sets of words below.

changeable	unlikely	misfit
unchanged	likable	fitting
unchanging	unlikelihood	fitness

- Can you find the base words?
- Which base words have letters dropped or changed?

Try Your Skill Find the base word in each word listed below. On your paper, write the base word. Remember that the spelling of the base word might change when a word part is added.

1.	traveler	11.	nonviolent
2.	careful	12.	rebuild
3.	prewash	13.	unwanted
4.	nonstop	14.	eventful
5.	harmless	15.	magician
6.	worrier	16.	preschool
7.	misspell	17.	unforgettable
8.	comfortable	18.	natural
9.	reopen	19.	sensible
10.	defensive	20.	unlawful

Keep This in Mind

- Word parts can be added at the beginning or end of base words to make new words.
- The spelling of a base word may change when an ending is added. Often the final letter is changed or dropped.

Now Write Open one of your textbooks to any page. Find five words that contain base words. Copy these words. Then write the base words. Be sure to spell them correctly. You may use a dictionary. Then put the paper into your folder.

First Things First

Learning Word Parts: Prefixes

Here's the Idea In the last lesson you learned about base words and how to recognize them in longer words. A word part added to the beginning of a base word is called a **prefix**. For instance, the word part *un-* is the prefix in *uncertain*.

There are many different prefixes. The meaning of the prefix changes the meaning of the base word. The prefix *un-* means "not," so *uncertain* means "not certain, doubtful."

Some words may seem to have a prefix but they really do not. The word *under*, for example, does not contain the prefix *un-*. How do you know this? Look at the word. If you cover the letters you think make a prefix, do you have a base word? No, you have only a nonsense syllable, *-der*. Therefore, the word *under* does not have a prefix. Not all words do.

Look at this list of common prefixes. If you learn these prefixes, you will be able to figure out what many words mean.

Prefix	Meaning	Examples
pre-	"before"	preschool
non-	"not"	nonsense
un-	"not"	unhappy
mis-	"wrong"	mistreat
re-	"again"	reappear

Check It Out Notice how these prefixes and base words work together to make new words.

precook	—	"to cook before"
nonfiction	—	"not fiction"
uneasy	—	"not easy"
misjudge	—	"to judge wrongly"
renew	—	"to make new again"

- Does every prefix change the meaning of the base word?
- What is the base word in each example?

Try Your Skill   On your paper, number from 1 to 20. Look at each word below and decide whether it has a prefix or not. If the word does have a prefix, write the meaning of the prefix plus the base word. For example, next to the word *unhappy* you would write this: not + happy.

1.	replay	8.	unity	15.	unnecessary
2.	misty	9.	prerecord	16.	prejudge
3.	unfair	10.	misplace	17.	recipe
4.	pressure	11.	unskilled	18.	nonviolent
5.	none	12.	reelect	19.	rebuild
6.	receive	13.	nonswimmer	20.	miserable
7.	mispronounce	14.	ready		

Keep This in Mind

- A prefix is a word part added at the beginning of a word.
- Each prefix has its own meaning or meanings. The prefix changes the meaning of the base word to which it is added.
- Some words appear to have a prefix but do not. Check to see if the base word makes sense without the prefix.

Now Write   Find five new words that contain the five prefixes you have learned in this lesson. Use a dictionary to help you. List the new words on your paper.

Write five sentences, each one using one of the five new words. Finally, study the new words so that you can add these words to your vocabulary.

When you have finished, put your paper into your folder.

Last, but Not Least

Learning Word Parts: Suffixes

Here's the Idea   A word part added at the end of a word is called a **suffix**. In the word *wonderful,* the suffix is *-ful.* Like a prefix, a suffix has a meaning of its own. Each suffix also changes the meaning of the base word to which it is added.

In this lesson you will study only five of the most common suffixes. There are many more. However, when you learn the meanings of these five, you will have made a good start toward understanding many new words.

Suffix	Meaning	Examples
-er (or **-or**)	"a person or thing that does something"	helper, reflector
-less	"without'"	fearless
-able (or **-ible**)	"having this quality, able to be"	washable, sensible
-ful	"full of, having"	hopeful
-ous	"full of, having"	dangerous

When some suffixes are added to base words, the spelling of the base word changes. A letter may be dropped from the base word. For example, *cure,* becomes *curable.* Sometimes the final letter of the base word will be changed. For example, *beauty* becomes *beautiful.* At other times, the final consonant may double. For example, *swim* becomes *swimmer.* If you are not sure how to spell words when adding suffixes, check in a dictionary.

Check It Out   Look at the following words and their definitions. Notice how the suffix and base word work together to make a new word.

winner	—	"a person or thing that wins"
operator	—	"a person who operates"
worthless	—	"without any worth"
reasonable	—	"having the quality of reason"
horrible	—	"having the quality of horror"
useful	—	"having a use"
famous	—	"having fame"

- Does every suffix change the meaning of the base word?
- In which words is the spelling of the base word changed?

Try Your Skill   On your paper write each word below. Next to each, write the base word and the suffix. For example, next to the word *famous,* you would write this: fame + ous. Remember that there may be spelling changes in base words.

1.	dryer	7.	thriller	13.	lovable
2.	tearful	8.	actor	14.	pitiful
3.	joyous	9.	homeless	15.	runner
4.	counselor	10.	admirable	16.	poisonous
5.	penniless	11.	breakable	17.	generator
6.	readable	12.	carrier	18.	glamorous

Keep This in Mind

- A suffix is a word part added at the end of a base word.
- A suffix changes the meaning of the base word.
- A letter may change, drop, or double in the base word when a suffix is added.

Now Write   Write five words that contain the five suffixes you have learned in this lesson. You may use a dictionary. Then write five sentences, each using one of the five words. Finally, study these words. Make them part of your vocabulary. When you finish, put your work into your folder.

Writing Better Sentences

Put It Together

Learning About Sentences

Here's the Idea   You have seen how a good vocabulary enables you to express ideas clearly. You know that the right word in the right place can make a big difference.

Now you are ready to put your words together in the most effective way. You are ready to create sentences.

A **sentence** is a group of words that expresses a complete thought. With a sentence, you can express an endless variety of thoughts. In fact, a sentence can be a powerful tool. Look at these examples of powerful sentences.

> Common sense is not so common.—VOLTAIRE
>
> There is nothing permanent except change.—HERACLITUS
>
> Friendship is a sheltering tree.—SAMUEL TAYLOR COLERIDGE
>
> Colors fade, temples crumble, empires fall, but wise words endure.—EDWARD THORNDIKE

Not every writer can write a sentence that becomes famous. However, you can learn to write good sentences. A good sentence is clear, direct, and lively. It states an idea in a strong way.

Check It Out   Read the following sentences.

1.   Pitcher plants are meat eaters.
2.   The pale moon rose over the snow-capped mountains.
3.   We have a haunted telephone.
4.   Computers can do almost anything.
5.   The Mahoney family celebrates Christmas in July.

- Does each sentence express a single idea?
- Is each sentence clear and direct?

Try Your Skill   Choose five of the directions below to complete. Then, write a single sentence in answer to each direction. Try to make each sentence clear and interesting to a reader. You may use details from your memory or from your imagination.

1. Tell one event that happened in this class.
2. Describe your favorite object.
3. Explain how to cheer someone up.
4. Explain what a best friend is.
5. Explain why a person should get enough sleep.
6. Tell how you came to school this morning.
7. Describe how your head feels when you have a cold.
8. Explain what a broom does.
9. Explain why people should vote.
10. Tell one wish you'd like to come true.

Keep This in Mind

- A sentence is a group of words that expresses a complete thought.
- The purpose of a sentence should be clear to the reader.
- A good sentence expresses an idea strongly and directly.

Now Write   Now you are ready to write five original sentences. Write a sentence that tells how to do something. Write one that describes something. Write one that tells what something is. Write one that tells why something should be done. Finally, write one that tells about some action.

Try to write sentences that you would enjoy reading. When you've written your sentences, read them over. Are they clear and direct? Are they strong? If not, rewrite them. Put your work into your folder.

Getting Nowhere

Avoiding Empty Sentences

Here's the Idea Some sentences get nowhere. They may be written as sentences, but they may not say anything. Such groups of words are called **empty sentences.**

There are two different kinds of empty sentences. The first kind goes around in circles. It either repeats an idea from an earlier sentence, or states the same idea twice.

> I was thirsty and I wanted something to drink.

If you are thirsty, it is understood that you want something to drink. The sentence above needlessly repeats the same idea. This kind of sentence goes around in circles, getting nowhere. Such sentences can be revised by adding more information.

> I was thirsty because I had just eaten a handful of pretzels.

The second kind of empty sentence gives an unsupported opinion. The writer makes a strong statement that captures a reader's attention, but leaves the reader asking "Why?"

> Most TV news programs are second-rate.

Such strong statements are empty of meaning for a reader unless they are supported by facts, reasons, or examples. Supporting evidence may be given in the same sentence or in another sentence.

> Most TV news programs are second-rate because newscasters act like entertainers, not like journalists.

> Most TV news programs are second-rate. They devote too little time to explaining news events.

You must offer readers a reason for an opinion, or your writing will seem empty. They may not agree with you, but they will know why you think as you do.

Check It Out Read the following empty sentences.

1. The forest was quiet because there wasn't a sound.
2. You should always try to eat a good breakfast.
3. Exercising can be harmful.
4. I didn't like the movie because it was terrible.
5. This record is broken, and it is unplayable.
6. My old cat isn't young any more.

- Which sentences repeat an idea? Which sentences give an unsupported opinion?
- How could you improve these empty sentences?

Try Your Skill Decide why these sentences are empty. Write the empty sentences. Then write improved sentences.

1. The wind was freezing and I was cold.
2. My feet were sore from walking and they hurt.
3. The city is the best place to live.
4. We shouldn't waste our natural resources.
5. The book was so dull that it bored me.
6. Writing is the most important skill you will ever learn.

Keep This in Mind

- There are two kinds of empty sentences. One kind repeats an idea. The other kind states an opinion without supporting it.
- Improve sentences that repeat an idea by eliminating repetition. Complete sentences that give your opinion by stating reasons for the opinion.

Now Write Label your paper *Empty Sentences*. Find, or write, two examples of each kind of empty sentence. Improve them by eliminating repetition or by supplying reasons. Write the improved sentences. Put your paper into your folder.

Cut It Out!

Avoiding Padded Sentences

Here's the Idea   Every word in a sentence should contribute something to the idea. Some sentences will be longer than others, but a good sentence has no extra words.

Sentences that contain useless words or phrases are called **padded sentences.** Padded sentences are boring. The writer takes too long to get to the point. Such sentences can be improved by trimming. Look at the following example.

> Due to the fact that I didn't have shoes on, I couldn't go into the museum.

The phrase *due to the fact that* adds nothing to the sentence. It gets in the way of the main idea. The sentence could be improved by leaving out the padding.

> Because I didn't have shoes on, I couldn't go into the museum.

Such phrases as *you know, you see, what I mean to say is,* and *well, what I think is* are sometimes used in conversation. However, they add nothing to your ideas. You should avoid them when you write, as well as when you speak.

Keep in mind that padding gets in the way of your ideas. Good writers revise their work to eliminate unnecessary words.

Check It Out   Read the following pairs of sentences. Notice how each padded sentence has been revised.

> Padded   What I mean to say is that I agree.
> Improved   I agree.

> Padded   I am going to write about whales, which are not fish, but mammals.
> Improved   Whales are not fish, but mammals.

Padded	What I want to do is catch the four o'clock bus.
Improved	I want to catch the four o'clock bus.

- Do you notice how much clearer and stronger the improved sentences are?

Try Your Skill Decide which sentences in each group are padded. Write each padded sentence. Draw a line through any unnecessary words or phrases. Then write improved sentences, making any necessary changes.

1. What this paper is going to be about is bees. Bees are social insects. They live together in large groups. Each insect in the group has one special job to do.

2. Never go to bed angry. The reason that you shouldn't is because your anger may give you bad dreams. Then your night will be as bad as your day was.

3. What I think is that Willie Mays was one of the greatest ballplayers of all time. He played 22 seasons in the major leagues. Mays had a career batting average of .302 and hit 660 home runs.

4. During World War II, Navajo Indians sent secret messages in their native language for the U.S. Marines. They used a code that assigned the names of animals to military terms. On account of the fact that the Navajo language is so varied, the code was never broken by the enemy.

Keep This in Mind

- A padded sentence has more words than necessary to express an idea.
- Omit words and phrases that contribute nothing to the idea in a sentence.

Now Write Label your paper *Padded Sentences*. Find, or write, four padded sentences. Write improved sentences by omitting any unnecessary words. Keep your work in your folder.

A Look at Paragraphs

What Is It?

Learning About Paragraphs

Here's the Idea What is a paragraph? A **paragraph** is a group of sentences that work together. They deal with one main idea.

Read each of the following groups of sentences. See if the sentences in each group work together.

1   I was torn between panic and pleasure when Pete offered to drive me to school on his new motorcycle. Suppose I fell off? With fingers shaking, I buckled on the helmet Pete offered and climbed up behind him. With a roar like a jet, we took off down the street. By the time we reached school, all my fears had been blown away by the force of the wind around us. The motorcycle seemed like an old friend, and I had been the first girl in school to ride on it.

2   The young boy turned over on the thin mattress as the summer sun edged its way over the East River. The sun moved slowly. It spread a soft, gray light down the boy's face, and he was awakened. His eyes opened quickly, hurrying sleep away. He lay still a moment, smelling and hearing the morning all around him.

3   You can create your own T-shirt design. Use a plain T-shirt, a piece of cloth, an apple, a stiff paintbrush, and textile paint in any colors of your choice. Begin by slicing an apple in half lengthwise. Brush a thick layer of textile paint over the cut side of the apple halves. Press the apple, paint side down, on a piece of cloth. Keep practicing until you have it just right. Then print your T-shirt.

Check It Out Look again at the three groups above. The first group tells a story. The second group describes a person. The third explains a process. Are they all paragraphs?

- Does each group of sentences deal with one idea?
- Does every sentence in each group say something about the main idea?

Try Your Skill Below are three groups of sentences. One is a paragraph. Two are not. Read each group and decide which are not paragraphs. Write a sentence or two explaining why the group of sentences does not make a good paragraph.

1   I'll never forget the championship game of the baseball season. That night our family had fried chicken for dinner. Chicken is my favorite food. There were two outs in the last inning, and I was batting. We were behind, but the tying run was at third base. I popped the ball up to the infield for the final out.

2   To change a flat tire, first secure the emergency brake, then loosen the nuts on the wheel rim. Next use the jack to raise the car. Then replace the flat and turn the nuts until they are almost tight. Finally, lower the car and tighten the nuts.

3   The hot air balloon rocked gently overhead. It was red, green, and white, with a tan basket below. Light-bulb-shaped, it moved among the clouds. In fifth grade I did a report on hot air balloons. My teacher liked my report. There was no sound at all as the balloon slowly descended.

Keep This in Mind

- Each paragraph should deal with one main idea.
- Every sentence in the paragraph should say something about the main idea.

Now Write Find one of the groups of sentences that does not make a good paragraph. Look it over, using **Keep This in Mind** as a guide. Find the sentences that do not belong. Copy the remaining sentences in the form of a paragraph. Put your paragraph into your folder.

United We Stand

Recognizing Unity in a Paragraph

Here's the Idea You want your reader to understand what you have to say. Your reader will understand your ideas if you organize them well. The basic tool for organizing ideas in writing is the paragraph.

Remember that a paragraph is a group of sentences that work together. A paragraph expresses one main idea. All the sentences in the paragraph should relate to that main idea. When they do, the paragraph has **unity.**

Check It Out Read this paragraph:

In 1973 Billie Jean King beat Bobby Riggs in the most talked-about tennis match ever played. News reports called it the Battle of the Sexes. King, a leader in the fight for women's equality in sports, played against Riggs, a critic of women athletes. King had played her first tennis game when she was eleven years old. King's victory over Riggs was witnessed by 30,000 fans in Houston and by millions of television viewers around the world.

· Do all of these sentences work together? Do they all deal with one main idea? Does this paragraph have unity?

Try Your Skill Here are four paragraphs without unity. In each, one sentence does not work with the others. Write each sentence that does not belong.

1   I guess I've been on every kind of diet ever invented or thought of. Many books on diets have been published recently. I remember the time I resolved to eat only fruit and cottage cheese. I gained three pounds, and to this day I hate the sight of cottage cheese. Then there was the B diet: boiled eggs and bananas. I ate so many bananas that I felt like King Kong. The trouble was, I was still shaped like him, too.

2   Thomas Jefferson and Alexander Hamilton did not get along. The tall, red-headed Virginian had little use for the ideas of the smaller, dark-complexioned former lawyer from New York. The two disagreed on the idea of democracy. Jefferson was in favor of it, Hamilton against it. They disagreed, too, on which group the national government should favor—farmers, or those who owned factories and businesses. Hamilton was killed in a duel.

3   My cousin and I learned most of our family's history by playing in Grandmother's attic. In one corner stood a brass-bound trunk, filled with forgotten dolls once treasured by aunts and mothers. Grandfather's World War I uniform hung proudly on a metal rack, along with once-stylish dresses. The clothing now is much more comfortable than it was thirty years ago. When we played with the toys our mothers had played with, or dressed up in the old-fashioned clothes, we felt that the past was truly part of our lives.

4   Senses are so basic that all animals have them, but not all animals use their senses in the same way. Many people have lost their sense of hearing. A frog's eye, for instance, does not see a fly as we see it—in terms of legs, shape of wings, and number of eyes. In fact, a frog won't spot a fly at all unless the fly moves. Put a frog into a cage with freshly killed insects, and it will starve.

Keep This in Mind

- All of the sentences in a paragraph should work together; they should all relate to the main idea. Then a paragraph has unity.

Now Write   Choose one of the paragraphs that does not have unity. Look at the sentence on your paper that does not belong with the others. Now write the paragraph so that it has unity. Put your work into your folder.

What's It All About?

Using a Topic Sentence

Here's the Idea If a paragraph has unity, it must have a **topic sentence.** The topic sentence is usually the first sentence in a paragraph. It tells what the paragraph is about. It states the main idea in a clear and interesting way.

When you write a paragraph, there are two good reasons for using topic sentences:

First, the topic sentence helps you keep track of your ideas. By making sure that your sentences work with the topic sentence, you will not make the mistake of bringing in unrelated ideas. All your sentences will work together.

Second, the topic sentence helps your reader. By stating what the paragraph is going to be about, it acts as a guide.

Check It Out Read the following paragraph.

> When Manolo was nine he became aware of three important facts in his life. First, the older he became, the more he looked like his father. Second, he, Manolo Oliver, was a coward. Third, everyone in the town of Arcangel expected him to grow up to be a famous bullfighter, like his father.—JAMES RAMSEY ULLMAN

- Does this paragraph have a topic sentence?
- Does the topic sentence state what the paragraph is about?

Try Your Skill Write the topic sentence from each group.

1. (a) My toes became numb inside my boots.
   (b) As I walked home, the biting cold pierced my body.
   (c) Even under a heavy jacket, my skin had goosebumps.
   (d) My face felt as if it would never thaw.
   (e) I exhaled in huge bursts of steamy fog.

2. (a) In first-class sections, there were elegant dining cars, parlor cars, and sleepers.

   (b) However, dust from the plains swept over the passengers.

   (c) Railroads brought new speed to travel.

   (d) In addition, floods and blizzards often destroyed sections of track.

   (e) Early railroads were both enjoyable and unpleasant.

3. (a) She applied it to everything I did.

   (b) Sometimes she'd say it barely loud enough to hear, and I'd stop and think about what I was doing.

   (c) Other times she'd write it on a piece of paper and put the paper where I'd be sure to find it.

   (d) "An ounce of prevention is worth a pound of cure" was my grandmother's favorite saying.

   (e) I used to tease her about her "all-purpose" advice, but I never questioned the wisdom of that advice.

Keep This in Mind

- Be sure that every paragraph has a topic sentence.
- Be sure that the topic sentence states clearly what the paragraph is about.

Now Write Look at the six topic sentences below. Most of the sentences are too vague or unclear. Another is too narrow to be a main idea. Decide which one gets right to a main point. Write it on your paper. File the paper in your folder.

1. I think lighthouses have something to do with sailing.
2. Did you ever see a lighthouse?
3. Lighthouses help sailors in several ways.
4. I'm going to write about a topic I like—lighthouses.
5. One lighthouse had 262 steps to the top.
6. My cousin wrote a report about lighthouses, too.

Follow the Leader

Developing a Paragraph

Here's the Idea The sentences that follow a topic sentence should support the main idea of the paragraph. Supporting ideas can be developed in three ways. You can use details. You can use examples. You can use facts and figures. You will see that one of the three ways will be the best way to develop an idea.

Using details can be a lively way to develop a paragraph:

> The tension within Dick grew. He felt for the spare pair of goggles around his neck and made certain they were in place. If the pair he was wearing should shatter, mist up, or become oiled, he must be able to make the change immediately. He pushed in the clutch, selected first gear, returned to neutral.
> —JEFFREY ASHFORD

Using an example is often a way to develop a paragraph that begins with a general statement:

> Dolphins can solve simple problems. At Marineland of Florida, gates separate the dolphins' small pools from the big show pool. One night some dolphins must have wanted to play in the big pool. They figured out how to use their snouts to open the gates.
> —*National Geographic World*

Using facts and figures is a way to prove a point or make an idea clear in a paragraph:

> The open mouth of a killer whale is a frightening sight. An adult may have as many as fifty teeth. The teeth are cone-shaped, three inches long and one inch in diameter. They curve inward toward the throat and interlock when the jaw is closed. The teeth are used for grasping, ripping, and tearing food, but not for chewing. The food is swallowed whole or in large chunks.
> —SEYMOUR SIMON

Check It Out   Read this paragraph about snakes:

Garter snakes are not good mothers. The day I discovered that my garter snake had unexpectedly given birth to thirty babies, I was sure I had a gold mine right there in my aquarium cage. The next day, however, only twenty babies were left in the cage. The snake supply dwindled daily. By the time the little snakes would have been big enough to sell, Mother Garter Snake had gobbled every one for breakfast, lunch, and dinner.

Is the topic sentence developed by details? Is it developed by an example? Is it developed by facts and figures?

Try Your Skill   Find and write the topic sentence. Write whether it is developed by *Details, Example,* or *Facts and Figures.*

There are millions of hungry people in India and Southeast Asia, Africa, and Latin America. Hundreds of millions of people in Asia have starved to death in the past. Ten million died in 1769–70 in the Great Famine of Bengal, India. More recently, in the winter of 1966–67 parts of India had the worst drought in a hundred years.—ELIZABETH S. HELFMAN

Keep This in Mind

- The main idea of a paragraph can be developed by using details, an example, or facts and figures.

Now Write   Reread the topic sentence that you selected in **What's It All About?** under **Now Write.** The following sentences develop that main idea. Write whether the sentences develop the paragraph with *Details, Examples,* or *Facts and Figures.*

First of all, lighthouses flash beacons at night to guide ships near the coast. During the day, the tall, light-colored structures are land markers that can be seen from far away. Lighthouses also warn ships of dangerous places, and they have special fog-warning signals. They have safeguarded sailors since early times.

What's in a Name?

Recognizing Three Kinds of Paragraphs

Here's the Idea   When you write, you may want to tell a story. You may want to describe someone or something. You may want to explain. For each of these times you would use one of the three kinds of paragraphs: narrative, descriptive, or explanatory.

A **narrative** paragraph tells a story about something that happened in the order that it happened.

A **descriptive** paragraph is a word picture. It appeals to your senses. You describe things as you see them or hear them.

An **explanatory** paragraph explains, as clearly as possible. It may tell "how" or "why." In a "how" paragraph, you explain what is to be done first, what is to be done next, and so on through all the steps in a process. The "why" paragraph gives reasons why something is so. It begins with an idea or opinion. Then it is expanded with your reasons why the idea or opinion is true.

Check It Out   Read the following paragraphs.

1   The storm struck like an enemy. It exploded on the countryside with violent, shuddering force. Cold rain attacked, while fierce winds drove against the small homes. Lightning and thunder shot down from above. Throughout, the sky was an angry black.

2   Bobby was suspicious when he opened the front door. No one was supposed to be home, but he had heard strange, shuffling noises. Then some lights in the kitchen went off. Bobby was worried. He headed towards the door. Suddenly his friends burst into the room. "Surprise! Happy birthday!" they shouted. Then Bobby laughed.

- Do these paragraphs tell stories or describe or explain? Are they narrative or descriptive or explanatory?

Try Your Skill   Read these paragraphs. Write whether they are *Narrative, Descriptive,* or *Explanatory.*

1   Dean had invented a new kind of pizza. On the bottom was a thick, crispy crust. On top of the crust were tangy tomatoes, then juicy sausage and pepperoni. Next came a second layer of tomato-covered crust to make a double-decker pizza. Thick, gooey cheese topped the creation.

2   All people would be happier as pet owners. Whether the pet is a dog, a rabbit, or a hamster, it is fun to watch and to play with. In its own way, a pet shows affection. In addition, it can teach its owner how to care for other living things. Certainly, no one is lonely with a pet.

Keep This in Mind

- A narrative paragraph tells a story.
- A descriptive paragraph describes someone or some-thing.
- An explanatory paragraph explains "how" or "why."

Now Write   Below is a paragraph that explains how to make sand art. Copy this paragraph, filling in the blanks with words or phrases that will tie the paragraph together. They should show the order of the steps in the process.

     Sand art is a simple technique. _____, you need a clean container. _____, you need several colors of sand, a spoon, and a stick. _____, pour one color of sand into the container and _____ smooth it or contour it with the spoon. _____ pour and shape more layers of different colors. _____, you can make designs and even pictures by poking a stick down through the layers of sand.

Writing a Paragraph

In Focus

How To Narrow a Topic

Here's the Idea   Sometimes you may be interested in a subject that is too broad or too general to be covered in a single paragraph. If a topic is too general, you will find it hard to write a paragraph that is interesting and informative.

For example, if you started with a general topic like "vacations," you might end up with a paragraph as dull as this one:

> I like vacations. I like being out of school. I like being free to swim or ride or ski. I wish all vacations were longer.

One good way to narrow topics is to ask questions about them. Such questions might begin with *who, what, when, where, how,* or *why.* By asking such questions, you can make the topic more specific. Then you will be able to write a good paragraph.

For example, you could narrow a topic like "vacations" by jotting down ideas like this:

Who?	I
What?	learned to snow ski
When?	February, 1978
Where?	Stowe, Vermont
How?	lessons, practice, Toll House
Why?	outdoor fun? falling!

Narrowing your topic to such specifics as these might lead you to write a paragraph as lively as this one:

> I spent my winter vacation falling down. In February, my family spent a week in Stowe, Vermont. For five days I took ski lessons. Every day I climbed up and down the Toll House slopes. Unfortunately, I spent more time falling than I did skiing.

Check It Out This time, it's your turn to start with the idea of "vacations." Try to narrow that general topic to a more specific topic. Jot down your ideas.

- Can your topic be covered in one paragraph?
- Did you narrow your topic by asking *who, what, when, where, how,* or *why* questions?

Try Your Skill Choose two of the general topics below. On your paper, list the topic and the questions *who? what? when? where? how?* and *why?* Then narrow each topic by writing a short answer to each question.

Topics: my family   friends
         school   food
         pets   sports

Keep This in Mind

- Narrow general topics by asking *who, what, when, where, how,* or *why* questions.
- Choose a topic that you can handle in a paragraph.

Now Write In the next few lessons you will be writing a paragraph on your own. You will be completing one step of the process in each lesson. At the end of the section you will have a lively, well organized paragraph.

As your first step, write two general topics of your choice. Narrow each topic by asking *who, what, when, where, how,* and *why.*

Write the two new topics. Write the title of this lesson, **In Focus,** on your paper.

Put your work into your folder.

A Better Birdfeeder

How To Avoid a Sleepy Topic Sentence

Here's the Idea You learned about using a topic sentence in **What's It All About?** You know that a topic sentence should express the main idea of a paragraph. Now you will learn how to write a lively topic sentence.

Don't turn your readers off with a boring topic sentence. Make your topic sentence direct. Also make it snappy.

Make It Direct Avoid extra words that introduce *you* instead of your topic. Never write a sleepy sentence like "I am going to write about how to build a birdfeeder." Write a direct statement like "Building birdfeeders takes just three easy steps."

Make It Snappy You also want to make your topic sentence snappy whenever you can. Some topics are more serious than others are; you don't always need to be clever. When it is appropriate, try using humor. "Birdfeeders are for the birds" is a humorous variation of an old saying. Try using the same first letter for each word. "Don't buy a birdfeeder, build it!" Try using an unusual twist. "Birds of a feather eat together."

Check It Out Here's another topic sentence:

In this paragraph, I'm going to write about why I like sports.

- Does this topic sentence attract your attention? Is it direct? Is it snappy?
- Does this topic sentence avoid extra words that introduce you and not the topic?
- Does this topic sentence use humor, rhyme, or an unusual twist to pep it up?

Try Your Skill Below are six poorly written topic sentences. Rewrite three of them. Make each topic sentence direct. Try to make it snappy.

1. I want to tell you about my best friend George.
2. It is my opinion that school should be closed on Wednesdays.
3. My paragraph is going to be about the hardships of the early sailors.
4. I think I can tell you in this paragraph how to fry a fish.
5. I think I will write a paragraph about how the Grand Canyon was formed.
6. I would really like to write about the fact that adults should let kids listen to the kind of music they like, not just what the adults like.

Keep This in Mind

- A topic sentence should attract the reader's attention. It should be direct and snappy.
- Avoid extra words that introduce you and not the topic.
- When it is appropriate, use humor or rhyme or an unusual twist to pep up a topic sentence.

Now Write You're ready for the second step in the writing of your original paragraph. Turn back to the paper titled **In Focus** in your folder. Think about the topics you have selected. Now write topic sentences for each of your topics.

Writing your topic sentence may take some time. Be patient. Try to express your topic in several different ways. Experiment with your ideas until you discover something that works. Make your topic sentences direct. Also make them snappy.

Copy your two best topic sentences. Label your paper **A Better Birdfeeder.** Put the sentences into your folder.

The Main Course

How To Develop a Paragraph

Here's the Idea You know how to use a topic sentence to begin a paragraph. What should follow your direct and snappy sentence? How should you support your main idea?

In **Follow the Leader** you learned to recognize three main methods of paragraph development. You saw that using **details** creates a lively paragraph. You also saw that using an **example** is an effective way to develop a paragraph that begins with a general statement. Finally, you saw that using **facts and figures** helps to prove a point or to make an idea clear.

When you are writing your paragraph, you will have to choose a method to develop your main idea. Try to relate your choice to the topic sentence. Decide which method of paragraph development will complete the idea in your topic sentence most clearly.

Check It Out Read the following paragraph.

Riding the rapids on a raft is better than riding any roller coaster. Tumbling over bumps and around curves is a thrilling ride. In the excitement, riders often laugh, or shriek as they are sprayed by icy water. Sometimes a lucky passenger even gets a dunk! For some soggy fun, try a raft trip.

- Is the paragraph developed by details? Is it developed by an example? Is it developed by facts and figures?
- Does this method of paragraph development complete the idea in the topic sentence clearly?

Try Your Skill   Here are five possible topic sentences. Decide how the main idea of each topic sentence could best be developed. Write *Details, Example,* or *Facts and Figures,* to show the method of paragraph development you choose. Be prepared to explain your choice.

  1. Last year, paramedics assisted in an astounding number of emergencies.
  2. My neighbors' kitchen is the most comfortable room I have ever been in.
  3. Once, the audience outwitted the magician.
  4. The food at the Washington Avenue Cafeteria is worse than terrible.
  5. The world's largest aquarium is the John G. Shedd Aquarium in Chicago.

Keep This in Mind

- You can use details to develop a paragraph.
- You can use an example to develop a paragraph.
- You can use facts and figures to develop a paragraph.
- Choose the method of paragraph development that will complete your topic sentence most clearly.

Now Write   In your folder, review the steps you have completed in Parts 1 and 2 of this section. Now select your best topic sentence. Use it to begin your paragraph. Also, choose a method of paragraph development.

Write your paragraph. Keep working until you are sure that your idea is clearly expressed.

Write the title of this lesson, **The Main Course,** on your paper. Put all of your writing into your folder.

Saying Goodbye

How To End a Paragraph

Here's the Idea A good ending sentence should be based on what you've already written. You wouldn't end a paragraph on baseball by writing, "Hockey is my favorite sport." If you did, your ending wouldn't work with the rest of the paragraph.

A good ending sentence ties a paragraph together. You should sum up the main idea of your whole paragraph. Be careful not to add new information in your ending. Let's say you wrote a comparison of the ocean and a lake. Your ending sentence should sum up that comparison. It should not talk about ponds. One way to end it might be, "I prefer the unpredictable sea to the calm waters of inland lakes."

A good ending should be interesting. Put a new twist on your words. Use some of the techniques for writing lively topic sentences that you have learned. Try rhyme, or a humorous twist. Make your last words truly lasting.

Check It Out Read the following paragraph.

My friend George is a "gopher." George works during the summers for his father. They build houses and do odd jobs. Most of the time George's father does the carpentry. When he needs nails, he yells, "George go for the nails. " When he wants coffee, he says, "George, go for some coffee." *George is my best friend.*

- Does the paragraph have an ending?
- Does the ending sentence work with the rest of the paragraph? Does it add a new idea?
- Does the ending sentence sum up the idea of the paragraph?
- Is the ending sentence interesting?

Try Your Skill Revise these endings. Try to make them sum up the main idea. Try to make them interesting.

1   Susan joined the sea of subway riders. Clutching her purse, she descended into the darkness. The crowd pushed her first to the ticket booth and then to one of the screeching trains. Once inside, she saw that there was no chance of getting a seat. *The subway was powered by electricity.*

2   Homemade gifts are the best gifts. Not only are they less expensive than bought gifts, but they can also be more personal. The variety of gifts that can be made, ranging from candles to jewelry, is endless. Homemade gifts show that the giver cares, because they require time, energy, and creativity. They are appreciated more than gifts that are bought from shelves. *I made my own Christmas gifts two years ago.*

Keep This in Mind

- A paragraph should have an ending.
- A good ending sentence works with the rest of the paragraph. It should not add a new idea.
- A good ending sentence sums up the main idea of the paragraph.
- A good ending is interesting.

Now Write You are ready to write a strong ending to your own paragraph. Review what you have written so far. Read your paragraph aloud, at least to yourself. Write an ending that works with the rest of your paragraph. Make it interesting. Make it sum up the idea of the paragraph.

Write your entire paragraph in a final form. Be as neat as you can. As a last step, proofread your writing carefully. This paragraph is the first full paragraph you have written in this book. Write the title of this lesson, **Saying Goodbye,** on your paper. Keep your paragraph in your folder.

A Writer's Choices

I Did It!

How To Use a Personal Point of View

Here's the Idea Whenever you write, you have many decisions to make. You have to choose a topic and narrow it. You have to create a lively topic sentence. You have to decide on a method of paragraph development. Another decision you have to make is what point of view to use.

Point of view means the eyes and mind through which something is written. As a writer, you have a number of choices. One possible point of view is personal, or **first-person point of view.**

Using first-person point of view means that you use the first-person pronoun *I*. When you write about something that is imaginary, you can let *I* be the main character, or any character. However, you can't let your reader know what anyone else in the story is thinking or feeling. If you use first person, you must stick to one character's view of the events.

When you write about something that really happened, you may also want to use a personal point of view. You may want to use *I* to tell what you yourself think or do or feel.

Check It Out Read the following paragraphs.

> I wished that my first day of school at Hunter Junior High had been my last. Because I had transferred from a school three hundred miles away, I knew no one. The large building with its maze of halls confused me. Worst of all, no one bothered to talk to me or even to smile. I wondered if I would always feel like a stranger.

- Can you tell through whose eyes this account is told?
- Do you see that this is told from first-person point of view?

Try Your Skill   In these paragraphs, the words that determine point of view have been left out. Copy them, filling in the pronouns needed to make them first-person point of view.

1   The most important day _____ remember in all _____ life is the one on which _____ teacher, Ann Mansfield Sullivan, came to _____. _____ am filled with wonder when _____ consider the immeasurable contrasts between the two lives which it connects. It was the third of March, 1887, three months before _____ was seven years old.—HELEN KELLER

2   All night _____ sat there with the body of _____ brother and did not sleep. _____ vowed that someday _____ would go back and kill the wild dogs in the cave. _____ would kill all of them. _____ thought of how _____ would do it, but mostly _____ thought of Ramo, _____ brother.
—SCOTT O'DELL

Now read each paragraph again. As a reader, notice how close you feel to the writer's point of view.

Keep This in Mind

- Point of view determines through whose eyes a story is told.
- In first-person point of view, what is written is seen through one character's eyes. The first person pronoun *I* is used.

Now Write   Use first-person point of view as you follow the directions given below:

1. Write a sentence about something you really did.
2. Pretend to be a character in a famous story. You may use someone from a book, movie, or television program. As that character, write a sentence telling what you did.

Proofread your sentences. Put your work into your folder.

Fly-on-the-Wall

How To Use an Outsider's Point of View

Here's the Idea First-person point of view is fun to use. You can write from your own viewpoint. Another point of view is called the **third-person point of view.** You can put yourself into another character's mind. You can look at the world through someone else's eyes. You can think about this point of view as a fly-on-the-wall viewpoint.

A fly on the wall is almost invisible. You probably wouldn't pay much attention to it. But if you looked through the fly's eyes, you would see everything that is happening around you. You would also hear everything that's said. You would not know exactly what anyone is thinking or feeling, however. All your information must come from observation.

Most often the third-person pronouns *he* and *she* are used in third-person point of view. Whether you write about something that really happened or about something imaginary, use the third-person pronouns to make your observations.

Check It Out Read this paragraph:

> When Jane spotted a glowing mass in the dark sky, she shouted a warning to her friend Anita. She dived to the ground and pulled the amazed Anita with her. The reddish disc seemed to come closer. The girls blinked. Then the painful light disappeared. As they got up, Jane said she had never believed in flying saucers.

- Can you see and hear everything? Do you know what the characters are thinking or feeling?
- Do you notice the third-person pronouns?

Try Your Skill In this paragraph, the words that determine point of view have been left out. Copy the paragraph. Fill in the pronouns needed to make it third-person point of view.

John Constantine Unitas had come a long way. Until _____ clicked with the Colts, _____ had always been the quarterback nobody wanted. The Colts, in fact, signed _____ for just the price of a long-distance phone call to _____ Pittsburgh home. Nowadays college quarterbacks sign pro contracts for hundreds of thousands of dollars. One of football's best professional quarterbacks, Johnny Unitas, signed merely for the opportunity to make the team.—DAVE ANDERSON

Now read the paragraph again. As a reader, notice how much you are able to see and hear from the observer's point of view.

Keep This in Mind

- Think of third-person point of view as a fly-on-the-wall viewpoint. You can see and hear everything. You can't know what any of the characters are thinking or feeling.
- The third person pronouns *he* and *she* are used in third-person point of view.

Now Write Use third-person point of view as you follow the directions given below:

1. Write a sentence about something you have actually seen or heard a friend of yours do or say.

2. Pretend to observe a character in a famous story. You may want to use someone from a book, movie, or television program. Write a sentence about what the character did.

3. Invent a new character. Name the character. Write a sentence telling what the character did.

Proofread your sentences and put them into your folder.

Believe It or Not!

How To Write About Something Real

Here's the Idea Sometimes you may choose to write about something real. You may want to write a story about something that actually happened. You may want to describe a person, place, or object that actually exists. You may want to explain a process that is actually used or an opinion that is really held.

Whether you use narration, description, or explanation, you need to be as *accurate* as you can. Make sure that the names of people, places, and things are spelled correctly. Make sure that any facts or figures are correct. Also make sure that all dates are correct. Check all information carefully. When you write about what is real, be accurate.

The following paragraph is an example of how a writer has used facts and figures to support the main idea. Notice also that the writer uses third-person point of view.

America has become an urban society. Seventy years ago more people lived on farms or in rural areas. At that time about 40 percent, or two out of every five persons, lived in the country. Now only 25 percent, or one person in four, live there.
—MARC ROSENBLUM

Check It Out Now read the following paragraph. Notice that this writer uses first-person point of view.

I prepared for my dive into the Caribbean waters. I checked my equipment. I had a shatterproof facemask, a knife, a camera, and a depth gauge. My rubber fins let me swim 50 percent faster. With my aqualung I could stay underwater for over an hour. I dived to thirty feet and photographed sixteen types of tropical fish. Although I had made thirty dives since I began skindiving in 1975, each one was a new adventure.

- Is this a narration, a description, or an explanation of something real?
- Is the writing factual? Can its accuracy be checked?

Try Your Skill Follow the instructions given below:

1. Find an object in the room that you can examine closely. On your paper, name the object. List five statements of fact about the object. Write sentences that are factual. Be accurate.

2. Think of a real person or place with which you are familiar. On your paper, write the subject you choose. Now list five statements of fact about your topic. Make sure your facts are accurate. Check any information that may seem doubtful.

Keep This in Mind

- You may choose to write a narration, a description, or an explanation based on something real.
- Be accurate. Check your facts.

Now Write Now you're ready to write an original paragraph about something real. You may choose to write a narration, a description, or an explanation.

Take a few moments to think about a particular person, place, or object that you know well. On your paper, write your subject. Briefly, list any facts, figures, dates, or details that relate to your subject.

Next, decide whether you want to tell a story, to describe your subject, or to explain it. Decide which way is most appropriate. Then organize the information you have listed. Decide to use either first-person or third-person point of view.

Write your paragraph.

Read the paragraph. Do whatever rewriting you think is needed. Write your paragraph in a final form. Proofread your work, and put it into your folder.

Once upon a Time

How To Write About Something Imaginary

Here's the Idea Everyone has created something imaginary. As a child, you may have created imaginary people in games of make-believe. In grade school, you may have created creatures of fantasy in pictures. Even now, when you dream, you have the ability to create imaginary worlds of every sort. How, as a writer, can you create something imaginary as easily?

Allow your imagination to do some of your work for you. It is a powerful creator, always active. Sit quietly for a few moments. Allow your mind to wander. What do you see? hear? feel? taste? smell? Notice what your senses reveal to you.

Think about whatever person, place, object, or action you imagine. You may want to create a story. You may choose to describe what you imagine. You may decide to explain it.

Whether you choose narration, description, or explanation, you need to use **details** to bring your creation to life. Be specific in order to make your reader see, hear, feel, taste, or smell whatever you imagine. Make your imaginary world come alive for your reader.

Check It Out Now read the following paragraph.

> As I awakened, the strange world came into focus. Smelly, slime-covered pools dotted the island. Jagged orange rocks surrounded me. I tripped over a rock and fell onto the wet, spongy ground. I heard a roaring explosion in the distance, and I saw flying fragments of metal. Then I knew my aircraft was gone. I would have to find another way to escape.

- Is this paragraph a narration, a description, or an explanation of something imaginary?
- What details make it come alive for the reader?

Try Your Skill   Imagine a place that seems new or strange to you. Then describe your imaginary place, with details, in the following ways:

1. Write a sentence about something strange you might see.
2. Write a sentence about a sound that is new to you.
3. Write a sentence about something unusual you can touch.
4. Write a sentence about something new you taste.
5. Write a sentence describing an unusual smell.

Keep This in Mind

- You may choose to write a narration, a description, or an explanation about something imaginary that you create.
- Use details based on the five senses to bring your creation to life.

Now Write   You're ready to write an original paragraph about something imaginary. You may choose to write a narration, a description, or an explanation.

Let your imagination wander for a few minutes. Then, on your paper, write the person, place, object, or event you imagine. List any details you imagine about your subject. Be as specific as you can.

Next, decide whether you want to tell a story, to describe what you imagine, or to explain it. Decide which way seems most appropriate. Then select and organize the details you have listed. Decide to use either first-person or third-person point of view.

Write your paragraph.

Read the paragraph. Do whatever rewriting you think is needed. Write your paragraph in a final form. Proofread your work and put it into your folder.

Prance or Trudge?

How To Choose the Right Verb

Here's the Idea You have learned about important choices that a writer makes. A writer chooses to write about something real or to create something imaginary. A writer chooses to express an idea through narration or description or explanation. A writer chooses a point of view that is appropriate for the idea. Finally, a writer needs to choose the right words to express an idea exactly. A writer especially needs to choose specific verbs.

A verb is a word that tells what *happened* or what *is*. Some verbs, like *trudge* and *prance*, are strong and show action. Others are weaker and are often called linking or state-of-being verbs. These are words like *is, become,* and *seem*. A fine way to strengthen your writing is to use the more active verbs. It is stronger to write "Mary *won*," than "Mary *was* the winner."

Another way to work with verbs is to find specific substitutes for general verbs. Specific verbs can create moods in paragraphs.

For example, think of all the ways to say *look* that are more interesting and more specific. In a mysterious paragraph, your detective might *spy, snoop, pry,* or *peep*. In a humorous paragraph, a bumbling private eye might *peer, blink,* or *squint*. In a suspenseful paragraph, the detective might *stare, survey, inspect,* or *examine*. Any one of these verbs is clearer and stronger than *look*. They also help to set the mood.

Check It Out Notice the verbs in this paragraph.

> The skydiver *ignored* fear. She *leaped* from the hatch of the plane and *arched* her body for a free fall. Her arms and legs *stretched* spiderlike. Suddenly, she *whirled* to the right, then the left, and *looped* backwards. She *had sailed* through a figure-eight stunt in twenty seconds. Instantly, she *released* her parachute.

- Are the verbs active?
- Are the verbs specific rather than general ones?
- Do the verbs help to create a mood?

Try Your Skill You are going to work with the verb *walk*. Imagine that you walked to school on Monday and Friday last week. On Monday you were facing a tough math test. On Friday you were looking forward to filming a class play. Copy the following two paragraphs. Use active verbs that expressed your moods on those two mornings.

1   On Monday morning, I _____ out the door on the way to school. I _____ around the corner and _____ down the street. When the light changed, I _____ across the street. I _____ up the school steps. The bell was ringing as I _____ into class.

2   On Friday morning, I _____ out the door on the way to school. I _____ around the corner and down the street. When the light changed, I _____ across the street. I _____ up the school steps. The bell was ringing as I _____ into class.

Keep This in Mind
- Choose active verbs.
- Choose specific verbs, not general ones.
- Choose verbs that help to create a mood.

Now Write Start with the verb *say*. Make a list of verbs that are more specific than *say*. You might use *scream* or *whisper*, for example. Then choose three verbs from your list. Write one sentence with each verb. Try to make your sentences create different moods.

Put your paper into your folder.

The Process
of Writing

The Process of Writing

From this point on, you will be learning, and practicing, the skills of writing. You will be able to write often about what is important to you. You will also be able to practice different kinds of writing.

There will be lots of variety in your writing experiences. Whenever you write, however, there will be something that remains the same: **the process of writing.** There are steps you can follow **before you write, when you write,** and **after you write.** As you follow these steps, you will be learning to write.

On these four pages you can follow the process of writing from beginning to end. First, read about each step in the process. Then look at the example that shows how one person might have followed each step.

Before You Write Sometimes you write in response to an assignment. Sometimes you choose to write in order to communicate something important to you. Whatever you write, and whenever you write, you will find the beginning steps, called prewriting, very important.

Before you write, you need to focus on your subject. Take your time at this point in the process of writing. Narrow the topic so that you can handle it in a given length.

Think about your audience. Think about whether you want to use a personal point of view or an outsider's point of view. Use all of your senses to bring your subject clearly into focus.

Make a list of interesting details. Jot down notes or ideas related to your topic. You don't have to use them all.

If you need to learn more about your topic, do that, too.

Before You Write

You list possible topics.

You select a topic.

topics

Bilbo to the vet   Red Sox win   the history test
the beach   moving day

specifics

hot July day
ninth time we
moved
moved from
Bedford
Allied Van Lines
packing boxes,
127 of them

green furniture pads
Mrs. McKenna's farewell lunch
mopping, sweeping, cleaning
7 rooms, empty one by one
watched van leave
van away to New Jersey
crying

You list, in any order, details about your topic.

notes

Try to create real scene
Kind of paragraph? narrative?
Point of view 1st 3rd person
What else happened?   Ask Mom, Dad, Linda

You plan what you want to write.

When You Write   At this point in the process of writing, you are ready to write. Simply put your pencil to paper and write. Don't fuss with the writing. Don't worry about organizing ideas. Don't fret about spelling or punctuation. Don't get trapped by trying to make anything perfect at this stage. Let whatever happens, happen. Just write.

When You Write

You write a paragraph about your topic.

When the orange van pulled into our driveway, Linda and I ran to meet it. Even Bilbo was barking with excitement. This was the ninth time our family had moved. All through most of the day Linda and I followed the moving men in and out of the house. With each trip, they carried two or three more of the 127 cartons out to the van. It almost seemed like a parade. Piece by piece, room by room, the house was emptied. By late in the afternoon, I didn't feel excited anymore. I felt sad. I couldn't watch the movers. I climbed my favorite elm. The van drove away. For the moment at least, I had no home.

Notice how this paragraph tells about the topic.

After You Write Stop. Read what you have written. At this stage of the process you will need to work more carefully and thoughtfully. You have to check what you have written. Did you include everything you wanted to? Do you like what you've written? Is it interesting? Think about your topic.

At this point, it is possible that you may not like what you've written. It is likely, though, that you generally like your idea. Then you can rewrite whatever you need to change or want to change. Concentrate on every word: Is your idea clearly expressed? Did you *show* your reader what you want to say?

Is your writing organized logically? Is there a beginning, a middle, and an end to the development of your idea?

Is the writing lively and direct? Is each word the right word? Take the time to read your writing and think about it carefully.

After You Write

You rewrite.	→ When the orange ^(Allied) van pulled into ~~the~~ ^(our) driveway at 7 AM. ~~Linda and I~~ ^(we) ran to meet it. ⌐My sister and I⌐ ~~We~~ wanted to be part of our ninth family move.⌐ From that moment
You express your idea in a different way.	on, ~~we~~ ^(Linda and I) followed the five movers in and out of the house. With each trip, they carried more of the 127 cartons out to the van. Piece by piece, room by room, the house was emptied. By the end of the ~~afternoon~~ ^(day), the only things left ^(in the house) were the broom, the mop, and ~~cleaning supplies~~ ^(an echo). I walked through ~~our~~ ^(the) house one last time. ~~to say goodbye~~. Then I climbed my favorite elm ^(tree) ^in the yard. ~~to sit and think~~ As the moving van pulled out of the driveway, I started to cry.

Notice how this lively paragraph shows your idea clearly

Now, you need to look at how you expressed your idea. It is important to make your writing correct as well as clear and lively. Check your spelling. Check capitalization and punctuation. Use whatever references you have available to check your work.

Finally, when you are satisfied that your writing is clear and correct, write it in its final form. Write carefully. Make your work as neat as possible.

When you have finished your final copy, proofread your work. Read your writing aloud, to yourself, one final time.

My sister and I wanted to be part of our ninth family move. When the orange Allied van pulled into our driveway at 7 A.M., we ran to meet it. From that moment on, Linda and I followed the five movers in and out of the house. With each trip, they carried more of the 127 cartons out of the van. Piece by piece, room by room, the house was emptied. By the end of the day, the only things left in the house were the broom, the mop, and an echo. I walked through the house one last time. Then I climbed my favorite elm tree in the yard. As the moving van pulled out of the driveway, I started to cry.

You can learn to write only by writing. In each writing section you will be learning an idea about writing, checking your understanding of the idea, practicing your skill, and then writing on your own. Whenever you write, try to follow the steps in the process of writing. Each time you write you will be learning something about writing, and about yourself.

The Narrative Paragraph

What Happened?

How To Use Chronological Order

Here's the Idea   In its simplest form a narrative tells a story. When you tell what you did over the weekend, or what happened on an imaginary planet, you are writing a narrative. As a narrator, you usually tell what happened in the order that the events took place. This is called **chronological order.** It is in the order of time. Using chronological order is a natural, logical way of speaking and writing.

Because the narrative paragraph is such a natural way of writing, you may not always begin with a topic sentence that tells the main idea. However, you should always try to begin your narratives with strong and interesting sentences.

Following your first sentence will be the other events of your story. Use a natural time sequence to organize the events of your story. Tell what happened first, what happened next, and so on. This will help the reader understand the story.

Look at this narrative paragraph. Notice that the events are told in the same way they might have happened.

> He crawled through the doorway. He pulled the ankle flaps of his new winter moccasins up and tied them tightly. He fastened the thongs of the snowshoes firmly around his toes and around his ankles. He moved out onto the snow with wide, swinging steps and flapped his arms to make his blood flow fast and warm. It was good to be out in the open again, not just to push to the stream for water or to the storehouse for food, but out in the open and free to swing anywhere throughout his canyon.—JACK SCHAEFER

Check It Out   Now read this narrative paragraph:

> Huck began to dig and scratch now. Some boards were soon uncovered and removed. They had concealed a natural chasm which led under the rock. Tom got into this and held his candle as far under the rock as he could, but said he could not see to the end of the rift. He proposed to explore. He stooped and passed under; the narrow way descended gradually. He followed its winding course, first to the right, then to the left, Huck at his heels. Tom turned a short curve, by and by, and exclaimed: "My goodness, Huck, looky here!"—MARK TWAIN

- Are the events of this narrative in chronological order?

Try Your Skill   Choose one of the topic sentences below to develop a narrative paragraph. Plan your paragraph. Then write your paragraph, organizing the events in chronological order.

1. When the fog lifted, we saw it.
2. Last summer I did something I had never done before.
3. In the old house, everything was still.
4. That day started out in celebration, but ended in disaster.
5. The animals seemed as frightened as I was.
6. I was so excited to be there.

Keep This in Mind

- In a narrative paragraph, use chronological order to organize events.

Now Write   Write a narrative paragraph using chronological order. Follow all the steps in the process of writing.

Before you write, plan your idea. List related details.

Organize details. Write your paragraph.

Read what you have written. Do any necessary rewriting.

Write your paragraph in a final form. Proofread it. Then put it into your folder.

Frame by Frame

How To Use Transitions

Here's the Idea In a narrative paragraph you are telling a story. If you tell a story as it happened, you need certain words and phrases to help you show time order. These words and phrases are called **transitions.**

Good transitions make writing clear. They show readers your thought process. Study this list of transitions:

first	now	at the beginning	before
then	soon	in the middle	after
next	later	at the end	by the time

This list shows some of the transitional words and phrases you might use. There are many more. In fact, you might use any period of time to show chronological order. You might write your narrative using minutes, hours, days of the week, months, or years.

You can see that there are many ways to show time sequence. There are still other transitions, too. When you write, use a variety of transitions to make your ideas clear.

Check It Out Read the following narrative paragraph.

Yesterday I headed the supermarket's "Ten Most Wanted" list. First, because I entered the store through the exit door, I set off the burglar alarm. Then I slipped and fell into a pyramid of citrus, sending grapefruit flying. Afterward, I was so nervous that I dropped a dozen eggs. Finally, I didn't have enough money to pay. Needless to say, I am not a favorite customer.

- Find the transitions. Do they help make the story clear?
- Do the transitional words show time order?

Try Your Skill You are learning to tell stories with words. Stories can be told with pictures, too. Comic strips usually combine words with pictures. Some comic strips tell stories in pictures only. Here is one.

You are going to add words to these pictures. Tell what happened, frame by frame. Describe the action. Try to keep the humor of the cartoon.

First, jot down notes on your sheet of paper for each frame. Number your notes to match the number of frames. Put down ideas about what might be said in each frame.

Now write a few good transitional words or phrases for each frame. These should help you tell the story in the correct order. Number them to match the numbers of the frames.

Circle the one word or phrase in each list that shows the time most clearly.

Keep This in Mind

· Transitional words help to make a narrative clear.
· Use transitional words that show time order.

Now Write Write a narrative paragraph. Use transitions to show chronological order. Underline each of the transitional words and phrases you use. Put your paper into your folder.

Little by Little

How To Develop a Narrative Paragraph

Here's the Idea   How do you develop a narrative paragraph? Once you have a topic, or beginning sentence, how do you expand it? The most effective method, almost always, is to use **details.** Details give life to your writing.

Using details can be an easy task if you ask the right questions. Newspaper reporters use questions to find the details of a story. Reporters ask *who? what? where? when? why?* and *how?* In the process of your writing, try to ask the same questions. Ask these questions about any story idea, real or imaginary. You'll see how easily the details come.

Suppose you were telling a first-person account of a real incident. You have just taken your first toboggan ride. You could ask a reporter's questions to develop vivid details. For example, look at these possibilities:

Who?	Chris, David, Drew, and I
What?	tobogganing for the first time
Where?	Bemus Woods, twenty-foot high slide, six-foot long toboggan
When?	last weekend, during subzero cold, −13°
Why?	to try a new daredevil challenge
How?	bundled like mummies, laughing and shrieking

Using these details, you would then be able to write a lively narrative paragraph.

Check It Out   Read this narrative about a toboggan ride.

Last weekend, I took my new toboggan and my best friends flying. Chris, David, Drew, and I found our adventure on the giant slide at Bemus Woods. Although the temperature was thirteen degrees below zero, we didn't let that stop us. Our first ride left us breathless and shrieking with excitement. We raced down the slide again and again. We felt as though we were flying. Being a little bit scared has never been so much fun.

- Is this narrative developed by details?
- Does this narrative show *who? what? where? when? why?* or *how?*

Try Your Skill Can you use a reporter's questions to develop details? In the following paragraph, a story has already been started. Create real or imaginary details to complete this story. Then, on your paper, write your paragraph in a final form.

I was terrified. (*when?*) _____.
I was (*where?*) _____.
(*what happened? how?*) _____

_____.

I think it happened because (*why?*) _____.
I hope I'll never be _____ again.

Keep This in Mind

- Develop narrative paragraphs by using details.
- The details of a narrative paragraph can be developed by asking *who? what? where? when? why?* and *how?*

Now Write Write a narrative paragraph using vivid details. Use either real or imaginary details. Choose either first-person or third-person point of view.

Follow all the steps in the process of writing.

Write your story in a final form. Proofread it and put it into your folder.

The Descriptive Paragraph

Just Common Senses

How To Use Your Senses in Description

Here's the Idea Using the senses of sight, hearing, touch, taste, and smell gives you information about the world. Using your senses also makes you feel more alive to the world around you.

Try to use all of your senses when you write a descriptive paragraph. Use your senses to supply the details of your description. These details are called **sensory details.** They will give you a more complete feeling of what you are describing. Using sensory details will also allow you to make your experience real to your readers.

Read this descriptive paragraph:

> Yesterday my five-year-old sister Jenny made the mistake of playing with makeup. She coated her face with flower-scented pink grease. She smudged one eye with blue and the other with green. A pool of sticky black muck topped each eyebrow. Flame-red lipstick was smeared in a jagged ring around her mouth. When Jenny came to show me, she was still giggling.

Notice how sensory details make you feel as if you had been there, too.

Check It Out Now read this description of finding a cool stream:

> Just as we were getting weary, we spotted a clear stream. Shallow water bubbled and gurgled as it rushed across rocks. We hurriedly filled our cups and found the water numbingly cold. It tasted as fresh as a liquid icicle. After dipping our burning feet into the blue water, we hiked up the hill along the dusty path.

· What sensory details does this description use?

Try Your Skill Use your senses to create specific, lively descriptions. Try to imagine each of the sensations listed below. Then write two vivid words or phrases to describe each one.

1. the smell of soap
2. the feel of your hairbrush
3. the sounds of a football game
4. the taste of potato chips
5. the smell of smoke
6. the way a basketball looks
7. the taste of a brownie
8. the way your room looks
9. the feel of a towel
10. the sounds of a fire

Keep This in Mind

· When you write a descriptive paragraph, use sensory details. Be as specific as you can using details of sight, hearing, touch, taste, and smell.

Now Write Think of a real place that you know well. Imagine that you are there. On your paper, write *Sight, Hearing, Touch, Taste,* and *Smell.* Thinking of your special place, list details of each of the senses.

When you have finished, review your lists. Decide which senses are the most important in describing your place. Then organize the details in a logical order.

Write a descriptive paragraph about your place.

Read your paragraph aloud. Do whatever rewriting you need to.

Write your paragraph in a final form.

Proofread your work, and put it into your folder.

Words Are Moody

How To Use Adjectives To Establish Mood

Here's the Idea   Whenever you write, you make choices about the words you use. You can create many different characters and scenes based on your choice of words. You can create a character who is "slim" or one who is "scrawny." You can show a scene that is "lively" or one that is "hectic."

Most words give us special feelings. Some of the most colorful words are adjectives. They describe things, like *slim* or *scrawny*, *lively* or *hectic*. They help to set a feeling, or **mood.**

When you write description you can use adjectives to create a mood that is peaceful. You can use adjectives to create a different mood, one that is mysterious. It's fun to work with the emotional effect that adjectives can create. Choose adjectives carefully so they create the mood you want.

This is another reason to be careful with adjectives. It's easy to overuse them. Too many adjectives will make your writing wordy and dull. There is no need to say "the dark, inky, black sky" when "the black sky" works well. In description, use adjectives but use them carefully.

Check It Out   Read the following description.

> The fog had crept through the closed and curtained windows of the dining room and hung thick on the air. The silence seemed as heavy and breathless as the fog. The atmosphere was more choking than in the other room, and very chilly, although the remains of a large fire still burned in the grate.—MARGARET IRWIN

- Are there adjectives that create a mood?
- Do all of the adjectives fit the mood?
- Are there too many adjectives?

Try Your Skill Look at the adjectives below. Beside each number, there are three adjectives that have similar meanings. Number your paper from 1 to 10. Arrange the adjectives from the weakest to the strongest. For example, you would rearrange the adjectives *frightened, uneasy, terrified* to *uneasy, frightened, terrified.*

1. hot, warm, blistering
2. cold, cool, freezing
3. loud, thunderous, noisy
4. soggy, moist, wet
5. shiny, brilliant, bright
6. big, monstrous, bulky
7. small, tiny, microscopic
8. quiet, silent, hushed
9. mean, disagreeable, vicious
10. exciting, fascinating, interesting

Keep This in Mind

- Use adjectives to create a mood in description.
- Choose adjectives that fit the mood you want.
- Be careful not to overuse adjectives.

Now Write You are ready to write a descriptive paragraph that creates a mood. First, decide on a mood you'd like to create. You may find it easier to start by thinking of a place that makes you feel something special.

Next, list a few adjectives that fit the mood. Third, list sensory details that fit the mood. When your lists are complete, try to organize them in a logical order.

Write your paragraph of description. Read it aloud.

Write your final description. Read it aloud.

Proofread your work and put it into your folder.

Up and Down

How To Use Spatial Order

Here's the Idea When you write a descriptive paragraph, you are trying to communicate a picture or mood in words. You may want to tell your reader how something looks, sounds, smells, feels, or tastes.

If you say that the Rocky Mountains are "beautiful," your listener's question will be, "What do they look like?" You might say this:

> The Rocky Mountains rise from gentle meadows at their base. They spring up suddenly from the plains with sheer, majestic walls. Rocky gray peaks are topped by fluffy snow. These sharp outlines contrast with the rounded clouds above them.

Now your listeners will be able to picture them.

To make ideas clear in a descriptive paragraph, be sure to use a clear order. That order usually shows a relationship of **space.** Space relationship means how the things you describe are placed in relation to each other. This is called **spatial order.** Use spatial order to organize a description, especially descriptions of places or objects.

Look at the example of a descriptive paragraph below. Notice how the word picture is ordered according to space.

> My family calls my dresser "Danny's dump." The top of the dresser is usually piled high with clothes, sports equipment, and a few leftover snacks. The top drawer is jammed so full of old comic books that I can't open it. The drawer below has socks and T-shirts spilling out over the sides. I leave the bottom drawer open for my dog's bones, toys, and scraps. My dresser might not be orderly, but I know where everything is.

Check It Out Read another example of description:

Professor Lookit invented a unique squirtgun. The barrel and trigger below it pump water like any other water pistol. From the bottom of the grip, a rubber tube runs down to a balloon-like tank, which is filled with water. At the side of the tank is a plug for filling. The main advantage of this gun is that it gives more squirts with fewer refills.

· How does this description use spatial order?

Try Your Skill Choose a photograph, chart, or poster that is displayed on the walls of your classroom. Think about the picture. Use as many of your senses as you can. Decide which parts of the picture are the most striking. Notice how the parts are related to each other in space.

Look at the sentence beginnings below. Use them as a guide to write a descriptive paragraph about the picture.

| The central part | On the left |
| On the right | What is most important |

Keep This in Mind

· Use spatial order to organize descriptions, especially descriptions of places or objects.

Now Write Think of an object or place you would like to describe in a paragraph. Your subject can be real or imaginary.

List the important details. Organize the details in a logical way. Decide where you will begin your description. The rest of your description should follow in an organized way.

Write your description. Read it aloud.

If your description is not clear, rewrite it.

Proofread your work and keep it in your folder.

In, Out, and All Around

How To Use Transitions

Here's the Idea You learned how one kind of transitional word shows chronological order in narrative paragraphs. You need to use another kind of transitional word for description. Since description usually uses **spatial order,** the transitional words show relationships of some things to other things.

Here are some examples of transitional words and phrases used in description:

in	ahead of	down	to the right
on	outside	by	back and forth
above	downstairs	front	at the end of
under	close to	north	side by side
behind	between	east	in back of

Look at how this description of a dog uses transitional words and phrases to show spatial order.

> My dog Duke came inside last night looking as if he had lost a major battle. On top of his head two patches of fur were missing. Over one ear was a long scratch, and his matted tail hung down behind him. He limped because he was holding his injured left rear leg up under his belly. Duke needed first aid and my kindly attention.

Check It Out Now read this description of a dungeon:

> The prisoner found himself in a dark, musty cell. A tiny vent high on the wall in front of him was the only opening. A leaky pipe above him dripped onto an iron cot, and a puddle of foul water stood in the center of the cell. Insects skittered around the edges of the dirt floor. He shivered in disgust, as the solid iron door slammed behind him.

- How does this descriptive paragraph use transitions to show spatial order?

Try Your Skill You are going to write a description of the picture on page 74. Spend some time looking at it. Look at all the details carefully. Study the relationship of the objects and people. What is in front of something else? What is behind? What is above, next to, or below?

Decide on some logical space order that would fit this picture. The easiest way is to find the main focus. What one thing first catches your eye? What does your eye focus on? That's what is called the main focus. Use that item and describe other objects in relation to it. You could move from one side to the other, or up and down. You can even move in a circle.

Decide what space order you are going to use. Then list the five most important items in the order you have chosen.

Now you are ready to write your descriptive paragraph. Use your notes. Use transitional words. Write your paragraph. Be sure to follow the space order you have chosen.

Keep This in Mind

- In a descriptive paragraph, use transitional words that show spatial order.

Now Write Write a descriptive paragraph of a place or object that interests you. Your description may be of something real or imaginary.

When you finish writing, read your paragraph aloud. See if your description is in a clear and understandable order.

Rewrite. Make a final copy.

Proofread your description and put it into your folder.

The Explanatory Paragraph
Telling *How*

What's Next?

How To Use Step-by-Step Order

Here's the Idea Everyone knows how to do something well. Chances are that someone would like to learn something you know how to do. Can you share what you know so that someone else can learn? You can if you can write a good explanatory paragraph.

An explanatory paragraph explains. Sometimes it explains *why*. Sometimes it explains **how.** Whenever you explain how to do something—how to play soccer, sew on buttons, or use a handsaw—you are writing an explanatory *how* paragraph.

In an explanatory *how* paragraph, you need to describe a process **step-by-step.** It is important to make each step in the process simple and specific. Begin with the first step and then explain each step in the natural time order of the process. If one step in the process affects another step, be sure to explain how the steps are related.

Check It Out Read the following paragraph.

> Sewing a button on clothing is a simple task. First, gather a needle, straight pins, scissors, and thread that matches the color of the clothing. Second, remove any loose threads where the button used to be. Thread your needle. Next, mark the space for the button with a straight pin. Then, put the button in place and hold it there with one hand. Now, with your other hand, sew in and out of the holes in the button until it is firmly attached. Finally, knot the thread on the underside of the clothing. Snip the thread close to the clothing.

- Does this explanatory *how* paragraph explain a process step-by-step?
- Are the steps listed in a natural, logical sequence?

Try Your Skill   A six-year-old child gave the following explanation of how to make pizza. Could you follow the steps?

Pizza
½ of white cheese
1 full thing of red gravy
A lot of dough

Get the dough into a circle about size 14. Then throw it up in the air over your head.

Cook the gravy for a couple of hours or minutes. Then put it on the dough with a cookin' spoon—and pat it all around.

Take your gold square thing that makes the cheese all crumble up.

Then put on the gravy and cook it for a real long time.

If you don't get it out on time, it gets kinda blackish, but you still have to eat it.

Have it in the summer with ice cream.—*Smashed Potatoes*

From what you have learned about an explanatory *how* paragraph, explain what is wrong with these directions. On your paper, list at least three errors you find.

Keep This in Mind

- In an explanatory *how* paragraph, explain a process step-by-step.
- Write the steps in the natural time order of the process.

Now Write   Think of a simple process you enjoy and perform well. Make a list of the steps you take to complete the process. Be as specific as you can.

Now organize your detailed list into paragraph form. Write an explanatory *how* paragraph in a final form. After you have proofread your work, put it into your folder.

Watch Your Step!

How To Use Transitions

Here's the Idea An explanatory paragraph that tells how to do something is ordered by the steps in the process. The explanation begins with the first step. Then it moves through the steps in the order that they happen. It tells what to do *first*, what to do *second*, what to do *next*, and so on. There are special transitional words and phrases for this kind of paragraph. Study these examples:

first	then	at first
second	now	to start with
third	when	after that
fourth	while	at the same time
next	until	the next step
last	finally	at last

There are many variations of these transitional words and phrases. Choose whichever transitions seem to work best for the process you are describing.

Check It Out Read the following paragraph.

Scrambled eggs make a delicious light meal that is easy to prepare. First, gather the necessary utensils. You need a mixing bowl, an egg beater or wire whisk, a spatula, and a frying pan. Second, collect the ingredients. You need eggs, milk, butter, salt, and pepper. The third step is to break the eggs into the bowl. Use one egg for each person you are serving. Next, add a small amount of milk, and beat the mixture until it is fluffy. Then, over low heat, melt a tablespoon of butter in the frying pan. Add the eggs. Cook the eggs slowly until they are firm. While they cook, mix them a few times with the spatula. Finally, season them with salt and pepper and serve hot.

- What transitional words and phrases in this explanatory *how* paragraph show step-by-step order?

Try Your Skill   The sentences below belong in a paragraph, but their order has been jumbled. First of all, find the topic sentence and write it on your paper. Then write the remaining sentences of the paragraph in step-by-step order. Finally, fill in the blanks with precise transitional words to show the order.

_____, get a group of hardy bikers together.

_____, enjoy the fresh air and scenery _____ you are traveling.

Bike trips are fun, but they require careful planning.

_____, have the group use maps to plan each day's routes.

_____ you set out, have the group check the brakes, gears, and tires on all the bikes.

_____, make a list of needed supplies and _____ gather them together.

Keep This in Mind

- In an explanatory *how* paragraph, use transitional words and phrases to show step-by-step order.

Now Write   Write an explanatory *how* paragraph explaining something you know how to do.

Before you write, list the steps in the process using specific details.

When you write the paragraph, underline the transitional words and phrases you use.

Write your paragraph in a final form and put it into your folder.

The Explanatory Paragraph

Telling *Why*

Present Your Case

How To State an Opinion

Here's the Idea   How do you feel about math, your Uncle Harry, spinach, softball, or the school lunch program? You would have no trouble expressing your opinions on these and many other subjects. Having strong feelings or beliefs about things that affect your life is only natural. Expressing your opinion is something you do often.

The purpose of an explanatory *why* paragraph is to present an opinion in writing. You may want to explain why something is so, or why something should be changed. You will want to be convincing. To do this, start by offering an opinion. Then use reasons or facts to support your opinion. Any facts you use must be checked for accuracy.

For example, suppose that you were arguing that basketball is more exciting than baseball. Your first statement might be that there is more action in basketball than in baseball. That's a good topic sentence, but it's not specific enough. You must continue by explaining why you think this way. Why is there more action in basketball? There's more action in basketball because the ball is in play more of the time. You can be even more specific. How is the ball kept in motion? The players are either dribbling, passing, or shooting the ball. Your specific reason could be written like this: "There is more action in basketball because the players are dribbling, passing, and shooting the ball most of the time."

When you write an explanatory *why* paragraph, begin by stating your opinion. Then anticipate the questions your readers might ask. Try to give the most specific reasons you can to support your opinion.

Check It Out Read the following paragraph.

Math students should use calculators. Calculators are not a form of cheating. Even with a calculator, a student must know what to do to solve a problem. The calculator simply saves time by doing the addition, multiplication, subtraction, or division. It does these processes quickly and accurately. Since electronics is the way of the future, today's students should keep pace. They should use the most efficient method, the calculator.

- Does this paragraph state an opinion clearly?
- Do specific reasons or facts support the opinion convincingly?

Try Your Skill Below are three opinions that could be developed in explanatory *why* paragraphs. Choose one opinion and write it on your paper. List at least three specific facts or reasons to support the opinion. Check your facts for accuracy.

1. Summer is the best time of year.
2. Smoking is dangerous to your health.
3. _____ is the best form of exercise.

Keep This in Mind

- In an explanatory *why* paragraph, present and explain an opinion.
- Use specific reasons or facts to support the opinion convincingly.

Now Write Jot down several strong opinions you have. You might consider your feelings about something you do at home or at school, or something that happens in your community.

Narrow one opinion to an opinion you can write about in a paragraph. State your opinion in a clear, strong sentence. Then list at least three reasons or facts to support your opinion. Be specific. When you finish, put your work into your folder.

Save the Best for Last

How To Support an Opinion

Here's the Idea To write a strong explanatory *why* paragraph you need convincing reasons to support an opinion. "That's how it is" and "because I say so" are not convincing reasons. Your reader will expect you to give specific reasons. Once you have good reasons, you will need to put them into some kind of order. An effective method is to save your strongest reason for last. Build your case from the weakest point to the strongest; that is, in order of importance. In that way, you leave your readers with your most convincing reason fresh in their minds.

For example, below are three reasons why private cars should be banned from large cities.

1. Pleasant pedestrian malls could replace some streets.
2. Energy is saved when people use public transportation.
3. Air pollution would be reduced, and cities would be healthier places to live.

The first reason is a good one, but it isn't as immediately important to the nation as the supply of energy. The last reason is probably the most important of all, since it affects people directly. We are all concerned about our health. You can see that these reasons have been listed in order, from the least important to the most important.

Check It Out Read the following explanatory paragraph.

More junior high schools should offer soccer. Soccer is inexpensive for a school, since it requires little equipment. Because soccer is popular worldwide, junior high students should have a chance to try it. A fast-moving game, soccer is fun to play and to watch. Most important, soccer is a wholesome sport that any-one of any size can play. Soccer would be a good sport for junior high school students.

- Is the opinion supported by specific facts or reasons?
- Is the evidence given in order of importance, from the least important to the most important?

Try Your Skill Below is an opinion supported by three reasons or facts. Write the opinion. Then list the three reasons in order of their importance, from the least important to the most important.

The capital of the United States should be moved to Kansas.
1. The new capital would be in the center of the country.
2. A new capital could be built fairly quickly.
3. The national government would be nearer to more citizens.

Keep This in Mind

- The most convincing way to organize an explanatory *why* paragraph is in order of importance. Start with the least important evidence and end with the most important.

Now Write Take out the work you did for the last lesson, **Present Your Case.** You should have one opinion for an explanatory *why* paragraph and at least three specific reasons or facts to support the opinion.

Arrange the reasons or facts for each opinion in order, from least important to the most important.

Use your notes to write a convincing, well organized explanatory *why* paragraph. Do any rewriting you feel is necessary.

Write a final copy of your paragraph. Proofread it carefully.

Finally, put your work into your folder.

Build Your Case

How To Use Transitions

Here's the Idea An explanatory *why* paragraph needs a strong topic sentence and a strong concluding sentence. The topic sentence should state the opinion as directly as possible. The concluding sentence should sum up the argument.

Two kinds of transitions help you organize an explanatory *why* paragraph. One kind helps you to state the reasons or facts. The other kind of transition helps you to put your reasons or facts in order of importance.

To State Reasons or Facts:	because, so, since, therefore, as a result, if (something) . . . then (something)
To Put in Order of Importance:	the first reason, second, more important, most important, finally

Check It Out Look at these notes for a *why* paragraph.

Opinion:	speed limit should not be raised from 55 mph.
Reasons:	relaxing pace, saves lives, saves fuel

In a second pre-writing step, the reasons can be written with the appropriate transitions and arranged in order of importance.

relaxing pace —	*since* it gives passengers chance to see country-side	= *the first reason*
conserves fuel —	*because* engines work more efficiently	= *more important*
saves lives —	*if* motorists drive more slowly, they have time to react to danger	= *most important*

Now read the completed paragraph.

Highway speed limits should not be raised from 55 miles per hour. The first reason is that passengers can see more and are more relaxed at slower speeds. More important, lower speeds save fuel because engines are working efficiently. Most important, if motorists drive slowly they have more time to react to dangerous situations and lives will be saved. The savings in headaches, fuel, and lives speak strongly for keeping the speed limit at 55 miles per hour.

- Does the topic sentence state an opinion clearly?
- What transitional words and phrases show the reasons and their order of importance?
- Does the concluding sentence sum up the argument?

Try Your Skill Below is a set of notes for an explanatory *why* paragraph. First, put the reasons in the best order. Then write a good topic sentence and a good concluding sentence.

Opinion: Everyone should learn to swim.

Reasons: may save a life, could be summer job, fun

Keep This in Mind

- State the opinion in the topic sentence.
- Use transitions that show the reasons and their order of importance.
- Sum up your argument in the concluding sentence.

Now Write Write an explanatory paragraph expressing an opinion important to you. Do whatever pre-writing, writing, and rewriting are necessary to write a convincing paragraph.

Proofread your final paragraph, and put your work into your folder.

A Look at Compositions

It's a Long Story

Learning About Compositions

Here's the Idea There are times when you cannot say everything you want to say in one paragraph. You may have a long story to tell or a lot of information to present. A subject too big for a paragraph may be right for a composition.

A **composition** is a group of paragraphs that deal with one idea. That idea can be one story, one description, or one explanation. A composition is useful for expressing ideas that require more than a few sentences. You could explain what skim milk is in a few sentences. It would take a whole composition to explain how it is made.

Some topics are so general that even a composition is not big enough to cover them. If you wanted to write about every kind of dairy product, you would need an entire book.

Check It Out Read the following composition.

The Garage Sale

Brenda Michaels went early to the garage sale. She always enjoyed poking through a collection of leftover odds and ends. That day she was hoping to find a tennis racket, or maybe even a catcher's mitt.

When Brenda saw the squat brass lamp, she was surprised. She'd never seen anything like it. It was tarnished and dented, but Brenda wanted it very much. She paid fifty cents for it and took her treasure home.

In her room, she examined the lamp carefully. She looked at it from all sides. On the bottom, there was some strange writing that was covered with dirt. She started to rub off the dirt.

Then there was a puff of smoke, and a Genie appeared.

"Bzovr snufl gretzle," said the Genie, bowing low.

Brenda didn't answer. She just stared at the Genie.

"Excuse me," said Brenda finally. "I can't understand a word you're saying."

"Bzovr snufl gretzle," said the Genie, louder this time.

Brenda was puzzled. She didn't know what the Genie was trying to say. What language was he speaking?

The Genie was shouting, "BZOVR SNUFL GRETZLE!"

Brenda finally found her voice. She asked the Genie if he could speak another language. The genie didn't seem to understand her, either. He shouted something else, stamped his foot, and disappeared in another puff of smoke.

Brenda thought for a long time about the Genie. What was he trying to tell her? Could his message have changed her life? Slowly she rubbed the bottom of the lamp again, but this time nothing happened.

- What is the central idea of this composition?

Try Your Skill   Read these topics. Number your paper from 1 to 5. Write *P* next to the number if the topic could be covered in a paragraph. Write *C* if the topic requires a composition.

1. how to draw a rectangle
2. the most memorable birthday I've ever had
3. why skateboarding is dangerous
4. careers in medicine
5. what a rainbow looks like

Keep This in Mind

- A composition is a group of paragraphs that deal with one main idea.

Now Write   Write the title of this lesson, **It's a Long Story.** Write five topics that would be suitable for compositions. Choose topics that you like and that you know you could write about at some length. Put the paper into your folder.

Three in One

Developing a Composition

Here's the Idea A composition has three parts: an **introduction,** a **body,** and a **conclusion.** The introduction is the part that tells what the composition will be about. The introduction is similar to the topic sentence of a paragraph.

The body of a composition is the part that develops the main idea. In a narrative, the body contains the events of the story. In a description, the body contains the details that make up the word picture. In an explanatory composition, the body contains steps in a process, reasons, or facts.

A composition needs a conclusion for the same reason that a paragraph does. The reader must know that it is over. The conclusion may be a summary; that is, a general statement about the story, description, or explanation. The conclusion may be a group of sentences, simple or striking, that clearly signals an ending to the idea you have developed.

Check It Out Read the following composition.

The Jacobs' Specialty

At first glance, there doesn't seem to be much that's special about the Jacob family. However, something sets them apart from every other family I know. It's their refrigerator.

From the outside, the refrigerator looks like a big, white box next to the sink. Open the door, though, and the inside is unlike anything you've ever seen before. Every shelf and space is always crammed with tempting foods. The top shelf has colorful containers of pickles, jelly, cold meats, milk, and juices. The middle shelf is always heaped with plates of sandwiches. The bottom shelf is packed with cheeses, homemade breads, cakes, and fruit of every kind.

Getting an invitation to the Jacobs' house is like being invited to a banquet. One day the snack might be ham and Swiss on rolls with sharp dill pickles on the side. Another day, it might be rich cream cheese on thick slices of rye bread. On a rainy Saturday, the feast might include homemade pizza.

Whenever I think of that refrigerator, I think of the Jacob family itself. Every member of that family is friendly, generous, and affectionate. Everyone seems to contribute something to the comfort of family and friends. I guess that makes the family special. Their hearts are as open as their refrigerator door.

- Which part is the introduction, which is the body, and which is the conclusion?

Try Your Skill Write which part of a composition you think this paragraph is. Write the reasons for your answer.

A good-luck charm may be anything from a rabbit's foot to a shiny penny. It's not the shape or size that matters. What counts is that the owner believes in the charm. That belief gives confidence, and confidence often assures success. In that respect, anyway, good-luck charms have really worked.

Keep This in Mind

- A composition should have three parts: an introduction, a body, and a conclusion.

Now Write On your paper, write the title of this lesson, **Three in One.** Then take out the topics you wrote in the last lesson. Choose one topic and think about how you would write a composition about it. On your paper, write three headings: *Introduction, Body,* and *Conclusion.* After each, write notes that tell what you would include in each part of the composition.

When you have finished, put your work into your folder.

Here's the Lineup

Recognizing Three Kinds of Compositions

Here's the Idea   When you studied paragraphs, you learned that there are three main kinds. A narrative paragraph tells a story. A descriptive paragraph creates a word picture. An explanatory paragraph explains something.

There are also three main kinds of compositions. They have the same names and the same purposes. A composition may be a narrative, a description, or an explanation.

A **narrative** composition tells a story. The story may be real or imaginary. The characters and people may be invented or real. The important feature of a narrative is what happens.

A **descriptive** composition focuses on sensory details. The writer tries to make the reader feel what the writer feels and see what the writer sees.

An **explanatory** composition explains *how* something should be done or *why* something should be believed. This kind of composition uses steps in a process, or reasons or facts.

Check It Out   Read the following composition.

Sprout Some Fun

For many years, bean sprouts have been a regular feature of the Oriental diet. Now they are catching on in this country. They taste good and are good for you. If you want to raise some food and have some fun, too, grow your own sprouts.

First, take a handful of mung beans or alfalfa beans and put them into a big jar. Cover the beans with warm water. Set the jar in a warm, dark place. The next day, drain off the water.

Then, every day for four days, rinse the beans in fresh, warm water. Rinse them twice a day, morning and night. Each time, drain off the water so the beans are damp but not soggy. Keep the top of the jar covered with a piece of cloth.

When the beans sprout, move the jar to a sunny place. The sprouts will turn green. Then, wash the beans well to remove the hulls, the outer coverings. The sprouts are ready to be used in sandwiches and salads. Keep them in the refrigerator.

Bean sprouts are easy to grow. It's fun to watch them change from seeds to greens. Growing them satisfies two basic urges, the desire to create and the desire to eat. Try it yourself and see.

- What kind of composition is this? How do you know?

Try Your Skill On your paper, identify the two kinds of compositions given as models in the last two lessons, **It's a Long Story** and **Three in One.** Write your reasons for thinking so.

Keep This in Mind

- There are three kinds of compositions. A narrative composition tells a story. A descriptive composition creates a word picture. An explanatory composition explains *how* to do something or *why* something should be done or believed.

Now Write On your paper, write the title of this lesson, **Here's the Lineup.** Take out the topics you wrote in **It's a Long Story.** Choose one topic that you could use for a narrative composition, one you could use for a descriptive composition, and one you could use for an explanatory composition.

Write down your three topics, leaving space between each one. In a few sentences, write what events you would tell in your narrative composition. Then write how you would describe your subject in your descriptive composition. Finally, write a sentence or two telling how you would explain the topic of your explanatory composition. Put the paper into your folder.

The Narrative Composition

Real Life

What's the Idea?

How To Find and Narrow a Topic

Here's the Idea Every writer has times when it's hard to come up with ideas. These are good times to have a book of ideas. An idea book can be simply a pocket-sized notebook. It is helpful to carry it with you. After all, real life is the source of most topics. When you hear an interesting phrase in conversation, write it down. If you see something interesting that is happening, jot down the facts.

You can add ideas to your book by recalling events in your own life. What times were the happiest or saddest? What has happened in your life that others would be interested in?

Newspapers and magazines report on important events of the day. Record facts that interest you in your idea book.

Once you find a topic to write about, you will need to narrow it. A narrow topic is one that is specific enough to be handled easily in a composition.

To narrow a topic ask *who? what? when? where? how?* and *why?* The answers to these questions will give you information to make your topic more specific.

Here is a topic that becomes narrower and more specific:

—A challenging adventure   (what?)
—Crossing the Atlantic Ocean   (how?)
—Rowing across the Atlantic in a small boat   (when? who?)
—In 1966, two Britons rowed from Cape Cod to Ireland in a 22-foot open boat

Can you see a pattern in the four topics? Each time more information is added, the topic gets narrower and more specific.

Check It Out See how a general topic is changed to a more specific topic by asking questions.

General topic —   an outdoor adventure

(what?) —   camping trip to Acadia National Park
(who?) —   Rob and I, with the Portland Hiking Club
(when?) —   summer vacation July, 1978
(why?) —   to see what living outdoors for a week is like

Specific topic —   My week-long camping trip to Acadia National Park with the Portland Hiking Club in July, 1978

- How is the specific topic different from the general topic?

Try Your Skill Each of these topics is too broad to handle in a composition. Choose one and write it. Next, ask *who? what? when? where? how?* and *why?* Write the answers below the topic. Then write a specific topic, using your notes.

a big surprise   a difficult challenge
a long, hard day   a new invention
a real accomplishment   a food

Keep This in Mind

- Keep a book of ideas and notes for possible writing topics. Gather facts about people, places, objects, and events that interest you.
- Narrow your topic so it can be covered in a composition.

Now Write Think of something interesting that happened at your school. Write the topic. Next, narrow the topic. Then write your specific topic. Write **What's the Idea?** at the top of your paper. Put your work into your folder.

Get the Facts

How To Develop a Narrative Composition

Here's the Idea   Narrative compositions are developed with details. One way to find or remember details is to ask *who? what? when? where? how?* and *why?* When you are relating a true account, you must be sure to be accurate.

Be specific when you give the time and place of a real narrative. Be sure that your details are accurate. For example, "The first human being walked on the moon on July 20, 1969."

Readers will want to know who is in the story. In a real narrative, include all the important people and spell their names correctly. For example, "Neil A. Armstrong and Edwin E. Aldrin, Jr. were the first human beings on the moon."

Tell what actually happened. Be specific. Make sure your account is accurate. For example, "Neil Armstrong was the first astronaut to climb down the ladder of the Eagle module."

Finally, how did the people in the story react to what happened? For example, "When Armstrong stepped onto the surface of the moon, he said, 'That's one small step for man, one giant leap for mankind.' "

When you are writing about a real event, check your facts. Look up information you are not sure of. Check your information by talking with, or reading about, people who participated in the event. Use reliable sources. Don't confuse your readers.

Check It Out   Read these notes for a narrative composition.

Specific topic: my week-long camping trip to Acadia National Park with the Portland Hiking Club in July, 1978
    —camped near pine grove on Mt. Desert Island
    —fished in Frenchman Bay, cooked our catch

—hiking expedition, swimming
—bad weather
—adventure at Thunder Hole
—more bad weather
—farewell feast

· What other details might be added?
· How could the accuracy of details be checked?

Try Your Skill   Look at the following lists of topics. Some are historical events. Others are events that you might have been involved in. Choose one topic, and list related details. Ask *who? what? when? where? how?* and *why?* questions to develop details. Write the topic and details on your paper.

last year's World Series   a time you won something
an important battle   a time you helped someone
a natural disaster   a time you learned something new

Keep This in Mind

· Narrative compositions are developed with details.
· When writing about a real event, be sure that your details are accurate.

Now Write   On a sheet of paper, write the topic you narrowed in the last lesson. At the top of your paper, write the title of this lesson, **Get the Facts.** Then list details of the event. Be as specific as you can.

Ask your teacher or another student for help in recalling details, if necessary. You may need to use other sources, such as books or newspapers, to check the accuracy of some details. Use whatever sources are available to you.

When your pre-writing notes and list details are complete, put your paper into your folder.

Tell Your Story

How To Use Transitions in a Narrative

Here's the Idea Narratives are usually told in **chronological order.** You begin with the first event and move through time to the last. To help your reader understand the sequence, you should use clear transitional words and phrases.

You have used transitional words for narrative paragraphs. Some of these are *first, then, next, later, soon,* and *afterwards.*

It is important to use transitions within paragraphs. It is also important to use transitions between paragraphs. The topic sentence of each paragraph should connect that paragraph to the one before it. These transitions help locate the events in time. This way the reader moves smoothly from paragraph to paragraph. Examples of paragraph transitions are *later that day, by noon,* and *when I got home.*

Check It Out Read the narrative composition below.

Back to Nature

I had always wanted to "rough it" for an entire week. Last July I got my chance. Our Portland Hiking Club camped in the rugged wilderness of Acadia National Park.

The first day, the twelve of us set up camp near a pine grove on Mount Desert Island. During the day we hiked the mountainous trails or swam at Sand Beach. We fished from ledges at Frenchman's Bay. Then we cooked our catch over an open fire. At night we told ghost stories as we nestled in sleeping bags.

The last three days of the trip were almost spoiled by bad weather. Because of heavy downpours and muddy ground, we had to move our campsite and limit our hikes. Between storms, though, we managed to see Thunder Hole, where the ocean explodes into a narrow gorge.

On the final day of the trip we sat under trees, dodging rain-drops, for a farewell feast. We had pooled all our canned and dried foods and made a giant stew. While we downed the hot food, we talked about our trip. Before we left Acadia, we had set the date for our next journey back to nature.

- What transitions are used within paragraphs?
- What transitions are used to show sequence between paragraphs?

Try Your Skill   Read the paragraph below. Notice that transition words and phrases have been omitted. Also, the time sequence is out of order. Rewrite the paragraph, and use transition words and phrases so that the time sequence is clear.

I put a sandwich and an orange in a bag for lunch. I woke up too late to eat breakfast. I was so hungry that my stomach growled in class. I saw that I had forgotten my lunch at home. My family was shocked to see how much I ate at dinner.

Keep This in Mind

- In a narrative paragraph, transitions show time sequence from sentence to sentence.
- In a narrative composition, transitions show time sequence from paragraph to paragraph.

Now Write   Take out your work from the last lesson. You should have a narrow, specific topic relating a true account and a list of supporting details. Arrange the details in chronological order. Add transitions to make the time order clear.

Write the title of this lesson, **Tell Your Story,** at the top of your paper. Using your notes, write a narrative composition.

Do whatever rewriting is necessary. Make a final copy of your composition. Proofread your work. Put it into your folder.

The Narrative Composition

Imaginary

Get Started

How To Plan a Story

Here's the Idea Some narrative compositions tell accounts of events that really happened. Others tell stories that happened only in the writer's imagination.

Ideas for stories can begin with a picture, a dream, or a real event. How those ideas take shape in a story is up to you. Invent dramatic details. Create characters. Use your imagination.

Both real and imaginary narrative compositions are developed with details. Use time order and time transitions for both. Plan them in the same way, too.

However, there are several special elements to an imaginary narrative. These elements include the setting, the characters, and the plot. You should keep them in mind when you are planning your narrative composition.

The **setting** is where and when a story takes place. The setting of a story may be an invented place or a real place. The setting may be any time in the past, present, or future. Your story might begin, "As night fell we were still 3,000 feet from the top of Mount Everest." Describing the setting of your story with specifics will help your readers see what you have imagined.

The **characters** are whoever takes part in a story. Show your readers your characters. What does a character look like? What does his or her voice sound like? How does the character behave? Your characters can be people or animals.

Show someone's character by his or her actions. Instead of saying "Debbie was quick-thinking," you might *show* that she was quick-thinking. For example, "One of the lower climbers slipped. Debbie looped her safety line around a rock and wedged herself into a crevice. By doing so, she prevented the entire party from tumbling down the mountainside."

The **plot** of a story means the events that happen, from a beginning action, through conflict, to an ending. *Action* is what happens. Tell what happened first, next, and so on.

The *conflict* means the problems and struggles the characters face in the story. How do the mountain climbers feel when they are halfway up the mountain? What do they do? Do they feel afraid? Do they think of turning back?

The *ending* is the conclusion. It's the place to tie up all the loose ends. If your mountain climbers are hanging from a cliff, get them down. Make sure you resolve whatever action or conflict started the chain of events for your characters.

Check It Out   Look at these pre-writing notes for a story.

Setting	downtown Milwaukee, a summer day, in a car
Characters	Melvin Marvel, world famous magician, and an enormous white rabbit
Plot	Melvin finds the rabbit in his back seat
Conflict	Melvin, frightened, wonders if rabbit is a ghost?
Ending	the rabbit's head comes off revealing—a surprise

• Could these details be used to create an imaginative story?

Try Your Skill   Find a picture in which people are doing something that captures your attention. Can you imagine a story involving them? Who are they? What will happen? Use your imagination to create a story. Write a set of notes for your story.

Keep This in Mind

• Develop your story by using your imagination.
• Develop details of setting, character, and plot.

Now Write   On your paper, write the title of this lesson, **Get Started.** Develop an idea for a story. Make notes of setting, characters, and plot. Put your work into your folder.

The Right Introduction

How To Write an Introduction

Here's the Idea The first thing you usually present to your readers in a narrative is the setting or characters, whichever seems more important in your story. You might want to begin with the setting if it is unusual or if it is important to the events of the story. You might want to begin with a description of the main character if an unusual character is at the center of your story. Your **introduction** depends on the emphasis of your story.

No matter what you decide to begin with, you must get the story going. By the end of the first paragraph, your reader should know whether it is a mystery or adventure or science fiction. The reader should feel the mood of the story.

There are exceptions, however. Some stories create suspense. In such stories, the important elements are developed later in a story. You might want to introduce your audience to an ordinary setting, and slowly add elements of danger or mystery.

Whatever your plan, remember to keep your subject and your audience in mind as you write your introduction.

Check It Out Read the introduction below.

It was a fine summer morning in downtown Milwaukee. The breeze off Lake Michigan was cool, and the air was surprisingly clear. Melvin Marvel, the world famous magician, was whistling to himself as he braked for a light. Looking in his rearview mirror, Melvin saw—or thought he saw—an enormous white rabbit sitting in the back seat.

- Which words and phrases introduce the setting? Which words and phrases introduce the main character? Which words and phrases get the story going?

- What kind of story do you think will follow this introduction?

Try Your Skill Everyone has been frightened at some time. What has happened in your life that has scared you? What has made you scream or get the chills? Have you ever been lost in the woods or the city? Have you ever been alone and heard strange noises? Have you ever been somewhere you shouldn't have been? Think of some frightening experience you have had that could be the basic idea for an imaginary story.

List three possible story ideas on your paper.

Star the one that you could write about most easily.

Write an introduction for a story about this event. You want to set the scene for a scary story. The scene doesn't have to be a gloomy castle or a deserted inn. It doesn't have to be a stormy night. Frightening scenes can take place in your own living room on a sunny afternoon. The important thing is to list details that fit the mood.

Keep This in Mind

- Introductions usually present setting or characters. Your introduction depends upon the emphasis in your story.
- The introduction should set a scene that makes readers curious enough to want to read on.

Now Write On your paper, write the title of this lesson, **The Right Introduction.** Using the idea and notes from the last lesson, write the introduction for your story. Be sure to set the mood and introduce the story idea.

Put your paper into your folder. You will need it later.

What's Your View?

How To Use Point of View

Here's the Idea You control your story. You decide who tells the story. In the **first-person point of view,** the story is told by the character identified by *I*. The reader knows only what the main character is thinking, feeling, seeing, or hearing. The reader can identify with the main character. You limit what your reader knows to what the main character knows.

The **third-person point of view** is limited, too. A story is told by someone describing other characters and their actions. The reader can see and hear everything. The reader cannot know what any character is thinking or feeling, however. You must show how characters are feeling through their words and actions. The third-person point of view works well for stories with many characters and much action.

Another point of view allows the reader to know everything. It's called **omniscient,** (om·ni′·shunt) which means "knowing all things." The reader knows what each character is thinking or feeling, and everything that is going on. You usually use the pronouns *he* or *she* with this point of view. The omniscient point of view can be useful in many stories. You can choose which details to emphasize and which to keep hidden.

Check It Out Read the introductions below. Each is written from a different point of view.

1   "What a fine summer morning," I thought to myself as I drove downtown. I could feel a cool breeze off the lake as I opened the car window and put out my elbow. Then I glanced in the rearview mirror. I wasn't ready for what I thought I saw in the back seat—an enormous white rabbit.

2   It was a bright summer morning in downtown Milwaukee. The breeze off Lake Michigan was cool, and the air was clear. Melvin Marvel, the world famous magician, was whistling happily to himself as he braked for a light. Looking in his rear-view mirror, Melvin saw an enormous white rabbit sitting in the back seat. Melvin's hands began to tremble and his mouth opened wide. He felt as if he had seen a ghost.

· What is the point of view of each paragraph? Look back at the example in **Check It Out** in the last lesson, **The Right Introduction.** What is the point of view of that paragraph? How does it compare with paragraph 2 above?

Try Your Skill   This paragraph uses the third-person point of view. Rewrite it twice, once using the first-person point of view, and the second time using the omniscient point of view.

> Steve sat on the stubbly grass surrounding the basketball court. Five other boys his age were playing on the court. They shouted and joked with each other, but paid no attention to Steve. Steve sat stiffly. He never took his eyes off the game.

Keep This in Mind

· In the first-person point of view, the reader knows only what the main character sees and feels.

· In the third-person point of view, the reader can see and hear everything that happens.

· In the omniscient point of view, the reader knows everything—thoughts, feelings, and actions.

Now Write   On your paper, write the title of this lesson, **What's Your View?** Read your introduction from the last lesson. Decide what point of view you used. Rewrite it twice, using two other points of view. Star the introduction that works best for your story. Put your work into your folder.

Thicken the Plot

How To Use Details To Develop the Plot

Here's the Idea Now you are ready to write the body of your narrative composition. Here you present the actions and reactions, the conflicts, of the plot.

Plot means the events of a story. How these events are arranged is important. The most common way is to arrange them in the order that they happened. This is called **chronological order.** This makes it easy for the reader to follow the action of your story. Be sure to include each important event.

Action arising from a conflict is the most important element in plot. The conflict may be between characters. It might result from something that happens naturally, like a hurricane or blizzard. The conflict might even be within a character who is struggling to make an important decision. An interesting story has an unusual, frightening, or dramatic conflict.

Once you have decided on the plot, you must develop it. Specific details give life and shape to the outline of your plot.

Imagine that you are writing about Melvin Marvel and the white rabbit he discovered in the back seat of his car. First, you would write an outline of your plot. Then you would develop it by using specific details.

Check It Out Read the body of the story below.

Shocked and shaken, Melvin stared at the furry figure. There was something odd about those pointed ears, that twitching mouth, those clear pink eyes. Melvin had seen many rabbits in his years as a magician, but this one definitely looked familiar. Melvin began to worry that this rabbit was seeking revenge for being stuffed into his musty old top hat.

"Where did you come from?" Melvin asked in trembling tones. "Who are you?" The rabbit was silent. Panicked by a terrifying thought, Melvin cried, "Are you a ghost?" The rabbit only wiggled his whiskers and pointed at the traffic light. It had turned green. Instead of moving, Melvin put the car into neutral.

"*Are* you? Answer me!" Melvin shrieked, ignoring the cars honking around him. "Why are you haunting me?" Melvin climbed into the back seat. He shook the rabbit. "Believe me!" he screamed. By this time people were gathering to investigate the cause of the traffic jam. A crowd surrounded the car, peering into the windows at the strange scene.

- What details are developed in the plot?
- Are the details developed in chronological order?
- What is the conflict?

Try Your Skill These story notes are too general. Rewrite them to include a dramatic conflict. Make up details.

> Plot: I decided to visit my friend in another city.
> I took the train to the city where he lives.
> When I arrived I called him on the phone.
> He came to pick me up.

Keep This in Mind

- Use specific details to develop the plot.
- Arrange details in the order they happened.
- Make sure your action arises out of conflict.

Now Write On your paper, write the title of this lesson, **Thicken the Plot.** Write an outline of the plot for the topic you chose in **Get Started.** Jot down specific details. Keep in mind the setting and mood of the introduction. Write a draft of your story, leaving out the ending. Put it into your folder.

Put the Lid on It

How To Write a Conclusion and a Title

Here's the Idea The final paragraph of your story is the **conclusion.** It's here that you end your story. Don't leave any ideas dangling. Make your conclusion fit with the rest of the story. Don't add anything that isn't part of the story.

Be consistent about time sequence, characterization, and point of view. If you have been describing an event in the past, don't leap to the present in your conclusion. If your character has been timid, don't make her or him aggressive in the conclusion. You *can* do this if the character change is part of a surprise ending, however. If you've been using the first-person point of view, use it in your conclusion. Make your conclusion interesting. It is the last impression you leave with your reader.

The **title** of your story is the first thing the reader will see, although it will probably be the last thing you write. A good title should catch the reader's attention. It might also point toward the main idea or even the mood of your composition. A title may be as simple as "Night Drive," or as startling as "A Man Who Had No Eyes."

After you have written a conclusion and a title, you will have completed a draft of a short story.

Check It Out Read the conclusion below.

Suddenly the rabbit reached up and pulled off its head. Melvin started to scream, but it came out as a roar when he recognized his assistant, Luna Rooney. Between fits of laughter, Luna confessed. She admitted that she had donned a rabbit suit and hid in the back seat just to scare the daylights out of him. She certainly had done that. To this day Melvin can't pull a rabbit out of a hat without remembering his unusual passenger.

- In what ways is this an effective conclusion?
- What would be a good title for this story?

Try Your Skill Read this story in need of a conclusion.

> Jim Allen leaped up the steps and bolted into the house.
> "What is it Jim?" his mother called.
> Jim moaned, "My telescope has to be mounted and ready for display in the science fair tomorrow morning."
> "You promised to cut Mr. McInnes's lawn after school today," Jim's mother said.
> From his room, Jim shouted that he just couldn't do it.
> Jim's mother said that he would have to keep his promise.
> Jim flopped on his bed to think. What should he do? Suddenly the phone rang. Jim ran to answer it. It was his friend Ken.
> Ken was in trouble. He was stuck five miles outside of town. He had spent his last dime on the phone call, and was at the Triangle Store. He begged Jim to come and get him.
> Jim tried to explain his own predicament.
> "Please, Jim," Ken interrupted. "I have to be at work soon."
> Jim turned to his mother. He had a difficult decision to make.

Write a conclusion and a title for this story.

Keep This in Mind

- A conclusion ties the elements of the story together.
- A title should be interesting and fit the story.

Now Write Take out your introduction and paragraphs of plot development from the previous lessons in this section. Read them carefully. Then write a conclusion and a title. Reread your story. Do any necessary rewriting. Make a final copy of your story. Proofread it carefully. Put your narrative into your folder.

The Descriptive Composition

Take a Good Look

How To Plan a Descriptive Composition

Here's the Idea   A descriptive composition paints a picture with words. For a topic, choose an object or scene with enough details to develop the composition fully. Also be sure that your topic is narrow enough to cover it well.

After choosing your topic, make pre-writing notes. Use your senses to find and list details.

Then, use spatial order to organize your notes. Know how the objects in the scene or background are placed in relation to each other. You may want to use such transitions as *behind, beside, in front of, inside, on top of, under,* and *to the left.*

The **introduction** is the first paragraph of your composition. The topic sentence of this paragraph will tell your reader what your entire composition is about. The paragraph should make your reader want to read the rest of it.

The **body** of your composition follows the introduction. Each paragraph will have a topic sentence that gives the main idea of that paragraph. Use details to develop each topic sentence.

The **conclusion** is the final paragraph of your composition. It will also have a topic sentence. It will pull together all the ideas from the body of your composition and bring it to a close.

Check It Out   Look at these pre-writing notes.

Topic	my science lab
Introduction	science lab, most exciting room in school
	odors of gas, chemicals
	lots of noise
	special equipment

Body   classroom
           teacher's demonstration table (front)
           supply cabinet (left), tropical fish tank (right)
       my table
           Bunsen burner (left), test tubes (right)
           sink, chrome faucets (center)
       balance
           horizontal bar, chains
           pans and weights

Conclusion   I like all experiments—challenging, exciting
           future career as research scientist
           spend every day in a science lab

- What will be the main idea of this composition?
- What main ideas will be used to develop the body of the composition? What details describe the science lab?
- In what order are the objects arranged?

Try Your Skill Write a set of notes for a descriptive composition about any classroom you like. Use the notes in **Check It Out** as a model. List notes under *Introduction, Body* and *Conclusion*. Include notes for spatial order.

Keep This in Mind

- Choose and narrow a topic for a description.
- Decide what main ideas and details you will use.
- Use transitions that show spatial order.

Now Write On your paper, write the title of this lesson, **Take a Good Look.** Choose and narrow a topic for a descriptive composition. Choose a topic that interests you. Write and organize notes for your composition. Label your paper *Notes* and put it into your folder.

Narrow the Field

How To Write an Introduction

Here's the Idea The introduction for a descriptive composition usually describes the setting. That is, you describe the location of your subject. If you are describing an object, describe its surroundings. If you are describing a scene, describe what the scene is like. This paragraph should be interesting enough to make the reader want to continue reading.

One sentence of the introduction must serve as the topic sentence for the whole composition. It informs the reader of the specific object or area that you are going to describe. For example, if you were writing about a football stadium, your topic sentence might be, "The Superdome in New Orleans is the most spectacular football stadium in the country."

Check It Out Read the two introductions below.

1   Our science lab is the most exciting classroom in school. Something is always happening there. As we work, we can smell the chemicals. We can hear gas hissing, water splashing, and test tubes clinking. Everywhere in the lab we are busy with special equipment, like Bunsen burners, test tubes, and balances.

2   The carnival was back in town. This year it completely filled the large vacant lot near the railroad bridge. The Ferris wheel and the roller coaster loomed in the background. Other rides were set up along the river to the left. I spent most of my time in the central area where the game booths were located.

· What is the topic sentence in each introduction?

- How does each introduction focus on its topic? Which introduction has an object for a topic? Which has a scene for a topic? Is each paragraph interesting?

Try Your Skill   Below are some pre-writing notes for an introduction to a descriptive composition. Using these notes, along with details from your imagination, write an introduction.

Topic   our home economics classroom

Introduction   home ec. room—4 superkitchens in 1
sounds—pots and pans, water, laughing
mouth-watering smells—blueberry muffins, bread
good tastes—pizza, apple pie
stainless steel sinks (along one wall)
storage cabinets (back)
wall of windows (to courtyard)
counter space (wall near door)
stove—where something good is cooking (?)

Keep This in Mind

- An introduction for a descriptive composition should describe the location of the scene or object. It should make the reader want to continue reading.
- One sentence of the introduction should serve as the topic sentence for the whole composition.

Now Write   Take out your composition notes from the last lesson. On your paper, write the title of this lesson, **Narrow the Field.** Use your notes to write an introduction to your composition.

Label your paper *Introduction.*

Put your work into your folder.

It Makes Sense

How To Use Sensory Details

Here's the Idea The **body** of a descriptive composition should present a clear word picture to the reader. The more vivid and specific your details are, the better your word picture will be. To find and create vivid details, use each of your senses.

Not every object or scene affects all the senses. Food can be tasted, but it is not always heard. You can see a tree, but wouldn't taste it. However, you should try to use as many of your senses as possible. Test each sense in turn. Here are some questions you might ask for each sense.

Sight: What is its color? its shape? its size?
Touch: Is it hot or cold? rough or smooth?
Sound: How does it sound when tapped? crumpled? stretched?
Smell: Is the smell strong or weak? pleasant or unpleasant?
Taste: Is the taste pleasant or unpleasant? Sweet, sour, salty, spicy, or bitter?

List all the details you can think of to describe the object or scene. Test all your senses. Then, cross out the weak details. When you finish, you should have a complete description.

Check It Out This is the body of the composition about the science lab. Notice the spatial order.

On Ms. Burnham's demonstration table in front of the lab, an experiment is often in progress. Above the green chalkboard to the rear is a huge periodic chart printed in several colors. In the cabinet to the left of the chalkboard are shelves of brown bottles filled with strong-smelling chemicals. To the right, the pump on the fish tank hums as the water in the tank bubbles.

On the left of my lab table, a Bunsen burner, attached to the gas jet, gives off a blue flame. A deep, stainless steel sink is in the center of my table. Above it arch two long-necked chrome faucets that spit thin jets of hot and cold water. The force of the water can make a beaker ring. Each of the test tubes in the rack to my right contains a different and colorful substance.

The balance is at the right front of my table. A thin black bar balances on a vertical pivot. Three fine, linked chains hang from each end of the bar and hold a polished brass pan. A small, varnished box nearby holds brass weights shaped like old-fashioned milk cans. The weights make a clinking sound when I put them onto the pans.

- Point out the sensory details in these paragraphs. Which senses are mentioned?

Try Your Skill Below is a descriptive paragraph about a motorcycle. It lacks vivid sensory details and a logical order. Ask yourself sensory questions about it. Use your imagination. Try to find vivid details for at least three senses. On your paper, rewrite the paragraph, supplying and organizing vivid details.

My sister's motorcycle is a beauty. It has rugged trail tires. There's a fancy instrument panel between the handlebars. The engine under the gas tank is powerful. The seat and passenger cushions are made of leather.

Keep This in Mind
- Use sensory details to develop a description.

Now Write Take out your notes and introduction from the last two lessons. Write the title of this lesson, **It Makes Sense.** Revise your notes by adding sensory details.

Then write the body of your composition.

Label your paper *Body* and put it into your folder.

How Do You Respond?

How To Conclude a Description

Here's the Idea Write a strong, clear ending to your descriptive composition. Your reader should know that it is finished.

First, look at the topic sentences for each of your paragraphs in the body of your composition. These are the main ideas that you used to develop your topic. Think about how you can pull all these ideas together to summarize the main idea of your composition. Try to say them in a different way. Don't merely copy them.

Second, think about why you are telling the reader about your topic. Why is it interesting or important to you? You can share your feelings in such a way that the reader will feel as close as you do to your subject. In this way, the conclusion will re-emphasize the main idea of your composition. This main idea was stated in the topic sentence of your introduction.

Sometimes it's possible to end your description on a light or humorous note. Let your attitude about your topic be your guide.

Check It Out Read the conclusion below.

> Each day in the science lab is a new experience. The sounds and smells are exciting. Working with all the special equipment is challenging. I'm improving my skills every day. Some day I hope to be a research scientist. Then I will be able to work in a lab every day.

- How does the writer feel about the place he has described?

- Does the conclusion pull all the main ideas in the composition together?

Try Your Skill Imagine that you are writing a descriptive composition about a place where you and your friends like to meet.

Why do you like this place?

How do you think you'll feel about it many years in the future?

Write a conclusion to an imaginary composition about this place. Use the ideas that reflect how you feel about your topic. Use your imagination. Try to make your readers feel what you feel.

Keep This in Mind

- In the conclusion to a descriptive composition, tell how you feel about what you are describing.
- The conclusion should pull all the main ideas together.

Now Write Read over the composition you have been writing in the past three lessons. Review the notes for your conclusion. On your paper, write the title of this lesson, **How Do You Respond?** Then write the conclusion to your descriptive composition.

Make any necessary revisions so that your introduction, body, and conclusion fit smoothly together. Proofread your work for spelling and punctuation. Write a title for your composition.

Make a final copy of your descriptive composition. Put your work into your folder.

The Explanatory Composition

Telling *How*

How Is It Done?

How To Plan an Explanation

Here's the Idea An explanatory *how* composition explains the steps in a process. You might explain how to do something, such as how to use a CB radio. You might want to explain how to make something, like a belt.

Plan a *how* composition as you would a *how* paragraph. That is, explain the steps in a process in the order that they happen. Start at the beginning and proceed to the end. It is important that your explanation be in the correct time order. It is equally important that your explanation be accurate.

The title of an explanatory *how* composition should indicate clearly what the composition will be about. Mention the topic in the title. You might use the word *how*. Suppose that you wanted to give a recipe for garlic bread. Your title might be "How To Make Garlic Bread." The reader will know right away what the composition is about.

Check It Out Read these pre-writing notes.

How To Make Vegetable Soup

1. Select firm, fresh vegetables.
   4 or 5 different kinds
   different colors, different flavors
2. Prepare vegetables.
   clean, peel, cut into bite-sized pieces
   use cutting board, sharp knife
3. Combine and cook ingredients.
   vegetables
   beef or chicken broth
   simmer one hour

4. Season and serve.
    season to taste
    serve with bread and cheese

- What process do these steps explain?
- How are these steps arranged?
- Are there details? Do they seem accurate?
- Is the title clear?

Try Your Skill   Below are titles and notes for two explanatory *how* compositions. However, the steps in the process are not listed in the correct order. Copy the titles on your paper. Below each title, list the steps in the correct order.

How To Build a Doghouse
   Assemble lumber
   Cut lumber
   Paint doghouse
   Measure lumber

How To Make Popcorn
   Shake ingredients over high heat
   Measure oil and popcorn
   Combine ingredients in pan
   Serve, with salt

Keep This in Mind

- Explanatory *how* compositions explain the steps in a process. They explain how to do something or how to make something.
- Arrange the steps in the order that they happen.
- Make sure your details are accurate.
- Use key words in your title to indicate clearly what the composition will be about.

Now Write   On your paper, write the title of this lesson, **How Is It Done?** List two processes you could explain in a composition. One should be about how to do something. One should be about how to make something. Write a possible title for each topic. Put your work into your folder.

One Step at a Time

How To Use Step-by-Step Order

Here's the Idea A good way to organize an explanatory *how* composition is to follow this plan: introduction, steps in the process, and conclusion.

One sentence of the introduction should serve as the topic sentence for the composition. If your topic is how to prepare vegetable soup, the topic sentence might be "Vegetable soup is nutritious, delicious, and easy to prepare."

In the following paragraphs, give a step-by-step explanation. For example, you might divide the preparation of vegetable soup into getting the ingredients, preparing the vegetables, and cooking the soup. Each of these steps would be discussed in separate paragraphs. You would develop each paragraph with details from your notes. You must be specific, accurate, and complete.

Develop the concluding paragraph from the final step, seasoning and serving the soup. Tie up any loose ends. Make sure your reader knows your composition is ended.

Check It Out Read the body of an explanatory *how* composition about making vegetable soup.

First, choose a variety of vegetables. Four or five vegetables of different colors and textures will make the soup good-looking as well as good-tasting. Different vegetables will supply the vitamins needed for a nutritious meal. Some choices are carrots, potatoes, beans, and onions. All vegetables you use should look bright, feel firm, and not be bruised or wilted.

After selecting the ingredients, you must prepare them. First, clean the vegetables in cold water. Carrots, potatoes, and onions should be peeled. Then slice or dice all the vegetables into bite-sized pieces. Use a cutting board and a sharp knife.

When the vegetables have been cut up, combine the vegetables in a deep pot. Then pour in chicken or beef broth. Next, add salt, pepper, and any other seasonings you like. After that, stir the soup over high heat. When it begins to boil, lower the heat, cover the pot, and simmer an hour.

- What steps are explained?

Try Your Skill Below is the body of a composition explaining how to take pictures of stars. However, these three steps are not organized correctly. Write them in correct step-by-step order.

Then point your camera at the stars. Center it on the North Star, which appears as the most stable star in the sky. Next, set your camera for a time exposure of one hour or more.

Begin by choosing a clear night for your photography. Find an open field that is away from lights and buildings. When you have a clear view of the stars, mount your camera on the tripod.

During the exposure, sit back and let the camera do its work. Your only job is to avoid bumping or shaking the camera.

Keep This in Mind

- In the introduction of an explanatory *how* composition, introduce your topic. Make one sentence serve as the topic sentence for the composition.
- In the body give a step-by-step explanation.
- Develop the concluding paragraph from the final step of the process. Tie up loose ends.

Now Write Write the title of this lesson, **One Step at a Time.** Look at the processes you listed in **How Is It Done?** Choose one you could explain easily. List details for each step in the process. Write the body of the composition. Give a step-by-step explanation. Put your work into your folder.

Bridge the Gaps

How To Use Transitions

Here's the Idea Transitional words and phrases are important for making the step-by-step order of an explanatory *how* composition clear. They are similar to transitions used for narratives. They indicate time order. Look at the examples below.

first	the next step	when	before
second	after that	finally	as soon as
then	at the same time	last	afterwards

Transitions are used within a paragraph to help make clear the order in the paragraph. Transitions are also used to link paragraphs. They work like a bridge to carry the reader from the main idea of one paragraph to the main idea of the next.

Check It Out Here are the introduction and conclusion of the composition on making soup. First, review the body of the explanation in the last lesson. Which transitions are used within each paragraph? Which transitions link the three paragraphs?

Now, read these two paragraphs. Notice how they are linked to the body of the composition.

Introduction

What food warms your insides and brings a smile to your face? What tastes great for lunch on a chilly day? Homemade soup. It's everyone's favorite. Vegetable soup is especially nutritious, delicious, and easy to prepare. You can make it by following a few simple steps.

Conclusion

In a short time, the vegetables will become tender and full of flavor. After you have adjusted the seasonings, serve this easy-to-make meal in big bowls. Crusty bread and cheese are good with this soup. Anyone who tastes this hot, hearty, healthful treat will want seconds. People everywhere love vegetable soup.

- Are any transitions used within the introduction or the conclusion? What are they?
- Are there any transitions that link the introduction or the conclusion to the body? What are they?

Try Your Skill Below is a paragraph about how clouds are formed. The transitions are missing. Copy the paragraph. Make the order in the paragraph clear by adding clear transitions.

_____ rain water soaks into the soil. _____ underground water seeps into small streams. _____ the streams empty into rivers. _____ the rivers flow into lakes and oceans. _____ the water from large bodies of water evaporates into the air.

Keep This in Mind

- Time transitions help make the order of explanatory _how_ compositions clear.
- Time transitions make the order of each paragraph clear.
- Some time transitions link the main idea of one paragraph with the main idea of the next paragraph.

Now Write On your paper, write the title of this lesson, **Bridge the Gaps.** From your folder take out the body of the composition you wrote in **One Step at a Time.** Add the transitional words you will need within each paragraph.

Write an introduction and a conclusion to your explanatory _how_ composition. Add transitions between paragraphs. Add a title. Do whatever rewriting is necessary. Make a final copy of your composition. Proofread your work. Put it into your folder.

Writing Letters

Hi There!

How To Write a Friendly Letter

Here's the Idea A **friendly letter** is one that you write to someone you know. It should be interesting, neat, and easy to read. A friendly letter should seem as natural as a conversation. Share your feelings. Ask questions. Comment in detail on subjects that interest you. Keep your language lively and specific.

The form for a friendly letter has five main parts: the *heading*, the *salutation* or greeting, the *body* or main part, the *closing*, and the *signature*.

The **heading** tells where you are. When you are writing, the heading appears in the upper right corner of the page. It usually includes two lines for the address and one for the date.

The **salutation** is the way you say "hello." It is written on the next line and begins at the left margin.

The **body,** the main part of the letter, starts on the next line. In the body of the letter you talk to your friend. If the letter is lively, it will make your friend feel as though you were there in person. The first word of the body is indented. Each new paragraph of the body is indented, too.

The **closing** says "goodbye." It is written on the line below the last sentence of the body. The closing should line up with the first line of the heading.

The **signature** is the last part of your letter. Skip a line after the closing and sign your name in line with the first word of the closing. When you are writing a friendly letter to someone you know well, use your first name as your signature. Otherwise, sign your full name.

Every main part begins with a capitalized word. The greeting and closing are followed by commas.

Check It Out Read the friendly letter below.

- What details make this letter interesting?
- Identify the five parts of this letter.

361 Newton Road
New York City, New York 10001
March 11, 1980

Hi Juan,

It sure was good to hear from you. I'm glad to hear you are doing so well in math this year. After the trouble you had with it last year, I'm sure you must be feeling relieved.

School has been hard for me this year. I have five main subjects, including French.

One bright spot has been the school paper. I have been doing drawings for it this year and am really enjoying it. Who knows, maybe next year I'll have my own comic strip. Keep in touch, and let me know when you're coming to New York again. I'll throw a big party for you when you visit!

Your friend,
Marty

Try Your Skill Here's a friendly letter that has some problems. Read the letter and decide what's wrong with it. Write a few sentences explaining what should be changed.

27 Whitcomb Street
Price, Utah 84501
January 5, 1980

dear Ronnie,
   Happy New Year. I miss you. I hope you can make it out here this year. School is OK. Not much news to tell. I just wanted to say hello.

Sincerely,
Gerry

Now Write Write **Hi There!** at the top of your paper. Then write a friendly letter to a friend or relative. Label each part. Put your labeled letter into your folder.

A Good Send-off

How To Prepare Letters for the Mail

Here's the Idea Once you've written your letter, fold it neatly. Use an envelope that matches the width of the stationery. Carefully insert the letter into the envelope. Seal the envelope.

Follow these steps for preparing your envelope:

1. Address the envelope. Add your return address.
2. Double-check all numbers to make sure they are in the proper order.
3. Include the correct ZIP code. To learn the correct use of ZIP codes and state abbreviations see page 447.
4. Put a stamp on your envelope.

Addressing the envelope accurately will get your letter to the right place. Get in the habit of checking your letters and packages for accuracy. Call your local post office if you need more information.

Check It Out Look at the envelope below.

Ms. Gwen Linehan
1607 Stratford Street
Big Sky, MT 59716

Dr. Samuel Collins
147 Barnes Road
Farwell, NE 68838

- To whom is the letter being sent? Who sent the letter?
- How could you check to be sure that the state abbreviations and ZIP codes are correct?

Try Your Skill Write each of the addresses below as it should appear on an envelope. Also write a return address.

1. Kate Lawrence, 24 Hampton Road, New Orleans, LA 70118
2. Mr. and Mrs. Peter Donovan, 7318 Skyline Drive, Washington, D.C. 20008
3. Anthony Colelli, 4325 Broadway Boulevard, Apartment 2-C, Oakland, CA 94602
4. Martha Woodworth, 7 Churchill Lane, Durham, NH 03824
5. James O'Shea, 281 Chestnut Street, Phoenix, Arizona 85040

Keep This in Mind

- Prepare your letter correctly. Fold your letter neatly, and use an envelope that matches the width of the stationery.
- Check addresses for neatness and accuracy. Check abbreviations of states and correct ZIP codes.
- Put your return address on the envelope.

Now Write Take out the friendly letter you wrote in the last lesson, **Hi There!**

On your paper, write the title of this lesson, **A Good Send-off.** Draw a rectangle to represent an envelope. Address it as though you were going to mail it to your friend.

Copy your work onto a real envelope. Fold your letter and put it into the envelope.

Mail your letter. Don't forget a stamp.

Keep your paper in your folder.

Thank You

How To Write Social Notes

Here's the Idea Invitations and thank-you notes are both short forms of friendly letters. They use the same five-part format. The heading may be shortened to include only the date.

An **invitation** should include all the information that the other person needs. Tell what kind of occasion you are inviting him or her to. Tell where and when the occasion will take place. If you wish to know if the person will attend, write R.S.V.P. at the bottom of the invitation. R.S.V.P. is an abbreviation for a French phrase that means "please reply."

If you receive an invitation, reply as soon as possible. Thank the person for inviting you. Then tell whether or not you can come. If you can't come, express your regrets and give a short explanation.

There are two kinds of thank-you notes. One kind of **thank-you** note is usually written after you have received a present. If a gift was mailed to you, the thank-you note tells the sender that the gift arrived. It also thanks the person for being kind. If you liked the gift, say so. If you didn't like it, you can still thank the sender for her or his thoughtfulness and effort.

Another kind of thank-you note is called a **bread-and-butter** note. This kind of letter thanks someone for his or her hospitality rather than for a gift. You would write a bread-and-butter note after you stayed overnight at someone's house.

Both kinds of thank-you letters should show your appreciation for what the other person has done for you. Also, both kinds of letters should be written as soon as possible after you receive a gift or someone's hospitality.

Check It Out Read the thank-you note below.

February 8, 1980

Dear Mr. and Mrs. Cullen,

You were very nice to let me spend last weekend with you. I want you to know how much I appreciate it. I had never been on roller skates before, and that by itself was a great treat.

I hope you get the chance to visit me in Jonesboro sometime. Then your family can stay here, and I can return the hospitality. Thanks for everything.

Sincerely,
Hank Reidell

- What type of social note is this? How is the form of this letter different from the friendly letter shown in **Hi There!** in this section?

- What words and phrases are used to express appreciation in this letter?

Try Your Skill Read the thank-you note on the next page. Then rewrite it, correcting any errors that you find.

Dear Ms. Bert,

Thanks for the sweater. It is not really my favorite color, but it's a nice sweater. I guess you didn't know that I don't like blue. Hope everyone is fine at your house.

Robin

Keep This in Mind

- Social notes, like invitations and thank-you notes, are short forms of friendly letters. They have a heading, salutation, body, closing, and signature, in that order.
- An invitation should tell *what*, *when*, and *where*.
- Thank-you notes thank people for the thoughtfulness of their gifts and their hospitality.

Now Write On your paper, write the title of this lesson, **Thank You.** Imagine that one of your relatives has sent you a pair of purple sneakers for your birthday. Another has sent you a book by your favorite author. Write a thank-you note to each relative.

Put your work into your folder.

Get Down to Business

How To Write a Business Letter

Here's the Idea Many times you will need to write a letter requesting information, ordering products, or complaining about a product. Such letters are called **business letters.**

The two types of business letter forms are *modified block form* and *block form.* In the modified block form the paragraphs are indented, and the closing and signature are in line with the heading, just as in a friendly letter. This form may be used for both handwritten and typed business letters.

The *block* form for a business letter is used only when the letter is typewritten. All the parts of the letter begin at the left margin. The paragraphs are not indented. Instead, there is a double space between paragraphs.

In both forms, the address you are writing to is placed above the salutation. Begin this address at the left margin. If you are writing to a specific person, use *Dear* and the person's name in the salutation. Otherwise, use a general greeting such as *Dear Sir or Madam.* All salutations begin two lines after the inside address and end with a colon (:).

Always be brief and to the point in a business letter. Also, it's a good idea to make a copy of business letters for your records. If you make a carbon copy, mail the original.

Check It Out Look at the business letter on page 155.

- What is the purpose of this business letter?
- Identify the six parts of the letter.
- In what form is this letter written?

39 Hastings Street
Dodge City, Kansas 67801
February 5, 1980

Sales Manager
Old West Nostalgia Shop
4736 Madison Street
Elko, Nevada 89801

Dear Madam or Sir:

My hobby is collecting items related to the American West. My favorite hero is Wild Bill Hickok, who, like me, spent most of his life in Kansas.

Please send me the catalog of your collection called "Heroes of the West." I am enclosing $2.95 for the catalog, plus $1.00 postage.

Yours truly,
Mary Lou Taylor

Try Your Skill Below are the six parts of a business letter. On your paper, write them in the correct modified block form. Use the correct punctuation.

Heading

14 Boundbrook Road
Nutley, New Jersey 07110
March 13, 1981

Signature

Thomas Presti

Body

Please send me two dozen personalized pencils. Use my full name on each. Enclosed is my check for $6.50 to cover the cost of the pencils, handling, and postage.

Closing

Yours truly

Salutation

Dear Sir or Madam

Inside Address

Sales Manager
Conway Stationery Company
2149 Northern Avenue
East Orange, New Jersey 07019

Keep This in Mind

- Business letters are written to request information, order products, or complain about a product. They should be brief and to the point.
- The six parts of a business letter are: *heading, inside address, salutation, body, closing,* and *signature.*
- *Block* and *modified* block are two forms for a business letter.

Now Write On your paper, write the title of this lesson, **Get Down to Business.** Use one of the two forms for a business letter to write to a company in your town. You might want to request information, order a product, or complain about a product. Keep your letter in your folder.

Please Send Me

How To Write a Letter of Request

Here's the Idea One type of business letter requests information. It should be brief and specific. The more precise your request is, the easier it will be for the reader to reply. However, be sure to include all the necessary information.

Explain *what*. Ask only for the information you need. If you want a timetable for flights between Chicago and Houston, name the two cities. If you also want a list of fares, don't forget to say so.

Explain *when*. If you plan to fly to Houston on June 19, say so.

Explain *why*. Sometimes you may want to tell briefly why you are writing, if it's important.

Always be polite and appreciative. Remember that you are asking someone for help.

Check It Out Look at the letter of request on page 158. Read it carefully. Then answer these questions.

- Is this letter of request brief and polite?
- Is all the necessary information requested? Does it explain *what, when,* and *why?*

Try Your Skill On page 159 is a letter of request. It has some problems. First, read the letter carefully. Then rewrite the letter. Use the correct form. Be brief, specific, and polite.

76 Linden Lane
Kankakee, Illinois 60901
April 14, 1980

Midwest Airways.
188 Lake Towers
Chicago, Illinois 60607

Dear Sir or Madam:
    Please send me your June 1980 timetable for flights between Chicago, Illinois, and Houston, Texas.   I also need a listing of all available rates.
    My local travel agency has run out of timetables.   They suggested that I contact you directly.
    Thank you for your help.

                                    Yours truly,
                                    Sarah Kaplan

Keep This in Mind

·   Business letters of request should be brief, specific, and polite.
·   Ask only for the information you need. Include *what*, *when*, and *why*.

Sales Manager
Kelly Flagpole Company
Morristown, New Jersey
07960

13 Ross Way
Prospect, Kentucky 40059
June 25, 1979

Dear Sir,

Well, we finally did it. We bought a flag that's too big for our pole. Now we need a new pole.

A guy at my V.F.W. post told me you sell aluminum and wooden poles. He said your prices were higher than your poles. How much would a thirty-foot pole cost?

If I ordered it right away, when could you guarantee delivery? I'll need it by the Fourth.

I'll expect your answer in three days at the latest, as I don't have much time to waste.

Edgar T. Welsh

Now Write On your paper, write the title of this lesson, **Please Send Me.** Write a letter requesting information about something you are interested in. Use a real address, or make up an address for the company, college, or organization to which you are writing. Keep your letter in your folder.

Using a Dictionary

Look It Up

How To Use a Dictionary

Here's the Idea English has over 600,000 words, more than any other language. Few people know more than a small fraction of them. Everybody needs a dictionary.

What is a dictionary? It is a reference book containing both a list of words in a language and information about the words. The listing itself is valuable because it shows you that a word exists. The information is valuable because it helps you determine how to use words correctly.

The words in a dictionary are listed in alphabetical order. In a dictionary, words that begin with *a* come before words that begin with *b*, and so on. If two words begin with the same letter, they are alphabetized by the second letter. If the first and second letters are the same, look at the next letter. The following columns of words are in alphabetical order:

admire	hold	schedule	yank
always	holdout	scheme	yarn
at	holiday	school	yawn

Not all dictionaries are alike. Some dictionaries list only words in special fields like music or medicine. Bigger dictionaries may contain more words and a more detailed explanation of each word. The biggest dictionaries, like those on stands in the library, are unabridged. That means they contain just about all the words in the language. An unabridged dictionary is useful when you need to look up an uncommon word.

Most of the time, though, a desk- or pocket-size dictionary, which is abridged, will suit your needs. It's helpful to keep one of these handy when you're reading or writing. It will help you understand difficult words when you're reading. It will also help you use words correctly when you're writing.

Dictionaries also vary in organization, symbols, and abbreviations. For this reason, it's a good idea to become familiar with the dictionary that you will use most often. Learn how the information for each word is organized. Study the explanatory material in the front of the dictionary to learn what the abbreviations and symbols stand for.

Check It Out   Look at this portion of a dictionary page.

fire·fly (-flī′) n., pl. **-flies′** a small, flying beetle whose lower body glows with a light that goes off and on

☆**fire·house** (-hous′) n. same as FIRE STATION

fire insurance insurance against loss or damage resulting from fire

fire·light (-līt′) n. light from an open fire

fire·man (-mən) n., pl. **-men** 1. a man whose work is fighting fires 2. a man who tends a fire in a furnace, locomotive engine, etc. ☆3. U.S. Navy a nonrated enlisted man whose duties are concerned with the ship's engines, etc. ☆4. [Slang] Baseball a relief pitcher

Fi·ren·ze (fē ren′dze) It. name of FLORENCE, Italy

fire·place (fīr′plās′) n. a place for a fire, esp. an open place built in a wall, at the base of a chimney

fire·plug (-plug′) n. a street hydrant to which a hose can be attached for fighting fires

fire·pow·er (-pou′ər) n. Mil. 1. the effectiveness of a weapon in terms of its accuracy and the number of shots it can fire 2. the number of shots a given unit can fire in a short time

fire·proof (-proof′) adj. that does not burn or is not easily destroyed by fire —vt. to make fireproof

☆**fire sale** a sale of goods damaged in a fire

fire·side (-sīd′) n. 1. the part of a room near a fireplace; hearth 2. home or home life

fire station the place where fire engines are kept and where firemen stay when on duty

fire·storm (-stôrm′) n. an intense fire over a large area, as one caused by an atomic explosion

fire tower a tower, usually in a forest, where a lookout is posted to watch for fires and give the alarm

fire·trap (-trap′) n. a building that would be unsafe in case of fire because it will burn easily or does not have enough exits

☆**fire wall** a fireproof wall for preventing the spread of fire, as from one room to the next

☆**fire·wa·ter** (-wôt′ər, -wät′ər) n. [prob. transl. of AmInd. term] alcoholic liquor: now humorous

☆**fire·weed** (-wēd′) n. any of various plants that grow readily on cleared or burned-over land

fire·wood (-wood′) n. wood used as fuel

fire·works (-wurks′) n.pl. 1. firecrackers, rockets, etc. used, as in celebrations, to produce loud noises or a fancy show of lights:

FIREFLY
(to ½ in. long)

highest in pitch or the leading part —adv. 1. a) before any other person or thing [guests are served first] b) before doing anything else [first we had soup] 2. as the first point [first, let me say this] 3. for the first time [I first met him yesterday] 4. sooner; preferably [when told to beg, he said he'd starve first] —n. 1. the first person, thing, class, place, etc. 2. the first day of the month 3. the beginning; start [at first, I believed him] 4. a first happening or thing of its kind 5. [pl.] the best quality of merchandise 6. the winning place, as in a race 7. the first or lowest forward gear ratio of a motor vehicle

first aid emergency treatment for injury or sudden illness, given while waiting for regular medical care —first′-aid′ adj.

☆**first base** Baseball the base on the pitcher's left, the first of the four bases a runner must touch in succession to score a run

first·born (furst′bôrn′) adj. born first in a family; oldest —n. the firstborn child

first-class (-klas′) adj. 1. of the highest class, rank, quality, etc.; excellent 2. of the most expensive kind [a first-class cabin on a ship] ☆3. designating or of mail that is sealed and that carries the highest regular postage rates —adv. 1. with the most expensive accommodations [traveling first-class] 2. as or by first-class mail

first cousin the son or daughter of one's aunt or uncle

first finger the finger next to the thumb

first·hand (-hand′) adj., adv. from the original producer or source; direct [a firsthand report]

☆**first lady** [often F- L-] the wife of the U.S. president

first lieutenant a U.S. military officer ranking above a second lieutenant

first·ling (-liŋ) n. 1. the first of a kind 2. the first fruit, produce, offspring, etc.

first·ly (-lē) adv. in the first place; first

first mate a merchant ship's officer next in rank below the captain: also **first officer**

first offender a person found guilty for the first time of breaking the law

first person that form of a pronoun (as I or we) or verb (as do) which refers to the speaker or speakers

first-rate (-rāt′) adj. of the highest class, rank, or quality; excellent —adv. [Colloq.] very well [I feel first-rate]

☆**first sergeant** U.S. Army & Marine Corps the noncommissioned officer, usually a master sergeant, serving as chief assistant to the commander of a company, battery, etc.

☆**first-string** (-striŋ′) adj. [Colloq.] Sports that is the first choice for regular play at a specified position [our first-string quarterback]

- How are the words listed?
- What special symbols are used?
- What words are new to you?

Try Your Skill On your paper, write each of the following lists in alphabetical order. Then look up one word from each list in a dictionary and write the first meaning given.

1.	2.	3.	4.
cake	goat	none	stick
easy	give	now	still
army	get	noon	stitch
friend	great	note	stiff
barn	glum	nob	stir
duck	ghost	nose	sting

Keep This in Mind

- Dictionaries are reference books that list words alphabetically. They give explanations for each word.
- Have a dictionary nearby when you're reading and writing.
- Become familiar with the organization, symbols, and abbreviations of the dictionaries you use.

Now Write Imagine you are a person who compiles dictionaries. On your paper, write the title of this lesson, **Look It Up.** Write ten words that begin with the first letter of your last name. Then put the words into alphabetical order.

Write a short definition for each word. Check your work in a dictionary.

Put your work into your folder.

Show Me the Way

How To Use Guide Words

Here's the Idea In most dictionaries there are two **guide words** at the top of each page. They are in large, bold print. The left guide word is the same as the first word at the top of the page. The right guide word is the same as the last word at the bottom of the page. All the other words on the page are arranged alphabetically between the guide words. Look at the top portion of the dictionary page shown below.

grew   417   **gripe**

where, formerly, many eloping English couples went to be married   **2.** any similar village
grew (grōō) *pt. of* GROW
grew·some (grōō'səm) *adj. same as* GRUESOME
grey (grā) *adj., n., vt., vi.* Brit. *sp. of* GRAY
Grey (grā) **1. Charles,** 2d Earl Grey, 1764–1845; Eng. statesman; prime minister (1830–34) **2.** Sir **Edward,** Viscount Grey of Fallodon, 1862–1933; Eng. statesman; foreign secretary (1905–16) **3.** Lady **Jane,** Lady Jane Dudley, 1537–54; queen of England (July 10–19, 1553): beheaded
grey·hound (grā'hound') *n.* [OE. *grighund*] any of a breed of tall, slender, swift hound with a narrow, pointed head and a smooth coat
grid (grid) *n.* [short for GRIDIRON] **1.** a framework of parallel bars; gridiron; grating **2.** a network of crossing parallel lines, as on graph paper **3.** a metallic plate in a storage cell for conducting the electric current **4.** an electrode, usually a wire spiral or mesh, for controlling the passage of electrons or ions in an electron tube —☆*adj.* [Slang] of football
☆**grid·der** (grid'ər) *n.* [< GRID, *adj.* & GRIDIRON] [Slang] a football player
grid·dle (grid'l) *n.* [< Anglo-Fr. *gridil* < OFr. *graïl* < L. < *craticula*, gridiron < *cratis*: see CRATE] a flat, metal plate or pan for cooking pancakes, etc. —*vt.* **-dled, -dling** to cook on a grid-

GREYHOUND (28 in. high at shoulder)

grill·room (gril'rōōm') *n.* a restaurant that makes a specialty of grilled foods
grill·work (-wurk') *n.* a grille, or something worked into the form of a grille
grilse (grils) *n., pl.* **grilse, grils'es:** see PLURAL, II, D, 2 [<? OFr. dim. of *gris*, gray] a young salmon on its first return from the sea to fresh water
grim (grim) *adj.* **grim'mer, grim'mest** [OE. *grimm* < IE. base *ghrem*-, angry] **1.** fierce; cruel; savage *[war is grim]* **2.** hard and unyielding; relentless; stern *[grim courage]* **3.** appearing stern, forbidding, harsh, etc. *[a grim face]* **4.** frightful or shocking; ghastly *[grim jokes about death]* —see SYN. at GHASTLY —**grim'ly** *adv.* —**grim'ness** *n.*
gri·mace (gri mās', grim'əs) *n.* [Fr. < OFr. *grimuche*, prob. < Frank.: for IE. base see CHRIST] a twisting of the face in fun or in a look of pain, disgust, etc. —*vi.* **-maced', -mac'ing** to make grimaces —**gri·mac'er** *n.*
gri·mal·kin (gri mal'kin, -môl'-) *n.* [earlier *gray malkin* (cat)] **1.** a cat; esp., an old female cat **2.** a spiteful or harmful old woman
grime (grīm) *n.* [prob. < Fl. *grijm:* for IE. base see CHRIST] sooty dirt rubbed into or covering a surface, as of the skin —*vt.* **grimed, grim'ing** to make very dirty or grimy
Grimm (grim), **Ja·kob (Ludwig Karl)** (yä'kôp), 1785–1863 & **Wil·helm (Karl)** (vil'helm), 1786–1859; Ger. brothers who worked in language studies and together made a collection of fairy tales

Guide words help you find words quickly. Look at them as you flip the pages searching for your word. The trick is to keep looking for guide words that are more and more like the word you need. Say that the word is *newt*. First, look for guide words beginning with *n*. Next, look for guide words beginning with *ne*. After that, look for guide words beginning with *new*. Sooner or later, you'll come to a page where the left guide word comes alphabetically before your word. Now you can look for *newt*.

Check It Out Look at the portion of a dictionary page on page 165.

· What are the guide words for this page? Would you find the word *grin* on this page? Which way would you turn the pages to find *great*?

Try Your Skill At the top of a sheet of paper, write the following sets of guide words: *back/boat, break/but, tab/tall,* and *tame/tax.* Look at the list of words below. Find the words that go below each set of guide words. Write them under the correct set in alphabetical order.

brave	tan	tape	bite
tag	take	bark	target
tarnish	brink	tactic	beef
blue	big	tacky	tax
break	breath	bring	taste

Keep This in Mind

· Dictionary guide words show the alphabetical range of words on each page. The left guide word is the same as the first word on the page. The right guide word is the same as the last word on the page.

Now Write Imagine that you are writing a composition about airplanes. You need to look up the following words: *aileron, elevator, fin, fuselage, landing gear, rudder, stabilizer,* and *wing.*

On your paper, write the title of this lesson, **Show Me the Way.** List the words above. Find each word in the dictionary. Next to each word, write the guide words that appear at the top of the page where the word is found.

Put your work into your folder.

It's All There

How To Read a Dictionary Entry

Here's the Idea   You know that a dictionary entry shows the meaning of a word. It also shows a great deal of other helpful information about a word. Take a look at all the information a dictionary entry can give you.

The **entry word** itself is in bold type and divided into syllables. For example, *mathematics* is entered as **math·e·mat·ics.**

The **pronunciation** of the word is often put inside parentheses. An accent mark tells which syllable to stress. Symbols are used to help you sound out the word. *Science,* for example, appears as (sī′əns).

The **part of speech** is given by an abbreviation in bold type. For example, *noun* is abbreviated **n.,** *adverb* is abbreviated **adv.** If you do not recognize an abbreviation, look in the front of the dictionary for an explanation. You will usually find a complete list of abbreviations used in the dictionary.

If a word can be used as more than one part of speech, the other parts of speech will be given elsewhere in the entry, usually at the end.

If a word has **special forms** or **endings,** they will be included next in the entry. For example, the entry for the irregular verb *swim* would include the forms **swam, swum,** and **swimming.** Plural forms are given for nouns.

The **origin,** or **history,** of a word is given next, often in brackets. Symbols and abbreviations are used. The symbol < means "came from." The abbreviations *ME., Gr.,* and *L.* stand for "Middle English," "Greek," and "Latin." Look up unfamiliar abbreviations in the complete list at the front of the dictionary.

Definitions are given in a numbered list. Usually, the most common definition is given first. The most common definition of the verb *guard* is "to watch over and protect." Sometimes a word will have a special meaning in a particular field. The dictionary will indicate this by naming the field. For example, one definition of *guard* is "*Sports*—to keep an opponent from making a gain or score."

A word may have a meaning that is generally used in conversation or in informal writing. This is a colloquial meaning. The dictionary indicates this by using an abbreviation. For example, one definition of *story* is "[Colloq.]a falsehood or fib."

Synonyms and **antonyms** may also be listed. For some words there may also be a *synonymy*—a group of synonyms and their shades of meaning. Or, the notation "**SYN.** *see*" may refer you to another entry.

Are you surprised by all that a dictionary entry can tell you? You can see how helpful a dictionary can be.

Entries may be somewhat different in different dictionaries. Become familiar with the way an entry is given in the dictionaries you use.

Check It Out   Look at the dictionary entry below.

fam·i·ly (fam′e lē, fam′lē) *n., pl.,* **-lies** [L. *familia*, household < *famulus*, servant] **1.** orig., all the people living in the same house; household **2.** *a*) a social unit consiting of parents and their children *b*) the children of the same parents **3.** a group of people related by ancestry or marriage; relatives **4.** all those claiming descent from a common ancestor; tribe or clan; lineage **5.** a group of things having a common source or similar features; specif., *a*) *Biol.* a category that is used in classifying plants or animals and that ranks above a genus and below an order *b*) *Linguis.* a group of languages having a common ancestral language *c*) *Math.* a set of curves, etc. with some shared property —*adj.* of or for a family

• How many syllables are there in *family*? How many pronunciations are given? What part of speech is *family*? Is it used as any other part of speech? From what language did the word come? What is the most common definition? Are there meanings used in special fields? Are any synonyms given?

Try Your Skill Turn back to the sample dictionary page in the last lesson, **Show Me the Way.** Answer the following questions.

1. How would you pronounce *grimace?* What does it mean?
2. What are the parts of speech of *grid?*
3. What are the other forms of the adjective *grim?*
4. Where does the word *greyhound* come from?
5. What is the most common definition of *grid?*
6. Where would you find synonyms for *grim?*

Keep This in Mind

- A dictionary entry contains the meanings of a word. It also contains other helpful information.
- Dictionary entries may be different in different dictionaries.

Now Write On your paper, write the title of this lesson, **It's All There.** Find the words *back, gorilla,* and *uniform* in a dictionary.

Copy two definitions that give two different meanings of the word.

Then write one sentence telling any other information you find about the word.

Put your work into your folder.

Does It Fit?

How To Find the Meaning of a Word

Here's the Idea If you see a word you don't know, you look it up in a dictionary. What if the word has several different meanings? Which would be the right one? Usually the sentence in which you found the word, the context, will help you out.

In each sentence below, the context helps you to know the meaning of the word *glass*.

1. Where did I leave my *glasses* this time? (In this sentence, *glasses* means "eyeglasses, spectacles.")
2. Would you like a *glass* of strawberry milk? (In this sentence, *glass* means "a quantity" of something.)
3. She smiled at her reflection in the *glass*. (In this sentence, *glass* means "a mirror.")

When you look up a word in the dictionary, read through all the definitions given. Try to find the meaning that best fits the word in a particular context.

Check It Out Here is part of a dictionary entry. Study it. Then read the sentence that follows.

> **court** (kôrt) *n.* [OFr. <LL. <L. *cohors:* see COHORT] **1.** an uncovered space wholly or partly surrounded by buildings or walls **2.** a short street, often closed at one end **3.** *a)* an area for playing any of several ball games [a tennis *court*] *b)* a part of such an area ☆**4.** a motel: in full, **motorcourt** **5.** *a)* the palace of a sovereign *b)* the family, advisers, etc. of a sovereign, as a group *c)* a sovereign and his councilors as a governing body *d)* any formal gathering held by a sovereign **6.** attention paid to someone in order to get something **7.** courtship; wooing **8.** *a)* a person or persons appointed to examine and decide law cases, make investigations, etc.; judge or judges *b)* a place where trials are held, investigations made, etc. *c)* an assembly or meeting of the judge or judges, the lawyers, and the jury in a law court

We reserved a handball **court** for four o'clock.

- Which definition of *court* fits the context of this sentence?

Try Your Skill Look at the dictionary entry below for the word *plug*. Some meanings are for *plug* as a noun, and some are for *plug* as a verb.

Write the number of each sentence. After it, write the meaning that matches the use of the word *plug*.

> **plug** (plug) *n.* [MDu. *plugge*] **1.** an object used to stop up a hole, drain, etc. **2.** *a*) a cake of pressed tobacco *b*) a piece of chewing tobacco **3.** a device, as with prongs that stick out, for fitting into an electric outlet, etc. to make electrical contact **4.** *same as:* *a*) SPARK PLUG *b*) FIREPLUG **5.** [Colloq.] a defective or shopworn article ☆**6.** [Slang] an old, worn-out horse ☆**7.** [Colloq.] a boost, advertisement, etc., esp. one slipped into the entertainment part of a radio or TV program, a magazine article, etc. —*vt.* **plugged, plug'ging 1.** to stop up (a hole, etc.) with a plug (often with *up*) **2.** to insert (something) as a plug *[*he *plugged* the putty in the hole*]* **3.** [Colloq.] *a*) to promote (a song) by frequent performance ☆*b*) to promote with a plug (*n.* 7) **4.** [Slang] to shoot a bullet into —*vi.* [Colloq.] to work or study hard and steadily; plod —plug in to connect (an electrical device) with an outlet, etc. by inserting a plug in a socket or jack —**plug'ger** *n.*

1.   The painters *plugged* putty into the holes.

2.   Carlton Fisk chews a *plug* of tobacco during every Boston Red Sox game.

3.   Although math is difficult for Rob, he *plugs* away at it.

4.   The performer *plugged* her new album.

5.   A mechanic replaced the *plugs* and points on the car.

Keep This in Mind

- If you don't know the meaning of a word, look it up. Read all the definitions. The context of the sentence will help you find the right meaning.

Now Write Look up the word *strike* in your dictionary. On your paper, write the title of this lesson, **Does It Fit?** Copy four different meanings of *strike*. For each meaning, write a sentence. Put your work into your folder.

Using the Library

A Good Place To Go

How To Use the Library

Here's the Idea Almost anything you might want to read for pleasure or research is available to you in your school or public library. Do you know where to find what you need? Do you know how materials are arranged?

The books in the library are divided into two groups, **fiction** and **nonfiction.** Fiction books are arranged alphabetically on the shelves according to the author's last name. For example, *Johnny Tremain,* written by Esther Forbes, would be shelved under **F.**

Most libraries arrange nonfiction books according to the **Dewey Decimal System.** This system puts books into ten major categories. Each category has its own set of numbers. Nonfiction books are arranged numerically on the library shelves by their Dewey Decimal number. The ten categories are listed below.

000–099	**General Works**	(encyclopedias, almanacs)
100–199	**Philosophy**	(conduct, psychology)
200–299	**Religion**	(the Bible, mythology)
300–399	**Social Science**	(economics, law, education, government)
400–499	**Language**	(languages, grammar, dictionaries)
500–599	**Science**	(mathematics, biology, chemistry)
600–699	**Useful Arts**	(farming, cooking, sewing, television, business)
700–799	**Fine Arts**	(music, photography, games, sports)
800–899	**Literature**	(poetry, plays)
900–999	**History**	(biography, travel, geography)

On the spine of each nonfiction book is its **call number.** This number includes the Dewey Decimal number and other information. Look at the example on the next page.

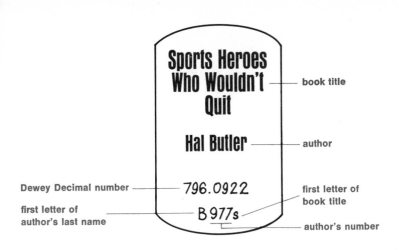

Sports Heroes
Who Wouldn't
Quit — book title

Hal Butler — author

Dewey Decimal number — 796.0922

first letter of
author's last name — B 977s

first letter of
book title

author's number

Check It Out Look at the spines of the books represented below.

The Contender	Summer of Fear	Soup for President	The Pinballs	The Loon in My Bathtub	The Story of Baseball in Words and Pictures	The Birth of the United States	Your Career If You're Not Going to College
Robert Lipsyte	Lois Duncan	Robert Newton Peck	Betsy Byars	Ronald Rood	John Durant	Isaac Asimov	Sarah Splaver
				591.5 R671ℓ	796.35709 D932s	973 A51	371.425 Sp51y

- How can you tell which books are fiction and which are nonfiction?
- How can you tell what the general category of each nonfiction book is?
- How can the call numbers and authors' names on the spines help you find these books?

Try Your Skill Decide which of the following books are on the fiction shelves and which are on the nonfiction shelves.

1. *May I Cross Your Golden River?* Paige Dixon

2. *Facts About the Presidents,* Joseph Nathan Kane, R973.0992 K131f

3. *Fitzgo: The Wild Dog of Central Park,* Paul Wilkes, 636.7 W625f

4. *Dear Lovey Hart, I'm Desperate,* Ellen Conford

5. *The Cay,* Theodore Taylor

6. *Riders of the Wind: The Story of Ballooning,* 629.13322DW1

Keep This in Mind

- Library books are divided into two groups, fiction and nonfiction.
- Fiction books are filed alphabetically by the author's last name.
- Nonfiction books are classified in ten major categories. Each nonfiction book has its own call number to show where it can be found on the shelves.

Now Write Do you have a favorite fiction author? If so, write his or her name on your paper. If not, find the name of an author. Ask your teacher, a librarian, or a friend for some help. Write the author's name on your paper.

Next, think of a subject you're interested in. It might be a hobby, a sport, or an art form. Write it on your paper.

Use your school or public library to find books by the author you have chosen and on the subject you have chosen. Try to find at least three fiction books and three nonfiction books.

Write their titles on your paper. Write the title of this lesson, **A Good Place To Go,** at the top.

Put your work into your folder.

Pick a Card

How To Use the Card Catalog

Here's the Idea When you're looking for a book in the library, the **card catalog** is the place to start. Every book in the library is listed there, at least three times.

Every book is recorded on an **author card,** a **title card,** and a **subject card.** All three cards give the call number of the book in the upper left corner. The same number appears on the binding of the book. The number determines where the book is located on the shelves.

All three cards contain the same information, but the information is arranged differently. All three cards tell the publisher, the date of publication, and the number of pages in the book. There is also a notation telling whether the book has illustrations. Sometimes, there is a short description of the book or mention of other books on the same topic.

On an **author card,** the author's name is at the top. The author's name is written with the last name first. Author cards are arranged alphabetically by the author's last name.

793.8
R972g   **Rydell, Wendy**
   The great book of magic: including
150 mystifying tricks you can perform/
   by Wendy Rydell, with George
Gilbert.—New York: H. N. Abrams,
c. 1976.
      271 p.: ill. (some col.); 28 cm.
   Bibliography: p. 264

O

On a **title card,** the title comes first. Title cards are alphabetized according to the first word of the title. However, if A, An, or The appears as the first word in a title, look for the title card under the first letter of the second word in the title. For example, you would find *The Great Book of Magic* filed under the letter G.

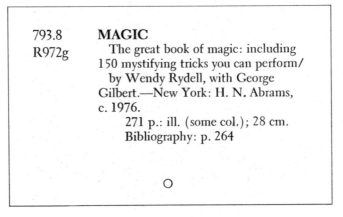

```
793.8        The great book of magic
R972g           The great book of magic: including
             150 mystifying tricks you can perform/
                by Wendy Rydell, with George
             Gilbert.—New York: H. N. Abrams,
             c. 1976.
                    271 p.: ill. (some col.); 28 cm.
                    Bibliography: p. 264


                         O
```

On a **subject card,** the subject is at the top. In the card catalog, the subject card is arranged alphabetically by the first word of the subject. The subject may be written in capital letters or in red.

```
793.8        MAGIC
R972g           The great book of magic: including
             150 mystifying tricks you can perform/
                by Wendy Rydell, with George
             Gilbert.—New York: H. N. Abrams,
             c. 1976.
                    271 p.: ill. (some col.); 28 cm.
                    Bibliography: p. 264


                         O
```

Check It Out   Look at the three sample cards shown. Answer the following questions.

- Under what letter of the alphabet would each card be filed?
- Where could you look for more books by Wendy Rydell?
- Where would you find more books on magic?

Try Your Skill   Below are the title, author, and call number for a book about magic. On a sheet of paper, draw three rectangles to represent file cards. Use the information below to make an author card, a title card, and a subject card.

> *The Illustrated History of Magic*, by Christopher Milbourne, 793.8 C4666m

Keep This in Mind

- Every book in a library is listed in the card catalog, on at least three different cards—author, title, and subject.
- Each card records the call number, the author, the title, and other important information about the book.

Now Write   On your paper, write the title of this lesson, **Pick a Card.** Draw three rectangles to represent file cards.

Choose a subject that interests you. It might be a hobby, a sport, a famous person, or an area of study, like biology or history. Write the subject on your paper.

In the library, go to the card catalog and find a subject card, author card, and a title card for books on your subject. Copy the information from the cards onto your paper.

Put your work into your folder.

Look Here!

How To Use an Encyclopedia

Here's the Idea A good way to begin any search for information is to look in an encyclopedia. An **encyclopedia** contains articles on a great many different subjects. The subjects of these articles are arranged alphabetically in numbered volumes. On the spine of each volume you will find a single letter or guide letters to tell you what subjects are in it. Look at the set of encyclopedias arranged below.

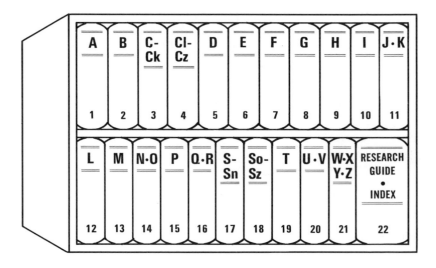

If you want to look up *magic*, for instance, first find the appropriate volume. You might use *Collier's Encyclopedia*, *Brittanica Junior Encyclopaedia*, or the *World Book Encyclopedia*. Then, look up the word *magic* in that volume, just as you would in a dictionary. Each page has guide words at the top, just as a dictionary does.

Different encyclopedias have different reading levels. Read a little in several to find the one that is easiest for you to understand. You may want to ask the librarian for an encyclopedia that would be best for you.

A major article in an encyclopedia is often divided into parts. Each part has a subtitle. When you need information on a specific topic, you usually don't have to read every word of the article. Just look under the appropriate heading. For example, you wouldn't need to study an entire article on the United States to find out about the Battle of Gettysburg. You might look in the section on *History* under *The Civil War*.

An article may also tell you where to look for further information on your topic, or provide a list of books for further reading.

Check It Out   Look at the sample encyclopedia shown at the left. Answer the following questions.

• In what volume would you find information about football? California? astronauts? television? Theodore Roosevelt?

Try Your Skill   Imagine that you are using the sample encyclopedia pictured in **Here's the Idea.** Suppose that you had to find answers to the questions below. Number your paper from 1 to 5. Write the key word in each question that tells you where to look in the encyclopedia. Next to the key word write the number of the volume in which you would look.

1. What is the name of the largest crater on the moon?
2. Was the game of lacrosse invented in North America?
3. In what year did Charles Lindbergh first fly across the Atlantic?
4. Do owls really have better vision at night?
5. Where does the tradition of Halloween come from?

Now Write On your paper, write the title of this lesson, **Look Here!** Write the same topic you chose for the last lesson, **Pick a Card.**

Find an encyclopedia article on your topic. List the following information: the name of the encyclopedia where you found the article, the number and guide letters of the volume, the guide words on the page, any related articles, and the titles of any books on the subject.

Put your work into your folder.

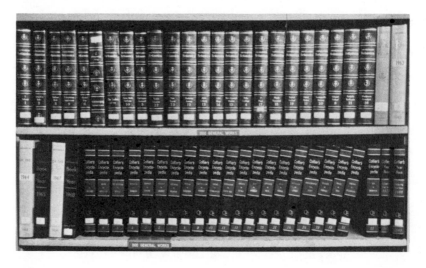

Write Again

In the preceding lessons, each Part taught you a new skill. In the following eleven pages you will find additional exercises to help you improve those skills. As you finish each lesson, your teacher may assign one of these additional exercises to give you more practice in writing. The exercises are interesting and you will most likely enjoy them. Give them your best effort.

Words: Building Your Vocabulary

Part 1 **It Grows on You**   What is your favorite meal? List names of several foods that you would include in the ideal dinner. Using a dictionary, check the history of each name. Have any been borrowed from other languages? Have any come from the names of people? Are any compound words?

Part 2 **Look Around**   List four special terms used in a sport you enjoy. Write a sentence using each term. Use context clues that would help a reader figure out what the word means.

Part 3 **Spell It Out**   List four words that are important to a job that you can do well. They might name special equipment or special skills. Write a sentence for each word, using definition or restatement in the context. Use a key phrase or punctuation to alert the reader to the context clue.

Part 4 **Look Again**   Here are six unusual words: *adze, flax, kohlrabi, lemur, terrapin,* and *weevil.* Look up three of the words in a dictionary. Then write three sentences, each one using one of the three new words. Use one or more examples as a context clue to the meaning of each of the words you have chosen.

Part 5 **Make It Clear**   List two synonyms for the word *happy.* Use a dictionary or thesaurus for help. Write a sentence for each synonym so that it fits the special meaning of that synonym.

Part 6 **Get Down to Bases**   In the articles on the front page of a newspaper, find five new words that contain base words. On your paper, copy the entire word as it appears in the news story. Then write the base word. Be sure to spell the base word correctly. Use a dictionary to help you if necessary.

Part 7 **First Things First**   List the prefixes *pre-, non-, un-, mis-,* and *re-* on your paper. Make a new word for each by adding the prefix to a base word. Write the new words. Then write five sentences, each one using one of the five new words.

Part 8 **Last, but Not Least** List the suffixes *-er* (or *-or*), *-less*, *-able* (or *-ible*), *-ful*, and *-ous*. Make a new word for each by adding the suffix to a base word. Write the new words. Then write five sentences, each one using one of the five new words.

Writing Better Sentences Section 2

Part 1 **Put It Together** What is your favorite sport? What equipment does it use? Think of one piece of equipment that it requires. Write a sentence telling what that piece of equipment is. Write a sentence describing it. Write a sentence telling how to use it. Write a sentence telling about some action in the sport. Write a sentence telling why more people should play it. Try to write sentences that you would enjoy reading. When you've written your sentences, read them over. Are they clear and direct? Are they strong? If not, rewrite them. Write your final sentences.

Part 2 **Getting Nowhere** Find, or write, two examples of each kind of empty sentence. Improve the sentences by eliminating repetition or by giving reasons. Write the sentences.

Part 3 **Cut It Out!** Find, or write, four examples of padded sentences. Improve the sentences by omitting any unnecessary words. Write the new sentences.

A Look at Paragraphs Section 3

Part 1 **What Is It?** Find a short paragraph in one of your textbooks. Decide what the main idea of the paragraph is. Now add one more sentence to the paragraph. Be certain that the sentence says something about the main idea. Copy the paragraph, including the sentence you added.

Part 2 **United We Stand** Find a short paragraph in one of your textbooks. Decide what the main idea of the paragraph is.

Be sure that the paragraph has unity. Write one sentence that is on the same topic as the paragraph but does not relate to the main idea. Write another sentence that does relate to the main idea.

Part 3 **What's It All About?** Pick an object in the room where you are working. Think about ways that you could write about it. Write two possible topics sentences for paragraphs about the object. Make certain that they are clear and direct.

Part 4 **Follow the Leader** Think of a someone you admire. List five *Details* or five *Facts and Figures* that tell about the person. Then give an *Example* of something this person did that earned your respect.

Part 5 **What's in a Name?** In a book or magazine, find one paragraph of each type: narrative, explanatory, and descriptive. Copy each paragraph. Label it to show its type.

Section 4 **Writing a Paragraph**

Part 1 **In Focus** Who is your best friend? Suppose that person were the topic for a paragraph. Write your friend's name on your paper. Narrow the topic by asking *who, what, when, where, how,* and *why.* Write the new topic.

Part 2 **A Better Birdfeeder** Think of your best friend. Write this sleepy topic sentence on your paper: (Name) is a wonderful friend. Use what you know about your friend to improve this sentence. Make it direct. Make it snappy.

Part 3 **The Main Course** Write a paragraph about your best friend. Make sure you have a narrow topic and a good topic sentence. Write the paragraph, using details, examples, or facts and figures to tell about your friend.

Part 4 **Saying Goodbye** Write a concluding sentence for a paragraph about your best friend. Decide what the main idea of the paragraph would be. Make the concluding sentence sum up the idea.

A Writer's Choices

Part 1 **I Did It!** Think of something you did as a child. Use first-person point of view to write three sentences about it. Proofread your three sentences. Put your work into your folder.

Part 2 **Fly-on-the-Wall** Use third-person point of view as you follow these directions: (1) Write a sentence about something that a friend did this morning. (2) Write a sentence about something you did this morning. Pretend that you observed yourself.

Part 3 **Believe It or Not!** Write a paragraph about something real. Choose any useful object in your home. Decide whether to write a narration, description, or explanation. If you write a narration, you will tell how the object came into your home. A description will describe the object. An explanation will tell how to use it. Write your topic. List details, facts, figures, or dates. Organize the information. Decide on the point of view. Write the paragraph. Read it, and rewrite as necessary.

Part 4 **Once upon a Time** Write a paragraph about something imaginary. Think about something that would be useful in your home, if it existed. It could be an animal, a machine, or a person with superhuman powers. Decide whether to write a narration, description, or explanation. If you write a narration, you will tell how the object came into your home. A description will describe the object. An explanation will tell how to use it. Write your subject. Imagine details, facts, figures, or dates. Organize the information. Decide on the point of view. Write the paragraph. Read it, and rewrite as necessary.

Part 5 **Prance or Trudge?** Start with the verb *run*. Make a list of verbs that are more specific than *run*. You might use *sprint* or *flee*, for example. Then choose three verbs from your list. Write one sentence with each verb. Try to make your sentences create different moods.

Section 7 The Narrative Paragraph

Part 1 **What Happened?** If you could spend a day in any way you wished, what would you do? List ideas for things you would do. Organize your list in chronological order. Write a paragraph based on your list of details. Read what you have written. Do whatever rewriting you think is necessary. Write your paragraph in final form. Proofread your paragraph.

Part 2 **Frame by Frame** Write a narrative paragraph telling how you got to school today. Use transitions to show chronological order. Underline each transitional word or phrase.

Part 3 **Little by Little** What has happened in the last year that made you happy? Write a narrative paragraph about whatever it is. Use vivid details. Follow all the steps in the process of writing. Write your story in final form. Proofread it.

Section 8 The Descriptive Paragraph

Part 1 **Just Common Senses** Choose a place that you can visit easily. You might choose the kitchen at home, for example. List what you *see, hear, touch, taste,* and *smell* there. Review your lists. Decide which senses are most important in describing your place. Then organize your lists of details in a logical order. Write a descriptive paragraph about the place. Proofread your work.

Part 2 **Words Are Moody** Suppose that your neighborhood were completely deserted for a whole day. What would it be like? Write a paragraph describing your deserted neighborhood. Decide on the mood you'd like to create. List a few adjectives that fit the mood. List sensory details that fit the mood. When your lists are complete, try to organize them in a logical order. Write your paragraph. Read it aloud. Rewrite and proofread.

Part 3 **Up and Down** Where do you get your mail? Is it delivered to your own mailbox? Do you pick it up at the post office? Describe the place where you get your mail. List the important details, and organize them. Decide where you will begin your description. The rest of your description should follow in an organized way. Write your description. Read it aloud to see if someone else can picture the place. Rewrite as necessary.

Part 4 **In, Out, and All Around** When you are with your friends, where are you most likely to be? What is your usual gathering spot? Describe it in a paragraph, using spatial order. Use transitions so that your description is in a clear, understandable order.

The Explanatory Paragraph Telling *How*

Part 1 **What's Next?** Think of your favorite sandwich. Make a list of the steps you follow to make it. Be as specific as you can. Now organize your detailed list into paragraph form. Write an explanatory *how* paragraph. Rewrite and proofread.

Part 2 **Watch Your Step!** Think of a tool that you know how to use. It might be an egg beater, a pencil sharpener, or a carpenter's level. Write an explanatory *how* paragraph explaining how to use this tool. Before you write, list the steps in the process using specific details. When you write the paragraph, underline the transitional words and phrases that you use.

The Expanatory Paragraph Telling *Why*

Part 1 **Present Your Case** What is your honest opinion of holidays? Narrow your opinion so that you can write about it in a paragraph. State your opinion in a clear, strong sentence. Then list at least three specific reasons that support your opinion.

Part 2 **Save the Best for Last** What skill do you know that would be useful to someone else? It might be frying an egg or playing the guitar. Think of reasons why this skill would be useful to someone else. List at least three. Arrange the reasons in order, from least important to most important. Use your list to write a well organized explanatory *why* paragraph.

Part 3 **Build Your Case** Look at the headlines in today's newspaper. Find an issue on which you have a strong opinion. Write a paragraph expressing this opinion. Do whatever pre-writing, writing, and rewriting is necessary.

Section 11 **A Look at Compositions**

Part 1 **It's a Long Story** Think about the things that have happened to you since you began this school year. From these things, list five topics that would be suitable for compositions. Choose topics that you know you could write about at some length. Choose topics that you would like to write about.

Part 2 **Three in One** From the things that have happened to you since this school year began, choose one topic and think about how you would write a composition about it. On your paper, write three headings: *Introduction, Body,* and *Conclusion.* After each heading, write notes that tell what you would include in each part.

Part 3 **Here's the Lineup** Think about something you learned to do when you were younger. Choose a topic broad enough for a composition. You could write a narrative composition telling what happened as you were learning this skill. You could write a descriptive composition about yourself at the age when you learned it. You could write an explanatory composition about how anyone else should do it. In a few sentences, write what events you would include in a narrative composition. Write how you would describe yourself in a descriptive composition. Write how you would explain the topic in an explanatory composition.

The Narrative Composition
Real Life

Part 1 **What's the Idea?** From time to time, all of us have to do things that we don't particularly want to do. Think about one of these times in your life. Choose an event that is fresh in your memory. Write the topic on a piece of paper. Next, narrow the topic. Then write your specific topic.

Part 2 **Get the Facts** On your paper, write the score of the last sports event you participated in, saw in person, or watched on television. Then list the details of the event. Be as specific as you can. Ask other witnesses for help in recalling details, if necessary. You may need to use other sources, such as newspapers, to check the accuracy of some details. Use whatever sources are available.

Part 3 **Tell Your Story** Think about the last sports event you saw. List details about the event. Arrange the details of your account in chronological order. Add transitions to make the time order clear. Using your notes, write a narrative composition.

The Narrative Composition
Imaginary

Part 1 **Get Started** Suppose that the main characters from two different television shows were in a story together. Use your imagination to develop an idea for a story. In your pre-writing steps, make notes about setting, characters, and plot.

Part 2 **The Right Introduction** Everyone has successes and failures. Think of some of your successes or some of your failures. One of these events could be the basis for an imaginary story. List three possible story ideas. Choose the one that you could write about most easily. Write an introduction for your story.

Part 3 **What's Your View?** Find a paragraph from the beginning of a short story you have enjoyed, and copy it. Decide what point of view has been used. Then rewrite it, using a different point of view. Label the point of view of each paragraph.

Part 4 **Thicken the Plot** A person loses a wallet. A student finds it. The student tracks the person down and returns the wallet. The person is grateful. These events could form the plot of a story. However, they are too general and lack conflict. Add details and rewrite the plot to include a dramatic conflict.

Part 5 **Put the Lid on It** With a friend, watch the first twenty minutes of a half-hour television drama. Take notes on the characters and plot as you watch. Do not watch the end. Review your notes and write a conclusion for the story. Have your friend tell you what actually happened.

Section 14 The Descriptive Composition

Part 1 **Take a Good Look** Look out one window of your home or school. Use what you see as the topic for a descriptive composition. Write and organize notes for the composition. List details. Use spatial order.

Part 2 **Narrow the Field** Take notes on what you see through one window of your home or school. Use your notes to write an introduction for a composition about the scene.

Part 3 **It Makes Sense** Carefully observe one part of a scene near your home or school. Use sensory details to write the body of a descriptive composition.

Part 4 **How Do You Respond?** Suppose that you are writing a composition about what you can see through one window of your home or school. Take notes on your reactions. Then write a conclusion for your description. Try to make your readers feel what you feel.

192

The Explanatory Composition
Telling *How*

Part 1 **How Is It Done?** What can you do that young children cannot do? It might be balancing on a skateboard or making a pillow. Make a list of the things you can do. Choose one. Write a possible title for a composition about this skill.

Part 2 **One Step at a Time** What do you do best? Are you happier in the kitchen, in a workshop, or on the basketball court? Choose something you know how to do well. List the steps involved in the process. Write the body of an explanatory *how* composition. Give a step-by-step explanation.

Part 3 **Bridge the Gaps** Write the steps involved in doing something you do well. Add transitions within each paragraph, and between paragraphs.

Writing Letters

Part 1 **Hi There!** Jot down notes on what you have done in the last week or so. Use these notes to write a letter to a friend.

Part 2 **A Good Send-off** On your paper, draw a rectangle to represent an envelope. Address the envelope to yourself.

Part 3 **Thank You** Imagine that a friend threw a surprise party for you on your birthday. Write your friend a thank-you note.

Part 4 **Get Down to Business** Use one of the two forms for a business letter. Write to the sales manager of an imaginary company asking for the latest catalog.

Part 5 **Please Send Me** Look through the advertisements in a magazine. Write a letter requesting more information about a particular product. Invent any details necessary to complete the six parts of the letter.

Section 17 **Using a Dictionary**

Part 1 **Look It Up** Write ten words that begin with the letter *n*. Put the words into alphabetical order. Write a short definition for each word. Check your work in a dictionary.

Part 2 **Show Me the Way** Imagine that you are writing a composition about nutrition. You need to look up the following words: *calorie, diet, digestion, mineral, protein,* and *vitamin*. List the words on your paper. Find each in a dictionary. Next to each word, write the guide words that appear at the top of the page where you found the word.

Part 3 **It's All There** Find the words *pickle* and *side* in a dictionary. Copy two different definitions of each word.

Part 4 **Does It Fit?** Look up the word *place* in your dictionary. On your paper, copy four different meanings of *place*. For each different meaning, write a sentence using *place*.

Section 18 **Using the Library**

Part 1 **A Good Place To Go** Think of an animal. Use your school or public library to find nonfiction books about that animal. Try to find at least three. Write their titles and call numbers.

Part 2 **Pick a Card** On your paper, write the title of a book you enjoyed reading or a book that someone has recommended to you. In your school or public library, find a title card and an author card for the book. Copy the information from the cards.

Part 3 **Look Here!** Find an encyclopedia article on your city or a city near you. List the following information: the name of the encyclopedia where you found the article, the number and guide letters of the volume, and the guide words on the page.

Handbook

A detailed Table of Contents for the Handbook appears in the front of this book.

Learning About Sentences

How would you invite a friend to a picnic? How would you identify yourself on the telephone? How would you ask for a certain shirt at a store?

Almost without thinking, you would put words together to make sentences. The clearest way to get your ideas across to someone else is to use sentences.

Part 1   What Is a Sentence?

Below are four groups of words. Each group of words expresses a complete thought or idea. Read the groups of words. Each group of words is a sentence. (Notice that each sentence begins with a capital letter.)

1. Greg is a goalie.
2. Richard made a belt by himself.
3. Laura was given the trophy.
4. The gym class practiced tumbling stunts.

A sentence is a group of words that expresses a complete thought.

Not All Groups of Words Are Sentences

Read these groups of words. Can you tell whether each of the groups is a sentence?

1. The girls went to the park.
2. Dominic and his brother.
3. Played in the snow.

Perhaps you are not sure if these groups of words are sentences. Here are two basic questions to help you decide whether a group of words is a sentence:

Who or what did something? Does the group of words tell who or what did something?
What happened? Does the group of words tell what happened?

If a group of words answers these two questions, it expresses a complete thought. The group of words is a sentence.

If a group of words does not answer the questions, it does not express a complete thought. The group of words is a **fragment.**

Making Sure Sentences Are Complete

Now return to the three groups of words shown earlier and test them for complete thoughts.

Example 1 | The girls went to the park

Who or what did something?	What happened?
The girls	went to the park.

This group of words answers both questions. You know, then, that it is a sentence. It expresses a complete thought.

Example 2 | Dominic and his brother

Who or what did something?	What happened?
Dominic and his brother	

Does this group of words answer both questions? No, it does not. You can see that it is not a sentence. It is a fragment. It tells only part of a thought. You can change this fragment into a whole sentence.

Who or what did something?	What happened?
Dominic and his brother	planted a garden.

Example 3 | Played in the snow

Who or what did something?	What happened?
	Played in the snow

Does this group of words answer both questions? No, it does not. Like Example 2, it is not a sentence. It is a fragment. You can also change this fragment into a sentence.

Who or what did something?	What happened?
The black kitten	played in the snow.

Exercises　Write complete sentences.

A. For each group of words you must answer the question *What happened* to make a complete sentence. Write the whole sentence. There are many possible correct answers.

1. The boy with the camera
2. An angry dog
3. My two sisters
4. The TV set
5. Most birds

B. For each group of words you must answer the question *Who or what did something* to make a complete sentence. Write the whole sentence. There are many possible correct answers.

1. talked on the phone
2. made brownies
3. found a sharp pencil
4. likes football
5. played in the band

C. Number your paper from 1 to 10. Write *Sentence* after each number that stands before a sentence. Write *Fragment* after each number that stands before a fragment.

1. We built a bookshelf
2. The lifeguard
3. An anthill in the yard
4. Our class planned a field trip
5. Carved the turkey
6. Rides a bike to school
7. Our hamster is loose
8. Alice dived into the lake
9. Makes jewelry out of tabs from pop cans
10. The cattle rancher

Part 2 Different Kinds of Sentences

You use sentences for several different reasons. Sometimes you want to tell something. Sometimes you want to ask something. Sometimes you want to tell someone to do something. Sometimes you want to show how strongly you feel about something. There is a different kind of sentence for each of these four purposes. Every sentence that you read or write is one of these four different kinds.

The Declarative Sentence

A declarative sentence tells or states something. Use a period **(.)** at the end of a declarative sentence.

> Tomorrow is my birthday.

The Interrogative Sentence

An interrogative sentence asks a question. Use a question mark **(?)** at the end of an interrogative sentence.

> Do you like to play basketball?

The Imperative Sentence

An imperative sentence makes a request or gives directions. Use a period **(.)** at the end of most imperative sentences.

> Pass the salt, please.

The Exclamatory Sentence

An exclamatory sentence shows strong feeling. Use an exclamation point **(!)** at the end of every exclamatory sentence.

> Our house is on fire!

A.   Number your paper from 1 to 10. Write *Declarative, Interrogative, Imperative,* or *Exclamatory* to tell what kind of sentence each is.

> Example: Are you going shopping Saturday?
>
> Interrogative

1. What good luck you always have!
2. Do you have a skateboard?
3. Tom has been taking piano lessons for two years.
4. When will the train arrive?
5. Aim for the target.
6. Tomorrow is my birthday.
7. Are you telling me the truth?
8. Guess the right number.
9. Oh, let me think!
10. Hurry up.

B.   Number your paper from 1 to 10. For each of the following sentences, write *Declarative, Interrogative, Imperative,* or *Exclamatory* to tell what kind of sentence each is. Then add the mark of punctuation that belongs at the end of each sentence.

1. The rocket took off on time
2. Have you ever seen the circus
3. What a terrific game it was
4. Ken erased the chalkboards
5. How dare you say that
6. Our family took a vacation in Virginia
7. What a mess we made with the paint
8. Have another piece of this delicious cake
9. Where does the bike trail end
10. Watch out

Part 3   Punctuating Sentences

Punctuation marks are important signals in reading and writing. Use the correct signals in your writing. Follow the signals when you read.

Remember these rules:

1. Use a period after a declarative sentence.

   We will have a school assembly tomorrow.

2. Use a question mark after an interrogative sentence.

   Do you enjoy reading?

3. Use a period after most imperative sentences. If the imperative sentence expresses strong feeling, use an exclamation point.

   Give me the hot chocolate, please. Don't spill it!

4. Use an exclamation point after an exclamatory sentence.

   The barn is on fire!

Exercises   **Punctuate sentences correctly.**

A.   Copy these sentences. Use the correct punctuation mark at the end of each sentence.

1. How funny the monkey looks
2. What is the name of that movie
3. Turn on the radio, please
4. Are you going on the bike hike
5. Henry, read a story to the class
6. Marcia hit a home run
7. What an exciting game it was
8. What time is it now
9. Our class went to the museum
10. Please open the window

B. Copy these sentences. Use the correct punctuation mark at the end of each sentence.

1. We went to a carnival
2. Can you answer the question
3. Stop it
4. Do you have a ballpoint pen
5. I found a birthday gift for Mother
6. Try the vanilla milkshake
7. Please come to my house after school
8. Does Ellen wear glasses
9. What a surprise this is
10. I watched the baseball game

Part 4 Parts of the Sentence

Every sentence has two parts. One part of the sentence is the **subject.** The subject answers the question *Who or what did something.*

Let's take another look at these sentences from **Part 1**.

1. Greg is a goalie.
2. Richard made a belt by himself.
3. Laura was given the trophy.
4. The gym class practiced tumbling stunts.

Can you find the subject in each of these sentences? Find the answer to the question *Who or what did something* or *What is the sentence about.*

Here are the subjects:

1. Greg
2. Richard
3. Laura
4. The gym class

The other part of the sentence is the **predicate.** The predicate tells something about the subject. The predicate tells *What the subject did, What the subject is,* or *What happened to the subject.*

First, see if you can find the predicates in the sample sentences by yourself. Then look at the following chart to find out if you were right.

Subject	Predicate
1. Greg (*who*)	is a goalie. (*what the subject is*)
2. Richard (*who*)	made a shirt by himself. (*what the subject did*)
3. Laura (*who*)	was given the trophy. (*what happened to the subject*)
4. The gym class (*what*)	practiced tumbling stunts. (*what the subject did*)

The subject of a sentence tells who or what did something, or what the sentence is about.

The predicate of a sentence tells what the subject did, what the subject is, or what happened.

A group of words is not a sentence unless it has a subject and a predicate.

Here are three new sentences. Decide by yourself which words belong in the subject. Decide which words belong in the predicate. Then check yourself against the chart that follows.

That big dog is a collie.
My older sister went to the movie.
Dave's math book fell into a puddle.

Subject	Predicate
That big dog	is a collie.
My older sister	went to the movie.
Dave's math book	fell into a puddle.

Exercises   Find subjects and predicates.

A.   Copy these sentences. Draw a vertical line between the subject of each sentence and the predicate.

> Example: The red wagon | makes squeaky noises.

1. My friends went to the beach.
2. The fierce tiger growled in his cage.
3. Don raced on roller skates.
4. Bill Lee is the pitcher.
5. Aunt Beth has many plants.
6. The baby reached for her bottle.
7. The first show began at two o'clock.
8. Our neighbors built a treehouse.
9. A baby robin flew from the nest.
10. Susan told a good joke.

B.   Copy these sentences. Draw a vertical line between the subject of each sentence and the predicate.

> Example: The girls | hiked through the park.

1. The small airplane landed in a field.
2. A team of horses pulled the wagon.
3. My brother's favorite holiday is Halloween.
4. The runners lined up.
5. Our family watched the fireworks from the porch.
6. Ms. Adams did a backflip for the class.
7. The old fisherman uses no bait.
8. Mark found a dollar in the hall.
9. My sister makes her own clothes.
10. Doug Henning performed many magic tricks.

Part 5 The Simple Predicate, or Verb

You have learned about the two parts of the sentence. When we divide a sentence into these two parts, we call the subject part the **complete subject.** We call the predicate part the **complete predicate.**

The complete subject may be short or long. It includes all the words that tell who or what did something.

The complete predicate may also be short or long. It includes all the words that tell what happened.

Complete Subject	Complete Predicate
The girl	played.
The tall girl with glasses	played basketball at the Y.

In each complete predicate, there is one part that is more important than the rest. This part is the **verb.** These two sentences have the same verb: *played.*

The verb is sometimes called the **simple predicate.** In the rest of this book, we will speak of it as the verb.

Finding the Verb

The underlined words in these sentences are the verbs.

The children <u>fell</u> on the ice.
The children <u>heard</u> the ice crack.

Some verbs tell of an action you can see.

Robert <u>fell</u> on his way to school.
The lion <u>jumped</u> through a hoop.

Other verbs tell of an action you cannot see.

> My mother heard the baby's cry.
> I remember all the words of that song.

- These verbs are called **action verbs.**

Another kind of verb tells that something *is*.

> I am a student.   Your desk is new.

- This kind of verb is called a **state-of-being verb.**

Here are some of the most common state-of-being verbs:

is	am	were	has been	seem
are	was	will be	have been	look

A verb is a word that tells of an action, or that tells what the subject is.

Exercises   Find the verb.

A.   Write the verb in each sentence.

1. Miss Morgan writes with a quill pen.
2. My uncle is a test pilot.
3. The Apollo rockets went to the moon.
4. Margie rested before the race.
5. Three penguins waddled to the water.
6. The sky looked pink and orange.
7. At noon the zookeeper feeds the lions.
8. The truck took garbage to the dump.
9. Our sewing class made T-shirts.
10. Adam hoped for better luck.

B.   Write the verb in each sentence. After the verb, write *Action* or *State of being* to tell what kind of verb it is.

1. That flag is colorful.

2. Valerie's dog performed a new trick.
3. Two girls paddled the canoe.
4. The lizard darted up a tree.
5. Our class wrote a newspaper.
6. Father seems impatient.
7. Eli used the microphone.
8. The Girl Scouts are at camp.
9. Indians made these beautiful necklaces.
10. The fans were happy about the victory.

Part 6   The Simple Subject, or Subject of the Verb

In each complete subject, there is one part that is more important than the rest. This is sometimes called the **simple subject.** Another name for it is the **subject of the verb.** In this book, we will call it the *subject of the verb.*

In the examples below, the subject of the verb is printed in *italics.*

Complete Subject	Verb
The *clock*	stopped.
The old *clock* on the shelf	stopped.

Finding the Subject of the Verb

To find the subject of the verb, first find the verb. Then ask *who?* or *what?* before the verb.

Examples: Monkeys escaped from the zoo.

Verb: *escaped*
Who or what *escaped?*   *Monkeys*
Monkeys is the subject of *escaped.*

Three young monkeys escaped from the zoo.

Verb: *escaped*

who or what *escaped?*   *monkeys*

Monkeys is still the subject of the verb.

See if you can find the verb, and then the subject of the verb, in this example.

The cake in the oven burned.

Did you find the action verb *burned?* The subject tells you *what* burned. What is the subject?

Did you say the *cake burned? Cake* is the subject of the verb *burned.*

In the next example, look for a state-of-being verb. Then find the subject of the verb.

Victor's blue jacket is on the chair.

Did you find the state-of-being verb *is?* The subject tells you *what* is. Did you say the *jacket is? Jacket* is the subject of the verb *is.*

Exercises   Find the verb and its subject.

A. Find the verb and its simple subject in each sentence. Write the subject and verb. Draw a vertical line between them.

Example: The ski slopes were crowded.

slopes | were

1. High waves tipped the sailboat.
2. Juanita added three books to her library.
3. Three jugglers in the main ring tossed hoops into the air.
4. My new gloves are waterproof.
5. Tom Sawyer found a secret hideout.
6. Jocelyn was her sister's bridesmaid.
7. A large group sang carols.

8. Six climbers from Nevada reached the mountaintop.
9. The desert seems endless.
10. Our parrot speaks Spanish.

Follow the directions for Exercise A.

1. Outside, hailstones fell.
2. Melinda leaped over the fence.
3. David is sick with the flu.
4. The American flag now has fifty stars.
5. The pickers handled the fruit gently.
6. Dr. Mendez taped my wrist.
7. One unusual vegetable in my garden is the rutabaga.
8. Today we had a fire drill.
9. A stray dog slept on our steps.
10. The sweater with yellow and orange stripes is mine.

Part 7 The Subject in Unusual Positions

In most sentences the subject comes before the predicate, but not in all sentences. Where is the subject placed in each of the sentences below?

Example 1 | The rocket soared toward the planet Venus.

> Verb: *soared*
> Who or what *soared?*   the *rocket*

Rocket is the subject of the verb. It is placed before the verb near the beginning of the sentence.

Example 2 | Toward the planet Venus the rocket soared.

Rocket is still the subject of the verb. It is still placed before the verb. It is now near the end of the sentence.

Example 3 Toward the planet Venus soared the rocket.

In this sentence, the subject is still *rocket,* but it has been moved again. Now it is placed after the verb.

When you are looking for the subject in sentences like examples 2 and 3, follow the usual steps. First, find the verb. (*What happened?*) Then ask *Who* or *What* before the verb.

> Example: During the movie we ate some popcorn.
> Verb: *ate*
> Who or what *ate? we* ate

Exercises   Find the subject in unusual positions.

A.   Find the verb and the subject in each sentence. Write the subject and verb. Draw a vertical line between them.

> Example: In the drawer are two pencils.
> pencils | are

1. Down the hill ran José.
2. In the early evening, fireflies appeared.
3. On the top branch sat a crow.
4. From the trees fell the colored leaves.
5. Down came the rain.
6. Into the hall the band marched.
7. Up into the tree sailed the balloon.
8. Into the water fell our money.
9. Out of the dark came a strange sound.
10. Across the range the cowboys rode.

B.   Follow the directions for Exercise A.

1. Around the barnyard waddled a goose.
2. Out into the storm went the cat.
3. After the storm a rainbow appeared.
4. Into the pond jumped a frog.

5. Over the apple trees my kite sailed.
6. In front of the store Mom waited.
7. Through the gate came a hay wagon.
8. Across the snow whisked a dog sled.
9. Above the clouds the jet soared.
10. At the front of the parade was a fire engine.

Part 8 The Subject in Imperative Sentences

An imperative sentence makes a request, or gives directions or orders. Study these examples of imperative sentences. Look for the subjects.

Switch off the light.	Don't throw the pencil.
Turn left at the gas station.	Finish your test.

In each of these sentences, the subject is not expressed. The subject is understood to be *you*. *You* is the person or group spoken to.

(*You*) Switch off the light.	(*You*) Don't throw the pencil.
(*You*) Turn left at the gas station.	(*You*) Finish your test.

Exercises **Find the subject.**

A. Write the verb in each of the following sentences. Beside the verb, write the subject. If the subject is not given in the sentence, write it in parentheses in the place where it is understood.

Example: Wait here for me.

(You) Wait

1. Try it again, please.

2. Wake up now.

3. Karen took the message.

4. Have a second helping of salad.

5. Stay in your seats.

6. I like chocolate ice cream.

7. Look at that fancy car.

8. Add one cup of flour to the mixture.

9. Read Chapter 2 for tomorrow.

10. Those boys need help with the ladder.

B. Follow the directions for Exercise A.

1. Astronomers watch for shooting stars.

2. Bait your hook this way.

3. Speak a little louder, please.

4. Hold the noise down.

5. Careful shoppers compare prices.

6. Keep up the good work.

7. Sing along with the music.

8. Rosa's friends go to McDonald's often.

9. Use fine sandpaper for this job.

10. Buy your tickets at the box office.

Part 9   Compound Subjects

Look at these two sentences:

Subject	Predicate
Jennifer	played softball.
I	played softball.

Since the predicates are the same, we can join the two sentences together. The new sentence will be:

Subject	Predicate
Jennifer and I	played softball.

Now the subject has two parts. When two or more subjects are used with the same predicate, they are called a **compound subject.** The word *compound* means having more than one part.

In the new sentence, the word *and* joins the two parts of the subject. The word *or* is also used to join parts of a subject. (A word that is used to join words or groups of words is called a **conjunction.**)

Look at these sentences with compound subjects:

> *Sausage* and *olives* taste good on pizza.
> *Carrie* and *Jake* left the movie early.

When three or more subjects are combined in a compound subject, use commas to separate them. The conjunction is placed before the last subject.

> Example: Our summer *cottage*, the *dock*, and a *rowboat* suffered damage in the hurricane.

Exercises **Find compound subjects.**

A. Find the verb and its compound subject in each of the following sentences. Write the subjects and verb. Draw a line between them.

> Example: Dan, Bob, and Ginny came to my house.
> Dan, Bob, Ginny | came

1. The horse and rider neared the highway.
2. Suzanne and Richard watched a horror movie.
3. Posters and lockers line the hallway.
4. Bacon, lettuce, and tomato make a tasty sandwich.
5. The brakes and seat on my bike are new.
6. Two chairs and a phone were the only props.

7. Karen and Joyce shared a milkshake.
8. The manager and the umpire disagreed on the call.
9. Jenkins, Tortini, and Owens scored runs.
10. Corn, wheat, and soybeans are the main crops of this farm.

B. Follow the directions for Exercise A.

1. Gymnasts and dancers performed at parents' night.
2. The principal and the teachers planned new courses.
3. Rain and fierce winds whipped the countryside.
4. Two ponies and a cow grazed in the field.
5. Radio, TV, and newspapers reported the crime.
6. Bob and Regina fixed breakfast for everyone.
7. Colorado, Utah, and Vermont have many ski resorts.
8. The policemen and paramedics raced to the scene.
9. Palms and cactus plants need a lot of light.
10. Vic, Al, and Kelly listened to a new album.

Part 10 Compound Predicates

When two or more predicates are used with the same subject, they are called a **compound predicate.**

By using a compound predicate and a conjunction, you are often able to combine two or more sentences.

Subject	Predicate
I	sat at the table.
I	ate my breakfast.

Subject	Predicate
I	sat at the table and ate my breakfast.

When three or more predicates are combined in a compound

predicate, commas are used to separate them. The conjunction is placed before the last predicate.

> **Example:** Jean *rehearsed the part, tried out,* **and** *won a role in the class play.*

Exercises Find compound predicates.

A. Find the compound predicates in each of the following sentences.

1. Laurie watched TV and did her homework.
2. Rob rode the bus and went to the zoo.
3. Ellen dropped the bat and ran to first base.
4. The car skidded on the ice and hit the sign.
5. Our cat caught a mouse and brought it in.
6. I grabbed my coat and ran to the store.
7. Tina drew a picture and gave it to her mother.
8. Beth raced down the court and shot a basket.
9. Mike read a story and wrote a report.
10. Tony learned a new dance and taught it to us.

B. Follow the directions for Exercise A.

1. The campers pitched their tent and cooked supper.
2. Ed writes folksongs and plays them on the guitar.
3. Jane cut her jeans and made them into shorts.
4. A friend took a brush and painted with me.
5. Joe gets his allowance on Friday and spends it right away.
6. Les took the test and passed it.
7. The tennis instructor explained a serve and then demonstrated it.
8. Joanie sorted the mail and delivered it.
9. Terry made a cake and cleaned the kitchen.
10. Tom joined the game and played third base.

Sentence Patterns Word Order and Meaning

A sentence is a group of words. However, not every group of words is a sentence. For example, read these word groups. Which one makes sense?

Pete fast ran.
Pete ran fast.
Ran Pete fast.

The only group that sounds right is the second group. Its words are in the order we are used to. We would say its words are in the right order for a sentence. A good sentence needs the right word order.

Sometimes a group of words has more than one right order. Read these two sentences. They have the same words. The words are simply in different orders.

Carrie told Brad.
Brad told Carrie.

Each word order sounds right. Each tells an idea. However, changing the word order changes the idea. The difference in word order makes an important difference in meaning.

Exercise   Change the word order and meaning.

Read each sentence. Then change the order of the words to change the meaning. Write each new sentence on your paper.

1. Herb called Sylvia.
2. The rug hid the dirt.
3. Some dogs chase cats.
4. Bob met my sister.
5. Jeanne saw a puppy.
6. The winner was Tom.

REVIEW   Learning About Sentences

The Parts of the Sentence   Write the verb and its simple subject for each sentence. Draw a vertical line between them.

> Example: The beginning skier fell many times.
>
> skier | fell

1. Katie left the radio on.
2. That store has a sale on T-shirts.
3. Our math teacher tells very funny stories.
4. Carolyn plays the drums.
5. Strawberry is my favorite flavor of ice cream.
6. The carnival seems crowded.
7. All over the walls Bob hung posters.
8. In the middle of the gym was a trampoline.
9. Down the path galloped a horse.
10. Begin with the third chapter.
11. Water those plants carefully.
12. Look for a good picnic spot.
13. James and Judy went to the concert.
14. The field and bleachers were wet.
15. My parents framed the drawing.

Kinds of Sentences   For each of the following sentences, write *Declarative, Interrogative, Imperative,* or *Exclamatory* to show what kind it is. Then add the punctuation mark that should be used at the end of each sentence.

16. Have you opened your presents
17. Try this new dessert
18. James forgot his social studies book
19. How deep the snow is
20. Where did you find that eraser

Using Sentences Correctly

You know that a sentence expresses a complete thought.

> The papers fell on the floor.

Some groups of words do not express a complete thought. They express only part of a thought. These groups of words are called **sentence fragments.**

> Example: The papers on the floor.

Sometimes two or more sentences that express complete thoughts are written as one sentence. These sentences are called **run-on sentences.**

> Example: The papers fell on the floor some blew away.

Now see how clear these ideas are when separate sentences are used.

> The papers fell on the floor. Some blew away.

When you write sentences, you should avoid confusion. You can see that you need to avoid fragments and run-ons. In this section, you will be able to practice writing sentences correctly.

Part 1 Avoiding Sentence Fragments

A sentence fragment may express any part of a thought. A fragment may only tell *who*.

Example: The tall boy in the band

A fragment may only tell *what happened.*

Example: Played the guitar for us

A fragment may tell any part of a thought.

Example: At the party

You can see that all of these sentence fragments express only part of an idea. Sentence fragments do not make sense.

A sentence that is clear and correct does make sense. A sentence expresses a complete thought.

Examples: The tall boy in the band played the guitar for us at the party.
The boy played the guitar.

Exercises Recognize sentence fragments.

A. Number your paper from 1 to 10. Read each of the following groups of words. Write *Sentence* or *Fragment* to tell what each group is.

1. The film crew set up the scenery
2. Taking photographs on vacation
3. A terrific hockey game

4. Three books on the library shelves
5. Our class went to the museum
6. Hanging from the ceiling
7. Ruby interviewed Steve Garvey
8. Drawings on the blackboard
9. We climbed a rope ladder
10. Margo looks like her older sister

B. Follow the directions for Exercise A.

1. A magazine about car racing
2. Several girls tried out for the role
3. When the bell rang
4. Appeared in a TV series
5. Scientists study cave drawings
6. Predicting the weather
7. Carla bought new jeans
8. A stranger peered through the window
9. Only one car in the parking lot
10. Making oatmeal cookies with raisins

C. Change these fragments to sentences by adding whatever is needed. Write each sentence on your paper.

1. ten pages in the math book
2. long, curly hair
3. turning cartwheels
4. the girls in the chorus
5. an art fair next week
6. the icy streets
7. eating a slice of watermelon
8. pasted into a scrapbook
9. one of the new tape recorders
10. the canoe in the water

Part 2   Avoiding Run-on Sentences

A run-on sentence has two or more sentences written as one. Sometimes sentences are written without capital letters and correct punctuation to show where each new idea begins. See how confusing this example is:

> The campers sat around a fire they sang songs.

Now see how clear the ideas are when each sentence expresses a single thought:

> The campers sat around a fire. They sang songs.

Whenever you write, be careful to put one complete idea in each sentence. Mark the end of each sentence with a period, question mark, or exclamation point. Begin each new sentence with a capital letter. Do not use *and* where it is not needed.

Exercises   Recognize run-on sentences.

A.   Some of the following sentences are run-on sentences. Some are correct. Number your paper from 1 to 10. Read each sentence aloud. For each sentence write either *Run-on* or *Correct.*

1. Three clowns were riding on one donkey, they pushed each other off.
2. Lillian and Darren raced to the car.
3. I had a piano lesson for one hour then my teacher played a piece for me.
4. Yesterday we played baseball Judy scored three runs.
5. At the beginning of the program, everyone recited the Pledge of Allegiance.
6. Melvin had tomato soup and a cheese sandwich for lunch.
7. It rained on the Fourth of July, we had our picnic inside.

8. Jeff answered an ad in the paper he got a guitar.

9. Adelle played chess with her father every night last week.

10. The 4-H Club met Tuesday after school, a speaker told about a contest.

B. Follow the directions for Exercise A.

1. I have two younger brothers, they are twins.

2. Janet has a paper route each morning.

3. My friends from camp exchange letters.

4. My brother catches fireflies he keeps them in a jar.

5. Last year we planted a maple tree it's in the back yard.

6. Sally rode a horse and she followed a trail guide, and she will go to the ranch again soon.

7. Aunt Meg knits sweaters for everyone in the family.

8. Rick knows the capital city of every state.

9. Luis likes corn and broccoli and he is a good cook.

10. Cassie filled the bookcase with mystery novels.

C. Read each sentence aloud. Then rewrite each one, using correct capitalization and punctuation.

1. Gary swam twenty laps, he felt tired.

2. Lisa trains animals she is quite good.

3. The Browns have a large family there are eleven children.

4. Ms. Lake has a ranch she breeds cattle.

5. Bees buzzed around the honeycomb and the beekeeper was working nearby and he was collecting honey.

6. The cat climbed a tree, we had to rescue him.

7. The group hiked near the stream they stopped for a swim.

8. Jody paddled the canoe, she went a mile downstream.

9. Do sharks swim close to shore have you ever seen one?

10. The race cars sped down the track and many people watched the race, and pit crews worked on the cars.

REVIEW   Using Sentences Correctly

Sentences, Sentence Fragments, and Run-on Sentences
Number your paper from 1 to 20. Write *Fragment, Sentence,* or *Run-on* for each of the following groups of words to show what each group is.

1. Vera hit a slapshot, it landed in the net
2. A strong current pulled us
3. An all-day bike trip
4. A red notebook with a picture of Charlie Brown on the front
5. Squeezing fresh orange juice
6. Fans lined up at the gates
7. The boys found a cave, they crawled in
8. The nurse gave me a shot it didn't hurt
9. A long pass from the forty-yard line
10. TV programs get Emmy awards, movies get Oscars
11. Recently cross-country skiing has become popular
12. Jenny rode the horse it needed exercise
13. Cathy wore her new clogs to school
14. The girls made ice cream for the party
15. Carol worked on the engine, she finally fixed it
16. Studied the chapters in the science book
17. The road with the narrow bridge
18. The jacket hanging in my locker
19. Are the bowling balls too heavy
20. Van takes piano lessons, George takes voice lessons

Using Nouns

Part 1   What Are Nouns?

The words you use to name things are called **nouns.**

Look around you. Think of things you use every day. The words you use to name all of these things are called nouns. The words that name people and places are nouns: Who is sitting near you? What is the name of your school? What street or road is it on? What city or town do you live in?

Nouns are words that name persons, places, or things. Look at these examples:

Persons: Luke Skywalker, firefighter, pilot, Diana
Places: frontier, Milwaukee, ranch, playground
Things: tree, robot, pizza, Frisbee

Some nouns, like those listed on page 226, are names of things you can see. Other nouns are names of things you cannot see. Here are some examples naming things you cannot see.

idea   courage   loneliness   peace

Exercises   Find nouns.

A. Number your paper from 1 to 10. List the nouns in each sentence.

1. Stacy saw the fireworks last July.
2. A surfer rode a huge wave.
3. A new band performed at the fair.
4. My brother has excellent eyesight.
5. My cousin lives on a farm in Iowa.
6. Jason plays the piano and the trombone.
7. The Dodgers will play in the World Series.
8. Keith has a picture of the Golden Gate Bridge on his notebook.
9. Ms. Mason told a story about the first Thanksgiving.
10. Robert does chores around the house and earns an allowance.

B. This exercise will help you see how frequently nouns are used in all kinds of writing and in discussion. On your paper, make four lists of nouns according to these directions.

1. Copy the names of five characters from short stories or novels.
2. Copy five nouns from your science book or math book.
3. List five names of foods.
4. List five names you have learned in your social studies class.

Part 2 Common Nouns and Proper Nouns

The noun *student* is the name for a whole group of persons. Your own name stands for one particular student.

The noun *city* is the name for a whole group of places. The name *San Francisco* stands for one particular city.

The noun *candy* is the name for a whole group of things. *Baby Ruth* is the name of one particular candy.

A common noun names a whole group of persons, places, or things. A common noun begins with a small letter.

A proper noun names a particular person, place, or thing. A proper noun always begins with a capital letter.

Many proper nouns are made up of two or more words, such as *Atlantic Ocean* and *Grand Canyon National Park*. When the proper noun has several words, capitalize all the important words. You do not have to capitalize *of, on,* or *the.*

Exercise   **Find common nouns and proper nouns.**

On your paper, label two columns *Common Nouns* and *Proper Nouns.* Write each word below in the appropriate column. (Remember to begin every proper noun with a capital letter.)

1. person	9. africa	17. dentist
2. city	10. lake superior	18. elm street
3. washington	11. maria	19. big mac
4. ms. steele	12. post office	20. new york
5. paper	13. england	
6. the bee gees	14. building	
7. principal	15. mr. ruiz	
8. college	16. chicago	

Part 3 Singular and Plural Nouns

What is the difference between the words in these pairs?

person	cake	idea	star
persons	cakes	ideas	stars

You can see immediately that the words are almost the same, but that they have different endings. The bottom word in each pair has an *s* added. What difference does that *s* make in the meaning of the words? The *s* changes the *number* of things.

A noun that names one person, place, or thing is called a **singular noun.** A noun that names more than one person, place, or thing is called a **plural noun.** (All the nouns in the top line of the word pairs are *singular.* All the nouns in the bottom line are *plural.*) Changing a word from singular to plural is called forming the plural of the noun.

Here are seven rules for forming the plurals of nouns:

1. **To form the plural of most nouns, just add an *s*.**

sticks	cows	bikes	drinks
stones	dogs	skates	snacks

2. **When the singular ends in *s*, *sh*, *ch*, *x*, or *z*, add *es*.**

buses	ashes	foxes
classes	lunches	buzzes

3. **When the singular ends in *o*, add *s*.**

studios	radios	stereos	banjos

   Exceptions: For the following nouns ending in *o*, add *es*:
   echoes heroes tomatoes potatoes

4. **When the singular noun ends in *y* with a consonant before it, change the *y* to *i*, and add *es*.**

fly → flies	penny → pennies
pony → ponies	candy → candies

5. For most nouns ending in *f* or *fe*, add *s*. For some nouns ending in *f* or *fe*, however, change the *f* to *v* and add *es* or *s*.

belief → beliefs	thief → thieves	leaf → leaves
chief → chiefs	knife → knives	half → halves
roof → roofs	wife → wives	shelf → shelves
dwarf → dwarfs	life → lives	elf → elves

6. Some nouns are the same for both singular and plural.

deer   trout   sheep   moose   salmon

7. Some nouns form their plurals in special ways.

mouse → mice	man → men	tooth → teeth
goose → geese	woman → women	foot → feet
	child → children	

Using a Dictionary To Find Plurals

Here is a dictionary entry for the word *echo*. Notice that the entry shows the plural ending, *-oes*. (The plural noun is *echoes*.) Most dictionaries show the plural forms of nouns if the plurals are formed in an irregular way.

---

ech•o (ek′ō) *n., pl.* **-oes** [< L. < Gr. *ēchō*] **1.** *a*) the repetition of a sound that occurs when sound waves are reflected from a surface *b*) a sound so made **2.** *a*) any repetition or imitation of the words, ideas, etc. of another *b*) a person who repeats or imitates in this way **3.** sympathetic response **4.** a radar wave reflected from an object, appearing as a spot of light on a radarscope —[**E-**] *Gr. Myth.* a nymph who pined away for Narcissus until only her voice remained —*vi.* **-oed, -o•ing 1.** to be filled with echoes [the long hall *echoed* with their laughter] **2.** to be repeated as an echo [his words *echoed* in the valley] —*vt.* **1.** to repeat (the words, ideas, etc.) of (another) **2.** to repeat or reflect (sound) from a surface

---

When you are in doubt about plurals, consult a dictionary.

Exercises   Form plurals.

A. Number your paper from 1 to 10. Copy each pair of nouns below. Then write the number of the rule that tells how the plural was formed.

1. piano → pianos
2. roof → roofs
3. doctor → doctors
4. tax → taxes
5. party → parties

6. tooth → teeth
7. tomato → tomatoes
8. life → lives
9. moose → moose
10. bench → benches

B. Write the plural form of these nouns.

1. woman
2. knife
3. sheep
4. girl
5. candy

6. dwarf
7. radio
8. watch
9. child
10. boy

11. trout
12. noise
13. half
14. potato
15. gas

16. copy
17. mouse
18. team
19. sandwich
20. leaf

Part 4   Making Nouns Show Possession

Study these examples.

> These are my sister's skates.
>   Who owns the skates?   my *sister*

> Sally's mother called.
>   Whose mother called?   the mother of *Sally*

> This is the boy's hat.
>   Who owns the hat?   the *boy*

What has been added to the nouns *sister*, *Sally*, and *boy*? Adding *'s* makes the nouns show ownership, or possession. We call *sister's*, *Sally's*, and *boy's* **possessive nouns**.

A possessive noun shows possession of the noun that follows.

Making Singular Nouns Show Possession

To make a singular noun show possession, add an apostrophe and s.

Singular Noun	Possessive Noun
mechanic	mechanic's
James	James's
Ms. Roberts	Ms. Roberts's

Making Plural Nouns Show Possession

There are two rules to remember for making a plural noun show possession.

1. If the plural noun ends in s, simply add an apostrophe after the s.

Plural Noun	Possessive Noun
workers	workers'
nurses	nurses'
dentists	dentists'

2. If the plural noun does not end in s, add an apostrophe and an s after the apostrophe.

Plural Noun	Possessive Form
men	men's
women	women's
children	children's

Adding the Apostrophe

Look at these words. See where the apostrophe is added.

the dancer's shoes   This means shoes belonging to one dancer.

the dancers' shoes   This means shoes belonging to more than one dancer.

If you are not sure where to add the apostrophe, write the word by itself first. Then follow the rules.

Exercises   Make nouns show possession.

A. Copy the following sentences. Make the underlined words show possession.

1. Rosa team beat Dwayne team yesterday.
2. In my uncle shop they sell men and ladies clothes.
3. The girls team won the spelling match.
4. Tammy little sister got lost in the store.
5. Where are the children toys?
6. My two brothers clothes were all over the floor.
7. The girl books fell out of the car.
8. The doctor gently felt the dog paw.
9. I left my sweater at the dentist office.
10. Richard hobby is collecting ballplayers autographs.

B. In each sentence one noun is underlined. Write the possessive form of each noun. (Write the word first. Then add the apostrophe or apostrophe and *s*.)

1. We found Ramon bike in the basement.
2. There are two girls coats in the closet.
3. One man hat blew into the street.
4. It was "ladies day" at Yankee Stadium.
5. The children library closes at five o'clock.
6. We found George mittens.
7. Which department sells babies cribs?
8. Where are the women tickets?
9. I lost my father pen.
10. Pam and Sue were wearing their mothers jackets.

Sentence Patterns The N V Pattern

In an English sentence, words are put together in a certain order to make sense. The word order in most sentences follows a pattern. In this book you will study four **sentence patterns.**

Every sentence has a subject and a verb. The subject is usually a noun. In this chart, N stands for the noun in the complete subject. V stands for the verb in the complete predicate.

N	V
Diana	stumbled.
My brother	waited.
This camera	works easily.

The word order in these sentences follows a pattern. That pattern is noun-verb, or N-V. This pattern is called the **N V pattern.**

Exercises   Use the N V pattern.

A. Make a chart like the one above. Label one column N. Label the other V. Write these sentences on the chart.

1. Rain fell.
2. Katy bats next.
3. The bus stopped.
4. Scott laughed.
5. The green vase shattered.
6. The train started slowly.

B. Copy this chart. Complete each sentence in the N V pattern.

1. _____ listened.
2. _____ worked carefully.
3. The sun _____.
4. _____ turned around.

C. Make a chart of your own for the N V pattern. Write five sentences in the N V pattern.

REVIEW   Using Nouns

Recognizing Nouns   There are common nouns and proper nouns in the following sentences. For each sentence, list the nouns. Capitalize every proper noun you list.

1. Leslie and mark play baseball with their friends.
2. Our family crossed the brooklyn bridge in new york.
3. The twins have brown hair and blue eyes.
4. Yesterday joan ate cereal with blueberries for breakfast.
5. In the last game, the pirates beat the yankees.
6. Kevin drove his chevy through the mountains.
7. That man crossed the atlantic ocean in a sailboat.
8. The train for atlanta leaves in the morning.
9. Ms. martin explained the long chapter.
10. Her family moved from louisville to chicago.

Forming Plurals   Write the plural form of each underlined noun.

11. Her brother visited the movie <u>studio</u>.
12. The <u>woman</u> owned the bookstore.
13. The woman searched the library <u>shelf</u> for the book.
14. The chef made the <u>sandwich</u> on rye bread.
15. The <u>baby</u> played with the toys.

Forming Possessives   Write the possessive form of each underlined noun.

16. the <u>teachers</u> meeting
17. <u>Jess</u> part in the play
18. <u>cartoonist</u> drawing
19. the <u>players</u> pictures in the paper
20. all the <u>boys</u> uniforms

Using Verbs

Part 1 What Are Verbs?

Read these sentences. What do the underlined words tell you?

Roberto <u>hit</u> a home run.   Vera <u>ran</u> to the store.

The underlined words tell what each person did. They tell about action. Words that tell about action are called **action verbs.**

Action Verbs

Some verbs tell about action you can see, such as *hit* and *ran*. Other verbs tell about action you cannot see, as in these examples:

Sarah <u>worried</u> about the test.   I <u>have</u> two dollars.
Tony <u>wants</u> a new jacket.   The jury <u>believed</u> the witness.

Exercises Find action verbs.

A. Write the action verb in each sentence.

1. The hikers lost their way in the fog.
2. Jennifer agreed with Mother.
3. Marty has two younger brothers.
4. Jim wished for a sunny day.
5. Members of Congress make laws.
6. Linda climbed the maple tree.
7. The four-year-old child expected a visit from Santa.
8. The band marched onto the field at half-time.
9. Jessica thought about her new school.
10. The actors painted their faces with makeup.

B. Think of an action verb that will complete each sentence below. Copy the sentences, filling in the blanks with your verbs. Many different correct answers are possible for each sentence.

Example: Toby _____ the ball.
Possible answers: Toby caught the ball.
Toby threw the ball.
Toby held the ball.
Toby hit the ball.

1. The class _____ at the joke.
2. Aunt Suzanne _____ a present.
3. Several people _____ on the beach.
4. A fox _____ over the fence.
5. Gina _____ her pen.
6. Anita _____ down the hall.
7. The two brothers _____.
8. The conductor _____ tickets.
9. We _____ for the signal.
10. The scientist _____ an Arctic expedition.

Verbs That State That Something Is

Not all verbs tell about action. Some verbs just state that something is. The underlined verbs in these sentences are often used just to say that something is. They are called **state-of-being verbs.**

I am a student.	The girls were happy.
John is my brother.	The weather has been bad.
We are late.	We will be on time.

The most common state-of-being verbs are these:

is	am	were	being
are	was	be	been

Other state-of-being verbs include these:

look	seem	become	taste	smell	feel

I feel sick.	The juice tasted good.
Jill became a dancer.	Ed seems surprised.

Verbs are words that tell action or state that something is.

Exercises   **Use action verbs and state-of-being verbs.**

A.   Write the verb in each of the following sentences. (Some are action verbs, and some are state-of-being verbs.)

1. The Dodgers are her heroes.
2. The boys were still hungry.
3. Aaron bought his ticket for the concert.
4. Pam argued with her sister about clothes.
5. The new hardware store opens tomorrow.
6. My cousin is a stunt driver.
7. Donny and Marie Osmond sang together.
8. Lisa climbed the spiral staircase.
9. Dan imagined a trip to Mars.
10. The butterfly had been a caterpillar.

B. Number your paper from 1 to 10. Write the verb in each of the following sentences. After the verb, write *Action* or *State-of-being* to tell what kind of verb it is.

1. Wes plays the drums in the school band.
2. Gino's parents own a toy store.
3. Gloria is the class clown.
4. I made a puppet for my niece.
5. The sparrow injured its wing.
6. "Studio See" is a children's news show.
7. Max hid in the basement during the thunderstorm.
8. The park seemed deserted.
9. *The Lord of the Rings* was a good movie.
10. The basketball landed in the bleachers.

C. Follow the directions for Exercise B.

1. This popcorn tastes too salty.
2. Mike's sister works at the Dairy Queen.
3. Your suitcase feels very light.
4. The hotel seems run-down.
5. George likes music by Earth, Wind and Fire.
6. Liz chopped wood for the fire.
7. A conch is a large shell.
8. Hutchinson was a fine player.
9. My brother collects arrowheads and fossils.
10. Joey and Mary planned the class trip.

Using Verbs in Sentences

Look at these groups of words. They do not express complete ideas. They are not sentences. What words are missing?

Kevin sick   We the zoo every year

These are not sentences because they do not have verbs.

When we add verbs, we can make sentences like these:

Kevin *was* sick.   We *visit* the zoo every year.

Remember that every sentence must have a verb.

Exercises   Use verbs in sentences.

A.   Number your paper from 1 to 10. If the word group is a sentence, write *Sentence.* If it is not a sentence, add a verb. Then write the complete sentence. (There are many correct ways to finish each sentence.)

1. The quarterback the ball.
2. Heidi a mountain girl.
3. A plane landed on the lake.
4. Rosy a yellow scarf.
5. The elevator wouldn't move.
6. Apples are my favorite fruit.
7. Amy her shoes in the closet.
8. We played a pinball machine.
9. *The Wiz* was a play and a movie.
10. The crowd the national anthem.

B.   Follow the directions for Exercise A.

1. Where the water fountain?
2. Al put posters on the wall.
3. A crabapple sour.
4. The Broncos in the fourth quarter.
5. The girls rode their bikes.
6. My collie sleeps near my bed.
7. The farmer the grain.
8. A tire makes a good swing.
9. Many people turkey on Thanksgiving.
10. The firefighters opened the fire hydrant.

Part 2 Main Verbs and Helping Verbs

Many of the verbs you have studied so far have been just one word: *hit, is, ran,* and *climbed,* for example.

A great many verbs are made up of two or three words. Notice the verbs in these sentences.

Betsy *walked* home.　　　　Steven *called* you.
Betsy *is walking* home.　　　Steven *was calling* you.
Betsy *has been walking* home.　Steven *might have called* you.

When a verb is made up of two or more words, the last word is the **main verb.** The other words are called **helping verbs.** In this way, one verb can have several parts.

Helping Verb	+	Main Verb	=	Verb
		walked		walked
is		walking		is walking
has been		walking		has been walking
		called		called
was		calling		was calling
might have		called		might have called

The most common of the helping verbs are the forms of *be, have,* and *do:*

be — am, is, are, was, were
have — has, have, had
do — does, do, did

These words can also be used by themselves as main verbs.

Used as Helping Verb	Used as Main Verb
Janet *was visiting.*	Janet *was* in Indiana.
Ralph *does like* math.	Ralph *does* his work.

These are several other helping verbs that can be used with main verbs.

be	been	shall	could	would	might
being	can	will	should	may	

A verb may be a single word or a group of words, made up of a main verb and one or more helping verbs.

Exercises **Find main verbs and helping verbs.**

A. Number your paper from 1 to 10. Make two columns. Head the first column *Helping Verbs*. Head the second *Main Verb*. Write the parts of the verb for each of these sentences in the correct column.

Example: That car should have stopped for the bus.

Helping Verbs	Main Verb
should have	stopped

1. Ernest has eaten some fudge.
2. Tomorrow we will be holding a field day.
3. One horse was leading the parade.
4. Laraine is wearing her catcher's mitt.
5. The trip should have ended sooner.
6. Stephanie does like the new apartment.
7. We may wash the car today.
8. They could have arrived on time.
9. Julio has been painting with poster paints.
10. Our teacher had explained the experiment before.

B. Write five combinations using the main verb *count*. Four examples are given below. You may use *counted* and *counting* as the main verb, too.

can count	might have counted
was counting	will have been counted

Some Verbs Need Helping Verbs

Look at these three sentences:

> We *ate* the cookies.
> We *eaten* all of them.
> We *eating* crackers now.

Something is wrong with the last two sentences. What can you add to make them sound right? You will add helping verbs.

> We **have** *eaten* all of them.
> We **are** *eating* crackers now.

Four of the verbs you use very frequently must be used with helping verbs. They are *been, done, gone,* and *seen.* Verbs with the *-en* ending, like *chosen* or *ridden,* must be used with helping verbs. Verbs with the *-ing* ending, like *sitting* and *talking,* must be used with helping verbs. There are many other verbs that must be used with helping verbs. You will learn more about them in **Section 5.**

Exercises   **Supply the helping verbs.**

A.   Number your paper from 1 to 10. If the sentence is correct, write *Correct.* If the verb needs a helping verb, write a helping verb and the main verb. There may be more than one right answer.

> Example: Ms. Lorne waiting at the bus stop.
>   was waiting

1. The groundhog seen its shadow.
2. A huge truck has swept the streets.
3. We playing hockey.
4. The vase broken by accident.
5. Superman rescued the trapped miners.
6. Babe Didrikson was a great athlete.

7. A lady walking the tightrope.
8. The girl was running down the alley.
9. We been listening to a John Denver album.
10. I using your ruler.

B.   Follow the directions for Exercise A.

1. Barb ridden a bronco.
2. Millions of years ago, dinosaurs lived.
3. The class learning about government.
4. Alec had a haircut.
5. My sister Carmen chosen the records.
6. A new movie theater opening soon.
7. We leaving for Boston tomorrow.
8. Costumes were stored in a trunk.
9. That dog bitten our mail carrier.
10. Listeners guessing the punch line.

Separated Parts of the Verb

Sometimes another part of the sentence comes between the helping verb and the main verb.

> Ezra **may** *not* **pitch** today.
> Joanne **will** *probably* **stay** for dinner.
> The gate **should**n't **have been locked** last night.

Not and the ending *n't* are never part of the verb, although they do change the meaning of the verb.

In questions, we very often use one or more words between the helping verb and the main verb.

> **Does** *this bicycle* **need** oil?   **Have** *you* **been listening?**
> **Were** *you* **looking** for me?   **Is** *Dad* **painting** in the garage?

Exercises   Find separated parts of the verb.

A.   Number your paper from 1 to 10. Make two columns. Head the first column *Helping Verbs*. Head the second *Main Verb*. Write the parts of the verb for each of these sentences in the correct column.

> Example: Joseph didn't see the curb.
>
> | Helping Verb | Main Verb |
> | --- | --- |
> | did | see |

1. Our goalie has not blocked any shots.
2. Vicky has never missed a Red Sox game.
3. Would you repeat your answer?
4. The floats were usually awarded prizes.
5. Donna will probably break the school record in the 100-yard dash.
6. Was the champ resting before the fight?
7. We shouldn't cross the railroad tracks.
8. Leo couldn't believe his eyes.
9. Prisoners have never escaped from that jail.
10. Didn't immigrants come to Ellis Island?

B.   Follow the directions for Exercise A.

1. I was only joking about your costume.
2. Will winter ever end?
3. Grandma has never missed my birthday party.
4. Winona could barely reach the swing.
5. Barry has almost finished his homework.
6. Have you ever sung in a choir?
7. When does your library card expire?
8. Can you still smell the fish in the kitchen?
9. I can't understand this language.
10. Shouldn't the movie start now?

Part 3　Direct Objects of Verbs

In many sentences, a subject and a verb are enough to express a complete thought.

> The child fell.
> The telephone rang.

In other sentences, the thought is not complete until other words have been added.

> Kirk spilled the **glue.**
> The class applauded **Jean.**

The word that is needed after the verb to complete the action of the verb is the **direct object of the verb.** *Glue* tells what Kirk spilled. *Jean* tells whom the class applauded. *Glue* and *Jean* are the direct objects in these sentences.

The direct object tells what receives the action of the verb.

Recognizing Direct Objects

To find the direct object in a sentence, first find the verb. Then ask *what?* or *whom?* after the verb. If a word answers *what?* or *whom?* after the verb, it is the direct object.

> Examples: John sharpened his pencil.
> John sharpened *what?*　his *pencil*
> The direct object is *pencil.*
>
> The hockey players cheered their coach.
> The players cheered *whom?*　their *coach*
> The direct object is *coach.*

Direct objects only answer *what?* or *whom?* after the verb. They do not tell *when* or *where* or *how.* You will see there are no direct objects in the following sentences.

Andrew plays in the afternoon.
His father drove to Tennessee.

However, there are direct objects in these sentences.

Andrew plays *football* in the afternoon.
His father drove the *truck* to Tennessee.

Exercises   Find direct objects.

A.   Copy the following sentences. Underline the verb twice. Draw a circle around the direct object.

Example: Della was riding her bicycle.

1. Teresa broke her ruler.
2. Tim liked the new coach.
3. The fielder should have caught that ball.
4. The conductor will collect tickets.
5. This computer will solve mysteries.
6. Did you call your parents?
7. My little brothers made a snowman.
8. Phyllis and Mandy were doing a puzzle.
9. Long ago, Indians hunted buffalo here.
10. Lyndon cut the cake into small pieces.

B.   On a sheet of paper, write sentences using the following verbs. Put a direct object in each sentence. Draw a circle around the direct object that you have added.

1. lost
2. was building
3. dropped
4. will fill
5. likes
6. was writing
7. covered
8. should have read
9. will eat
10. touched

Part 4 Linking Verbs

State-of-being verbs are often called **linking verbs.** Here are some examples:

> Rhonda's dress *was* blue.
> The stew *smells* delicious.
> Our players *looked* happy.

Linking verbs connect the subject with a word in the predicate. In the examples, they connect *dress* with *blue, stew* with *delicious,* and *players* with *happy.* The words in the predicate complete the meaning of the linking verbs.

The words *is, am, are, was, were, be, become* are often used as linking verbs. The words *seem, look, smell, taste,* and *feel* are sometimes linking verbs.

The words that follow linking verbs and tell something about the subject are either nouns or adjectives. These words complete the meaning of the linking verb.

Here are some examples of nouns that follow linking verbs. These nouns are called **predicate nouns.** See how each predicate noun is connected to the subject.

> My father *is* an **engineer.**
>
> Elvis Presley *was* a famous **singer.**
>
> She *will be* the **president** of our class.

Here are some examples of adjectives that follow linking verbs. These adjectives are called **predicate adjectives.** See how each predicate adjective describes the subject.

> Arthur *seemed* **nervous.**
>
> The snow-covered roads *were* **slippery.**
>
> Craig *is being* **stubborn.**

Exercises   Find the linking verbs.

A.   At the top of three columns write: *Subject, Linking Verb,* and *Word Linked to Subject.* Find the three parts in each sentence. Write them in the proper columns.

Example: The dancers in the marathon looked tired.

Subject	Linking Verb	Word Linked to Subject
dancers	looked	tired

1. Ansel Adams is a famous photographer.
2. The trail was rough in spots.
3. That comedian is very clever.
4. Everyone seems sorry about the mix-up.
5. That hot vegetable soup smells good.
6. My old winter coat looks shabby.
7. Our flight to Miami was smooth.
8. Larry has been president of the club.
9. Kris is a very good swimmer.
10. The coach feels confident about the playoffs.

B.   Follow the directions for Exercise A.

1. That new cereal tastes soggy.
2. My sister is the best speller in our family.
3. The radio is much too loud.
4. Toby felt nervous at rehearsal.
5. The people were tourists from Germany.
6. Logan Beach looks peaceful today.
7. Casey's aunt has been an aide to a Senator.
8. The topics for speeches seem interesting.
9. Lana was curious about the lineup.
10. The stairs to the attic are creaky.

Direct Objects or Predicate Words?

What are the differences between these two sentences?

Bob hit a home run.   Bob is an outfielder.

You have learned about two kinds of verbs. There are *action verbs* and *linking verbs*. You have also learned about two kinds of words that follow verbs and complete their meaning. There are *direct objects* and there are *predicate nouns* or *predicate adjectives*.

How can you tell which words are direct objects and which words are predicate words? First, find the verb in a sentence. Is the verb an action verb or a linking verb?

1. If an **action verb** is followed by a word, a noun, that tells *what* or *whom*, that word is a **direct object**.

Examples: Julie is studying *Spanish*.   We ate *lunch* early.

2. If a **linking verb** is followed by a word that tells about the subject, that word is a **predicate noun** or a **predicate adjective**.

Examples: Julie is a *student*. (predicate noun)
We are *hungry*. (predicate adjective)

Now compare these two examples.

Bob hit a home run.
Hit is an action verb.   *Home run* is a direct object.

Bob is an outfielder.
Is is a linking verb.   *Outfielder* is a predicate noun.

Exercises   Find direct objects and predicate words.

A.   Some of the verbs in the following sentences are linking verbs followed by predicate words. Others are action verbs followed by direct objects. Copy each of the sentences. Draw a circle around each linking verb. Underline each action verb.

1. The girls formed a band.

2. Phil made a metal sculpture.
3. Nicole is a student from France.
4. Roger will design the costumes.
5. *Freaky Friday* is an enjoyable book.
6. Vanessa is the bass player.
7. This new candy tastes fizzy.
8. Our family rented a cabin in the mountains.
9. The weather will be pleasant this spring.
10. That stray dog seems mean.

B. Follow the directions for Exercise A.

1. The dark movie theater was quiet.
2. Dave's favorite hangout is the corner.
3. We met our cousin for the first time.
4. Kate seems older than her sister.
5. The surrounding farms look deserted.
6. Josh paid three dollars for his ticket.
7. My brothers built an igloo last winter.
8. Todd feeds his dog table scraps.
9. Aaron fumbled the pass.
10. After the race, the runners were weary.

Part 5   Verb Tenses

Verbs are time-telling words. They do not just tell of an action or a state of being. They also tell *when* something takes place. By changing their forms, they tell whether the action or state of being is past, present, or future. These changes in form to show time are called **tenses.**

The **present tense** indicates an action or state of being happening now.

I *work* at school.   I *am* a student.

The **past tense** indicates an action or state of being completed in the past.

> I *worked* all last summer.   I *was* a library aide.

The **future tense** indicates an action or state of being happening in the future.

> I *will work* at the pool next year.   I *will be* a lifeguard.

Tense changes are made in three ways:

1. By a change in spelling: *know, knew, known*
2. By a change in ending: *look, looked*
3. By a change in helping verbs: *did work, will work*

Forming the Tenses

Present Tense.   In general, the **present tense** of the verb is the same as the name of the verb: *race, call, do, think* (I *race*, you *call*, they *do*, we *think*). Add *-s* or *-es* to the verb when it is used with a singular noun or with *he, she,* or *it* (he *races*, she *calls*, it *does*, Sara *thinks*).

Past Tense.   The **past tense** of most verbs is formed by adding *-d* or *-ed* to the present tense:

> race — rac*ed*   call — call*ed*

These verbs are called **regular verbs.**

The past tense of other verbs, called **irregular verbs,** is usually shown by a change of spelling:

> do → *did*   think → *thought*

Future Tense.   The **future tense** is formed by using the helping verbs *will* or *shall* with the present tense:

> *will* race   *shall* call   *will* do   *shall* think

Exercises Recognize and use verb tenses.

A. Number your paper from 1 to 10. Write the verb in each of the following sentences. Name the tense of each verb.

> Example: Superman will stop the runaway train.
>   will stop, future tense

1. We always watch the evening news.
2. The crew will build a new gym.
3. At midnight we raided the refrigerator.
4. Julie will have a slumber party on her birthday.
5. Some people dressed in costumes.
6. Ken's watch glows in the dark.
7. The bus will arrive late today.
8. Fresh blueberries taste great on ice cream.
9. Someone painted the lockers orange.
10. Gail tossed the ball to the catcher for the third out.

B. Number your paper from 1 to 10. Write the form of the verb asked for in each of the following sentences. Check by reading the sentence to yourself.

> Example: Bill Rodgers (past of *cross*) the finish line first.
>   crossed

1. Kara (future of *get*) two free throws.
2. My sister and I (past of *play*) miniature golf.
3. Vicky (present of *mow*) her neighbor's lawn.
4. The jury (future of *decide*) the sentence.
5. Dad (past of *plant*) pumpkins in the garden.
6. With snowshoes, I (future of *walk*) on top of the snow.
7. My friends (present of *want*) front-row seats.
8. Carol (present of *pitch*) with her left hand.
9. Steve (past of *joke*) about his haircut.
10. The weather service (past of *warn*) of a tornado.

Sentence Patterns

A sentence in the **N V N pattern** has three parts. The first N stands for the subject noun. The V stands for the verb. The second N stands for the direct object noun. Read the sentences in the following chart. They are in the N V N pattern.

N	V	N
Cora	writes	songs.
Snakes	lay	eggs.
My friends	planned	a party.
The plumber	fixed	the sink.
Donald	likes	his new bike.

Exercises   Use the N V N pattern.

A. Make a chart like the one above. Label the three columns *N*, *V*, and *N*. Write these sentences on the chart.

1. Therese plays the flute.
2. Phyllis called Terry.
3. My dog watches TV.
4. Andy took a deep breath.
5. We cheered our goalie.
6. Saturn has ten moons.
7. Both arrows hit the target.
8. Martina rode the train.

B. Copy this chart. Complete each sentence in the N V N pattern.

N	V	N
1. Angela	pushed	_____.
2. _____	measured	_____.
3. James	_____	carrots.
4. _____	answered	the phone.
5. This kitten	chases	_____.

C. Make a chart of your own for the N V N pattern. Write five sentences in the N V N pattern.

Sentence Patterns   The N LV N Pattern

A sentence in the **N LV N pattern** has three parts. The first *N* stands for the subject noun. *LV* stands for a linking verb. "Linking verb" is another name for "state-of-being verb." The second *N* stands for the noun that follows the linking verb.

N	LV	N
Janet	is	an artist.
Ralph	is	her brother.
The best speller	was	Linn.
Pine	is	a soft wood.
My skates	were	a birthday present.

Exercises   Use the N LV N pattern.

A. Make a chart like the one above. Label the three columns *N*, *LV*, and *N*. Write these sentences on the chart.

1. Tomatoes are fruits.
2. This game is a challenge.
3. Africa is a continent.
4. My partner was Reba.
5. The boys were friends.
6. Larry is a joker.
7. Nutmeg is a spice.
8. These dogs are poodles.

B. Make a chart like the one below. Complete each sentence in the N LV N pattern.

N	LV	N
1. The last batter	was	_____.
2. _____	are	insects.
3. Juan	_____	a good swimmer.
4. _____	was	_____.
5. _____	is	a new invention.

C. Make a chart of your own. Label the columns *N*, *LV*, and *N*. Write five sentences in the N LV N pattern.

Sentence Patterns

Sentences in the **N LV Adj pattern** have three parts. The N stands for the subject noun. LV stands for linking verb. Adj stands for adjective that follows the linking verb. The sentences in the following chart are in the N LV Adj pattern.

N	LV	Adj
The classroom	is	quiet.
Lemons	taste	sour.
Chris	was	fearless.
This record	sounds	scratchy.
These new boots	look	large.

Exercises   Use the N LV Adj pattern.

A. Make a chart like the one above. Label the three columns *N*, *LV*, and *Adj*. Write these sentences on the chart.

1. Connie looks happy.
2. These roads are narrow.
3. Your sweater feels furry.
4. Tacos are tasty.
5. The radio sounds loud.
6. The mail was late.
7. The oranges were ripe.
8. This radish tastes bitter.

B. Make a chart like the one below. Complete each sentence in the N LV Adj pattern.

N	LV	Adj
1. _____	is	funny.
2. _____	looks	sad.
3. Sandpaper	feels	_____.
4. The Haleys	_____	friendly.
5. _____	was	_____.

C. Make a chart of your own. Label the columns *N*, *LV*, and *Adj*. Write five sentences in the N LV Adj pattern.

REVIEW Using Verbs

Action Verbs and Linking Verbs Write the verb in each sentence. Beside the verb, write *Action* or *Linking* to show what the verb is. If an action verb is completed by a direct object, write the direct object. Or, write the predicate word that completes a linking verb.

1. That classroom will be a lunchroom next year.
2. Gary Trudeau is the creator of Doonesbury.
3. Carly made a bowl out of clay.
4. The doctor put a cast on Mandy's arm.
5. During the ride, Carl closed his eyes.
6. Alex wrote his report in the library.
7. The science experiment was a failure.
8. Nora was the best player on our team.
9. The tennis courts look wet.
10. We hung wallpaper with a thick paste.

Parts of the Verb Find the verb in each sentence, and write the complete verb.

11. The Bears are practicing for the first game.
12. Someone should have called the police.
13. Cindy may visit her grandmother in Minneapolis.
14. Tony was immediately sent to the nurse's office.
15. Ruthie has always liked sports.

Verb Tenses Write the verb in each of the following sentences. Beside each verb, write its tense.

16. The aquarium displays all types of fish.
17. Mr. Vito will change the date of the play.
18. Each cast member worked hard.
19. Sherry always plays pranks on her friends.
20. Larry asked for a different seat.

Using Irregular Verbs

Part 1 Principal Parts of Verbs

Every verb has many different forms. You have seen forms such as *talked, was talking, had talked, have been talking, will talk, would have talked,* and others. All of these different forms of a verb are made from just three parts. For this reason, the three parts of any verb are called its **principal parts.**

The principal parts of a verb are known as:

1. **Present**   2. **Past**   3. **Past Participle**

    talk   talked   talked

Here are some examples:

Present	Past	Past Participle
call	called	called
hurry	hurried	hurried
look	looked	looked
paste	pasted	pasted
stop	stopped	stopped
walk	walked	walked

The *present* part of the verb is its present tense. (Add -*s* or -*es* to the verb when it is used with a singular noun or *he, she,* or *it:* he *goes,* she *hurries,* it *looks.*) The present part used with *will* or *shall* forms the future tense.

The *past* part of the verb is its past tense.

The *past participle* is used with helping verbs to make other forms of the verb. Here are some examples of these other forms:

has called	was being called
have called	shall be called
had called	has been called
was called	will have called
were called	should have been called

Part 2   Regular Verbs

All of the verbs given in the list of principal parts are called **regular verbs.** Every verb that is *regular* forms its past tense by adding -*ed* (*call**ed***) or -*d* (*paste**d***) to the present form. The past participle is the same as the past form and is always used with a helping verb. Most English verbs are regular.

Exercises   Use principal parts of verbs.

A. Write the verb form indicated for the following regular verbs. Use one or more helping verbs with each past participle.

1. like (past)
2. notice (past participle)
3. arrange (present)
4. watch (past participle)
5. snow (past)
6. smell (present)
7. listen (past participle)
8. rock (past participle)
9. use (past)
10. explain (past)

B. Write a sentence for each of the verbs below. Use the verb form indicated.

1. turn (past participle)
2. paint (past)
3. chase (past participle)
4. juggle (present)
5. open (past)
6. weigh (present)
7. pound (past)
8. struggle (present)
9. help (present)
10. order (past participle)

Part 3   Irregular Verbs

Some verbs do not form their second and third parts in a regular way. These five verbs are examples:

Present	Past	Past Participle
feel	felt	felt
go	went	gone
know	knew	known
see	saw	seen
think	thought	thought

These verbs are not regular verbs. They are called **irregular verbs.**

Although there are only sixty irregular verbs in our language, they are important because many of them are verbs you use frequently. You cannot avoid them.

In order to use them correctly, you must know the correct past form, used alone to mean past action. You must also know the correct past participle, used with helping verbs. The best way to learn to use irregular verbs correctly is to study and memorize as many of these verb forms as possible. A list of the most commonly used irregular verbs is given on page 262.

When you are using irregular verbs, you should remember these two rules:

1. The past form is always used by itself, *without* a helping verb.
    We *went* to the library last Saturday.
2. The past participle is always used *with* a helping verb.
    We *have gone* to the library every Saturday this month.

Helping Verbs

The words most often used with the third principal part of all verbs are the forms of *be* and *have*. Here they are, so that you can refer to them when you need to.

		Be			Have	
		Present	Past		Present	Past
Singular:	I	am	was	I	have	had
	you	are	were	you	have	had
	he, she, it	is	was	he, she, it	has	had
Plural:	we	are	were	we	have	had
	you	are	were	you	have	had
	they	are	were	they	have	had

The forms *be, been,* and *being* are always used with one or more additional helping verbs.

I *could be*
she *has been*
they *were being*

Principal Parts of Common Irregular Verbs

Present	Past	Past Participle
begin	began	(have) begun
break	broke	(have) broken
bring	brought	(have) brought
choose	chose	(have) chosen
come	came	(have) come
do	did	(have) done
drink	drank	(have) drunk
eat	ate	(have) eaten
fall	fell	(have) fallen
freeze	froze	(have) frozen
give	gave	(have) given
go	went	(have) gone
grow	grew	(have) grown
have	had	(have) had
know	knew	(have) known
ride	rode	(have) ridden
ring	rang	(have) rung
rise	rose	(have) risen
run	ran	(have) run
say	said	(have) said
see	saw	(have) seen
sing	sang	(have) sung
sit	sat	(have) sat
speak	spoke	(have) spoken
steal	stole	(have) stolen
swim	swam	(have) swum
take	took	(have) taken
teach	taught	(have) taught
throw	threw	(have) thrown
wear	wore	(have) worn
write	wrote	(have) written

Using a Dictionary To Find Principal Parts

If you are not sure about a verb form, look it up in a dictionary. If the verb is regular, only one form will usually be listed.

If the verb is irregular, the dictionary will give the irregular forms. It will give two forms if the past and past participle are the same: *say, said.* It will give all three principal parts if they are all different: *sing, sang, sung.*

Dictionary Entry for *begin*

present

be•gin (bi gin′), ***v.*** to start being, doing, acting, etc.; get under way [Work *begins* at 8:00 A.M. His cold *began* with a sore throat.] —**be•gan′**, *p.*; **be•gun′**, *p.p.*

past participle

past

Part 4 Practice Pages on Irregular Verbs

There are a few irregular verbs that are especially troublesome. They cause problems in writing and in speaking. Many people get confused about which form is used alone to mean the past, and which form is used with helping verbs.

On pages 265–277, you will find practice sentences for irregular verbs used often. To find the verbs that are difficult for you, do the following exercise.

If the exercise shows that you do know these verbs, you may need only to review this section.

If the exercise shows that you need more practice with certain verbs, turn to those verbs on the following pages. For each verb there are many sentences that will help you to "say it right," "hear it right," and "write it right."

Exercise   Use irregular verbs.

Number your paper from 1 to 20. For each sentence, write the correct word from the two given in the parentheses.

1. A relief pitcher has (began, begun) to warm up.
2. That driver has (broke, broken) the law.
3. Joan has (took, taken) her books with her.
4. I have never (saw, seen) a funnier movie.
5. Has Bert (done, did) what he promised?
6. It (took, taken) a long time to find the right house.
7. Christopher has (ate, eaten) a whole box of candy.
8. Jake has (rode, ridden) his bike to the park.
9. Jennifer has (wrote, written) some exciting stories.
10. My brother (ran, run) to catch his bus this morning.
11. Dolores has (gave, given) an excellent report.
12. The Johnsons have (gone, went) on vacation.
13. The sunflower has (grew, grown) five feet high.
14. Barry (knew, known) the rules of the game.
15. The ranch hand (rode, ridden) a wild horse.
16. The students have (took, taken) two tests this week.
17. Your teammates have (ran, run) as fast as you.
18. I (seen, saw) you at the mall.
19. Jan (grew, grown) to like her new school.
20. The fog (began, begun) to clear last night.

Say It Right   Hear It Right

Say these sentences until the correct use of the verbs sounds natural to you.

1. The little boy *began* to cry.
2. Suddenly the airplane *began* flying in a circle.
3. My mother *has begun* her new job.
4. She *began* by washing the kitchen windows.
5. Alex *had* just *begun* packing for the trip.
6. *Have* you *begun* your social studies report?
7. Many forest fires *are begun* by careless campers.
8. I *have* finally *begun* to get along with my sister.
9. The film *began* with an eerie scene.
10. We *should have begun* the decorations sooner.

Write It Right

Write the correct verb from the two forms given. Check your answer by saying the complete sentence to yourself.

1. We have (began, begun) a new unit in science class.
2. My father (began, begun) cooking lessons last month.
3. By evening the hurricane had (began, begun) to lose force.
4. The next day people (began, begun) returning to their homes.
5. I have (began, begun) to think about a career.
6. Mr. Jansen, have you (began, begun) to correct our tests yet?
7. Eight people (began, begun) the race, but only three finished.
8. The mayor (began, begun) her speech with a joke.
9. While we were setting up the tent, it (began, begun) to rain.
10. The hamburgers were ready, so we (began, begun) eating.

Use the Right Word

Say It Right   Hear It Right

Say these sentences until the correct use of the verbs sounds natural to you.

1. What *broke* in the kitchen?
2. Paula *has broken* a plate.
3. My bike *broke* down on the way home.
4. Have you ever *broken* a leg?
5. I once *broke* a finger.
6. The clock radio *is broken*.
7. Ms. Berger *broke* up the argument in the hall.
8. Lorne *had* already *broken* his promise.
9. Carly *broke* the high jump record.
10. What *have* you *broken*?

Write It Right

Write the correct verb from the two forms given. Check your answer by saying the complete sentence to yourself.

1. The chick has (broke, broken) out of the shell.
2. My pencil (broke, broken) again.
3. The sand dollars on the beach are all (broke, broken).
4. The lamp was (broke, broken) into a hundred pieces.
5. His glasses (broke, broken) when he fell.
6. Mitch has finally (broke, broken) in his new hiking boots.
7. The second bus must have (broke, broken) down.
8. Has anyone ever (broke, broken) Babe Ruth's record for all-time home runs?
9. Yes, Hank Aaron (broke, broken) the record in 1974.
10. Jim (broke, broken) the eggs into the frying pan.

Say It Right   Hear It Right

Say these sentences until the correct use of the verbs sounds natural to you.

1. I *did* my homework before dinner.
2. Gerry *had* never *done* any woodworking before.
3. Denise *did* everything she could to help.
4. Who *hasn't done* the assignment?
5. The cast *did* an extra show.
6. *Have* you ever *done* needlepoint?
7. The cleanup crew *did* a great job.
8. What *was done* about the leaky faucet?
9. Cheryl's science project *has* never *been done* before.
10. Katie *did* her best on the balance beam.

Write It Right

Write the correct verb from the two forms given. Check your answer by saying the complete sentence to yourself.

1. I (did, done) all I could to pass my test.
2. What have you (did, done) with your report card?
3. Those pictures were (did, done) by Carlos.
4. Mary (did, done) the shoveling by herself.
5. I haven't (did, done) a thing about the broken window.
6. The racing car (did, done) 120 miles an hour.
7. Has Mike (did, done) his homework?
8. I should have (did, done) better on my painting.
9. Jack (did, done) more push-ups than anyone else.
10. Faith (did, done) an excellent science project.

Use the Right Word

Say It Right   Hear It Right

Say these sentences until the correct use of the verbs sounds natural to you.

1. What *have* you *eaten* for breakfast?
2. I *ate* eggs and toast this morning.
3. Skip *has eaten* all of the salad.
4. Paula *ate* a delicious ice cream sundae.
5. Johnny *had* never *eaten* oysters before.
6. Hot peppers *are eaten* in Mexico.
7. We *ate* a small lunch before the race.
8. *Have*n't you *eaten* yet?
9. Snails *are eaten* with butter and garlic.
10. Wendy *ate* four popsicles.

Write It Right

Write the correct verb from the two forms given. Check your answer by saying the complete sentence to yourself.

1. The squirrels have (ate, eaten) all the crumbs.
2. Teddy has (ate, eaten) the last piece of pie.
3. Shelly (ate, eaten) dinner with us last night.
4. Al had just (ate, eaten) breakfast when the phone rang.
5. We should have (ate, eaten) our lunch in a shady spot.
6. I dreamed that my sister was (ate, eaten) by a dragon.
7. By morning, the raccoons had (ate, eaten) all of our food.
8. Kevin has (ate, eaten) his lunch in a hurry.
9. Why haven't you (ate, eaten) your broccoli?
10. Ruth must have (ate, eaten) one of my cookies.

Say It Right   Hear It Right

Say these sentences until the correct use of the verbs sounds natural to you.

1. Who *gave* you that ice cream?
2. The roller coaster *has given* me a stomach ache.
3. Kim *gave* John some tips on ice skating.
4. The conductor *had given* me the wrong change.
5. Tom *gave* me a ride home yesterday.
6. *Haven't* you *given* your report yet?
7. Our team *gave* a cheer for Coach Long.
8. Ellen *has given* me her new address.
9. Only Susan *had given* the correct answer.
10. Bob *gave* the dog a shampoo.

Write It Right

Write the correct verb from the two forms given. Check your answer by saying the complete sentence to yourself.

1. My mother has (gave, given) me a dollar to buy lunch.
2. Officer Wendell (gave, given) a talk on traffic safety.
3. Calculators were (gave, given) as door prizes.
4. The manager (gave, given) my sister a raise.
5. Linda (gave, given) me a piece of chocolate cake.
6. I was (gave, given) a bike for my birthday.
7. Eric may have (gave, given) the book to Ms. Coleman.
8. The class (gave, given) Sandy a going-away party.
9. I have (gave, given) Bobby my best model car.
10. Has Lois (gave, given) you a copy of the contest rules?

Say It Right   Hear It Right

Say these sentences until the correct use of the verbs sounds natural to you.

1. Why *has* Laurie *gone* home early?
2. She *went* home sick.
3. My notebook *is gone* again.
4. Gilbert *went* to the band concert with his cousin.
5. I *had gone* sailing before.
6. Everyone but Pete *went* to the picnic.
7. *Have* you ever *gone* to Missouri?
8. Nina *went* on an errand.
9. Betty *must have gone* fishing in the motorboat.
10. Jeff *went* for a ride on a moped.

Write It Right

Write the correct verb from the two forms given. Check your answer by saying the complete sentence to yourself.

1. Do you know where Ken's family (went, gone)?
2. They have (went, gone) camping again.
3. Fortunately, the hurricane had (went, gone) out to sea.
4. Has Julie (went, gone) already?
5. We haven't (went, gone) to a basketball game lately.
6. Miss Jamison (went, gone) to the Smokey Mountains last year.
7. My family has always (went, gone) away for Christmas.
8. Last year, we (went, gone) to Washington.
9. The entire class has (went, gone) on a field trip.
10. When we looked, the deer was (went, gone).

Say It Right   Hear It Right

Say these questions until the correct use of the verbs sounds natural to you.

1. Hank's puppy *has* really *grown*.
2. The injured starfish *grew* a new leg.
3. *Have* you ever *grown* a cactus?
4. The farmer *grew* all sorts of vegetables.
5. The lioness *had grown* too old to hunt.
6. Delicious strawberries *are grown* in Michigan.
7. The noisy crowd *grew* larger and larger.
8. The tomatoes *have grown* rapidly.
9. Terry *grew* pleased with his new school.
10. Country music *has grown* in popularity.

Write It Right

Write the correct verb from the two forms given. Check your answer by saying the complete sentence to yourself.

1. The climbers had (grown, grew) too tired to continue their climb.
2. Mom has (grew, grown) impatient with Larry's practical jokes.
3. The thunder (grew, grown) louder as the storm continued.
4. I have (grew, grown) much closer to my dad.
5. Thick, green ivy has (grew, grown) all over the old house.
6. Rita had finally (grew, grown) tall enough to play baketball.
7. The pollution problem has (grew, grown) even larger.
8. I (grew, grown) weary of reading and fell asleep.
9. Some pineapples are (grew, grown) in Puerto Rico.
10. Palm trees have (grew, grown) all over the island.

Use the Right Word

Say It Right   Hear It Right

Say these sentences until the correct use of the verbs sounds natural to you.

1. Judy *knew* that she had passed the test.
2. Our family *has known* the O'Neills for years.
3. *Had* you *known* that Kurt was worried?
4. North Carolina *is known* for furniture making.
5. We *knew* that the snow would melt by morning.
6. I always *knew* about Frank's talent for painting.
7. How long *have* you *known* Susan?
8. Dogs *are known* for their loyalty.
9. The sportscaster *should have known* the score.
10. Everyone *knew* that the suspect was lying.

Write It Right

Write the correct verb from the two forms given. Check your answer by saying the complete sentence to yourself.

1. Only Gail (knew, known) how to repair the bicycle.
2. John Galvani is (knew, known) as Jackie to his friends.
3. I have never (knew, known) anyone as stubborn as Debra.
4. No one could have (knew, known) that answer.
5. Steve and Carlos have (knew, known) him for years.
6. Our cat Eleanor would have (knew, known) how to protect herself.
7. Dad never (knew, known) his cousin Rosemary very well.
8. If only I had (knew, known) you were home!
9. Everyone had (knew, known) that Mary Ellen was afraid.
10. I have always (knew, known) when I could do better.

Say It Right   Hear It Right

Say these sentences until the correct use of the verbs sounds natural to you.

1. *Have* you ever *ridden* a horse?
2. The surfer *rode* the waves.
3. We *should have ridden* to school on the bus.
4. Mom's new car *rode* well.
5. The cowboy *has ridden* off.
6. The gang *rode* their motorcycles on the highway.
7. Five people *have ridden* together on this sled.
8. Kevin *rode* a train across the country.
9. At night we *rode* with lights on our bikes.
10. In London horses *are ridden* by some police officers.

Write It Right

Write the correct verb from the two forms given. Check your answer by saying the complete sentence to yourself.

1. The executive (rode, ridden) in the first-class section.
2. Janet (rode, ridden) her bike on the nature trail.
3. Bo (rode, ridden) in his uncle's sailplane.
4. Even the cat (rode, ridden) along on the trip.
5. Ramon has (rode, ridden) the bronco.
6. Portia has (rode, ridden) the roller coaster.
7. Horses were (rode, ridden) by Pony Express carriers.
8. Some people in the parade (rode, ridden) unicycles.
9. The sailors had (rode, ridden) out the storm.
10. The entrants had (rode, ridden) their horses around the ring.

Say It Right   Hear It Right

Say these sentences until the correct use of the verbs sounds natural to you.

1. The meeting *ran* late.
2. The grocery store *has run* out of milk.
3. Michelle *ran* for class president.
4. *Have* you ever *run* a mile?
5. We think our cat *ran* away.
6. The old car *had*n't *run* for years.
7. Who *ran* up the stairs?
8. Marathon races *are run* in many cities.
9. Mary *ran* into a pole with her bike.
10. The quarterback *should have run* with the ball.

Write It Right

Write the correct verb from the two forms given. Check your answer by saying the complete sentence to yourself.

1. I have never (ran, run) a lawnmower before.
2. Mom stopped baking because she had (ran, run) out of flour.
3. Our gym class hasn't (ran, run) the fifty-yard dash yet.
4. Bicycle races are (ran, run) on a bowl-shaped track.
5. Paul (ran, run) the cotton candy machine at the school circus.
6. The team had (ran, run) out of energy.
7. Cara (ran, run) every morning last summer.
8. The stalled truck must have (ran, run) out of gas.
9. Franklin D. Roosevelt (ran, run) for President four times.
10. Many foreign airlines are (ran, run) by governments.

Say It Right   Hear It Right

Say these sentences until the correct use of the verbs sounds
natural to you.

1. *Have* you *seen* Billy?
2. I *saw* him in the gym an hour ago.
3. Angelina *has seen* three plays.
4. We *saw* a mysterious looking man.
5. I thought I *had seen* him somewhere before.
6. Darin *saw* him, too.
7. The suspect *was* last *seen* this morning.
8. Who *has seen* Cindy's pocketbook?
9. Astronauts *have seen* Mars.
10. Katie *saw* her mistake in the math problem.

Write It Right

Write the correct verb from the two forms given. Check your
answer by saying the complete sentence to yourself.

1. Joey says he once (saw, seen) a U.F.O.
2. Lana says she has (saw, seen) a Great White Shark.
3. I think they both have (saw, seen) too many movies.
4. We had (saw, seen) that card trick before.
5. Katy (saw, seen) deer and wild turkey on the island.
6. The Patriots game wasn't (saw, seen) on local TV.
7. Have you ever (saw, seen) Johnny Bench in person?
8. Terry (saw, seen) her guests to the door.
9. Has anyone (saw, seen) my pencil?
10. No one(saw, seen) Vincent run out the back door.

Say It Right   Hear It Right

Say these sentences until the correct use of the verbs sounds natural to you.

1. Kevin *took* the twins to the movies.
2. *Have* you *taken* your vitamins?
3. Tim *took* his sled to Squirrel Hill.
4. This seat *is taken*.
5. What *took* you so long?
6. Ginger *has taken* her sister to school.
7. I *took* first prize in the art fair.
8. Betty *had* often *taken* a streetcar before.
9. The prisoner *was taken* to a cell.
10. Lee *took* a course in wood working.

Write It Right

Write the correct verb from the two forms given. Check your answer by saying the complete sentence to yourself.

1. Shouldn't we have (took, taken) the Taylor Road bus?
2. Keith has (took, taken) out a book about tennis.
3. It has (took, taken) me an hour to get home.
4. Good friends are sometimes (took, taken) for granted.
5. Aunt Charlene (took, taken) me to a double-header.
6. Who could have (took, taken) the clothes to the cleaners?
7. It has (took, taken) you long enough to get ready.
8. Lucy (took, taken) many pictures on her trip.
9. Peter has (took, taken) the baby for a walk.
10. The injured boy was (took, taken) to the nurse's office.

Say It Right   Hear It Right

Say these sentences until the correct use of the verbs sounds natural to you.

1. Janie *wrote* the note in green ink.
2. *Has* anyone *written* to Uncle George?
3. I *wrote* to him the other day.
4. The report *was written* neatly.
5. *Have* you *written* your name on your paper?
6. Donna *wrote* another story about her brother.
7. Louis had never *written* a poem before.
8. Alexis *wrote* her name in the guest book.
9. The message *is written* in code.
10. Mr. Johnson *wrote* the instructions on the board.

Write It Right

Write the correct verb from the two forms given. Check your answer by saying the complete sentence to yourself.

1. I like the poems that you (wrote, written).
2. Everyone has (wrote, written) his or her name on my cast.
3. Lupé's letter was (wrote, written) in Spanish.
4. My neighbor has (wrote, written) a mystery story.
5. Ms. Jacobson (wrote, written) the year in Roman numerals.
6. Haven't you (wrote, written) to your pen pal?
7. Geraldo should have (wrote, written) in ink.
8. I had (wrote, written) so much that my hand hurt.
9. Have you ever (wrote, written) to a newspaper?
10. I must have (wrote, written) five letters to Sally.

REVIEW Using Irregular Verbs

Irregular Verbs Write the correct verb from the two forms given. Check your answer by reading the sentence to yourself.

1. A loud cheer (began, begun) the pep rally.
2. A thief has (broke, broken) into the safe.
3. Our class (wrote, written) a letter to the mayor.
4. Sherry (gave, given) away the answer to the puzzle.
5. Bart (did, done) a flip off the diving board.
6. The Davis family (went, gone) on a camping trip last summer.
7. Grandpa could have (ate, eaten) the whole pie.
8. Carrie and Jill (knew, known) how to plant the garden.
9. The usher has (took, taken) our tickets.
10. Kirk (ate, eaten) the rest of the grapes for lunch.
11. The commander (gave, given) an order to the troops.
12. The team has (gone, went) into a huddle.
13. Margie's sunburn (grew, grown) painful.
14. Cindy (knew, known) the magician's secret.
15. The shiek (rode, ridden) a camel.
16. Ed has (began, begun) to read an exciting book.
17. All the children have (ran, run) to the ice cream truck.
18. We (saw, seen) the movie at the drive-in.
19. Susan (did, done) a lot of work for the school play.
20. C. S. Lewis has (wrote, written) good science fiction.

Using Troublesome Verbs Correctly

When you write and speak, there are some verbs that are often troublesome. You have studied irregular verbs. In this section, you will learn about other verbs that cause problems. You will then be able to use these verbs correctly, too.

Read the following sentences.

> We was waiting for you.
> Here is some cookies.
> Rodney set down to watch TV.
> The Burtons don't have no pets.

Can you find the trouble spots?

Part 1 Using the Right Form of *Be*

You have already learned that the verb *be* has many forms:

is	was	am	being
are	were	be	been

Some of these forms may be used alone or as helping verbs. Others may be used only with helping verbs. There are also rules about the subjects that can be used with some of these forms.

Here are five important rules to remember in using the forms of the verb *be*. Each rule is followed by example sentences. Read each of the sentences aloud. When you hear the verbs used correctly, you will be able to remember the rules more easily.

1. If the subject names one person, place, or thing, use the forms *is* and *was*.

Christine *is* here.   She *is sitting* near me.
Teddy *was* here.   He *was called* away.

2. If the subject names more than one person, place, or thing, use the forms *are* and *were*.

The children *are* late.   They *are riding* their bikes.
The cookies *were* on that plate.   They *were eaten* at lunch.

3. When the subject is *you*, use the forms *are* and *were*.

You *are* my best friend.   Are you *coming* with me?
You *were* the fastest swimmer.   You *were doing* a good job.

4. When the subject is *I*, use the forms *am* and *was*.

I *am* here.   I *am studying* English.
I *was* at home.   I *was sleeping* in bed.

5. Use a helping verb before the forms *be*, *being*, and *been*.

Do not use one of these forms alone or as the only helping verb before a main verb.

> Karen *will be* here later.
> The patient *was being taken* to surgery.
> Jeff *has been looking* for you.
> These questions *have been* too hard!

Exercises   Use the right form of *be*.

A.   Number your paper from 1 to 10. Write the right form of *be* from the two given in parentheses.

1. George and Eileen (is, are) my neighbors.
2. I (is, am) a loyal friend.
3. (Is, Are) you the team captain?
4. The TV (been, has been) on for hours.
5. You (was, were) blocking my view.
6. (Was, Were) Craig and Janet tossing the beachball?
7. The Great Dane (being, was being) mean to the children.
8. Your backpack (is, are) loaded with books.
9. Nancy (be, is) twenty years old.
10. The boys (been, were) jumping over puddles.

B.   Follow the directions for Exercise A.

1. Tammy and I (is, are) building a bird feeder.
2. I (am, is) just guessing his age.
3. You (is, are) a good sport when you lose.
4. Jorge (be, is) feeding the fish.
5. I (am, be) helping by cooking dinner tonight.
6. Eric and Sam (been, have been) wearing suspenders.
7. The haunted house (was, were) scary to my little sister.
8. They (was, were) throwing snowballs.
9. You (was being, were being) silly.
10. (Is, Are) the passengers boarding the plane?

Part 2   Using the Right Verb After *There, Here,* and *Where*

Many sentences begin with the words *There is* or *There are.* How can you tell which words to use?

You must find the subject of the verb in order to tell. The word *there* is never the subject. When a sentence begins with *there,* the subject usually comes after the verb.

> There *is* a squirrel in the tree. (*squirrel* is the subject of the verb *is.*)
> There *are* the boats. (*boats* is the subject of the verb *are.*)

Can you decide which form to use in each of these sentences?

> There (is, are) a *motor* in that boat.
> There (was, were) *papers* on the floor.

First, find out whether the subject names one person, place, or thing, or more than one. Then follow the rules for the forms of the verb *be.*

The subject in the first sentence is *motor.* This names one thing. You should have chosen *is.* The subject in the second sentence is *papers.* Since this names more than one thing, you should have chosen *were.*

The words *here* and *where* are also used to begin sentences. They cause the same problem as *there.* When should you say *Here is* or *Where is?* When should you say *Here are* or *Where are?*

You can tell by finding the subject. *Where* and *here* are never the subject. In sentences beginning *Where is* or *Here is,* the subject comes after the verb.

> Here *is* the *trail.* (*trail* is the subject of the verb *is.*)
> Where *is* the *door?* (*door* is the subject of the verb *is.*)
> Here *are* the *pens.* (*pens* is the subject of the verb *are.*)
> Where *are* the *books?* (*books* is the subject of the verb *are.*)

A.   Copy these sentences using the correct form of *be.*

1. Where (is, are) your friends?
2. There (is, are) five magazines on the table.
3. Where (is, are) the two broken cups?
4. There (is, are) a strong wind from the west.
5. Here (is, are) the oldest trees in the park.
6. There (was, were) a letter in the mailbox.
7. There (is, are) several students in the library.
8. Where (is, are) the Big Dipper?
9. (Was, Were) there any more apples on the tree?
10. Here (is, are) the box of pencils.

B.   Follow the directions for Exercise A.

1. Where (is, are) my math book?
2. There (is, are) six chocolate cookies left.
3. Here (is, are) several old magazines.
4. Where (is, are) the keys for the car?
5. Here (is, are) a box of your old clothes.
6. There (is, are) a good reason for my mistake.
7. Here (is, are) the tracks of a big animal.
8. Where (is, are) my old blue jeans?
9. Here (is, are) the pencils you lost.
10. There (is, are) my two best friends.

Part 3   Some Confusing Pairs of Verbs

There are several pairs of verbs that cause trouble because they look alike. Others have meanings that people confuse. In this section you will learn how to use these verbs.

Learn and *Teach*

Learn means "to understand" or "to gain knowledge." Example: Everyone should *learn* to swim.

Teach means "to show how" or "to explain." Example: Can you *teach* me how to swim?

The principal parts of these verbs are:

learn, learned, learned   teach, taught, taught

Say these sentences until they sound correct and natural.

Learn

Present:	The students *learn* new words by reading.
Past:	Britt *learned* to read a compass.
Past Participle:	I *have learned* some of the customs of India.

Teach

Present:	Trained instructors *teach* diving.
Past:	Ms. Voss *taught* us science last year.
Past Participle:	My sister *has taught* me how to cut hair.

Exercise   Use *learn* and *teach* correctly.

Write the correct verb from the two given in parentheses. Check by reading each sentence to yourself.

1. Will you (teach, learn) me chess?
2. Ms. Casey (teaches, learns) eighth-graders.
3. I have (taught, learned) Shellie to fish.
4. Mr. Dior (teaches, learns) ballet classes.
5. My sister has (taught, learned) me to ride a horse.
6. Beginners can (teach, learn) a lot by watching.
7. By reading, Al has (taught, learned) about other lands.
8. Your parents (taught, learned) you good manners.
9. Ms. Fairbanks (taught, learned) our class about the stars.
10. These students have (taught, learned) about traffic safety.

Let and Leave

Let means "to permit." Example: Will you *let* me borrow two dollars?

Leave means "to go away from." Example: The bus *will leave* in an hour.

The principal parts of these verbs are:

let, let, let **leave, left, left**

Say these sentences until they sound correct and natural.

Let

Present:	The Masons *let* us play softball in their lot.
Past:	Tracy *let* her dog jump into the icy water.
Past Participle:	My parents *have let* me decide that myself.

Leave

Present:	The workers *leave* promptly at 5:00 P.M.
Past:	Kerry *left* the house in a hurry.
Past Participle:	The girls *have left* us with the clean-up chores.

Exercise   Use *let* and *leave* correctly.

Write the correct verb from the two given in parentheses. Check by reading each sentence to yourself.

1. Don't (let, leave) the cat get out.
2. Our guests will (let, leave) soon.
3. Sometimes Dad has (left, let) me win at cards.
4. (Let, Leave) your suggestions in the box.
5. Have you (let, left) your gym shoes at school?
6. (Let, Leave) Earl choose the music.
7. Will you (let, leave) your hair grow?
8. (Let, Leave) my books in the classroom.
9. Will Mom (let, leave) you come with us?
10. Ben and Molly have (let, left) their bikes in the yard.

May and *Can*

May asks permission. There are no principal parts. *May* is used as a helping verb only. Another form of *may* is *might*. Example: *May* I have a ride?

Can means "to be able to do something." There are no principal parts. *Can* is also a helping verb. Another form of *can* is *could*. Example: I *can* speak Spanish.

Say these sentences until they sound correct and natural.

May
You *may* check out only five books.
May we use the gym after school?
Might we have eaten earlier?

Can
This ladder *can* reach the roof.
The dolphins *could* jump through hoops.
That librarian *could* have helped Al.

Exercise **Use *may* and *can* correctly.**

Write the correct verb from the two given in parentheses. Check by reading each sentence to yourself.

1. (May, Can) I borrow your ruler?
2. Magnets (may, can) attract metals.
3. Doug Henning, an expert magician, (may, can) make things disappear.
4. Lionel (may, can) run very fast.
5. Yes, you (may, can) have some dessert now.
6. Cats (may, can) see in the dark.
7. (Can, May) you tell me what time it is?
8. You (may, can) try my new camera.
9. No one(may, can) shout in the library.
10. (May, Can) we please feed the animals?

Set and Sit

Set means "to place something somewhere." Example: *Set* the grocery bags on the counter.

Sit means "to rest in one place." Example: I usually *sit* in the front seat.

The principal parts of these verbs are:

set, set, set   **sit, sat, sat**

Say these sentences until they sound correct and natural.

Set

Present:	The machine *sets* the crates on end.
Past:	Chuck *set* his books on the water fountain.
Past Participle:	The stage crew *has set* the props in place.

Sit

Present:	Kyle *sits* in the back row.
Past:	Connie *sat* in an inner tube.
Past Participle:	The girls *have sat* in front of the fireplace all evening.

Exercise **Use *set* and *sit* correctly.**

Write the correct verb from the two given in parentheses. Check by reading each sentence to yourself.

1. I will (set, sit) the plates on the table.
2. Please (set, sit) in this chair.
3. We (set, sat) in the front row.
4. (Set, Sit) that heavy carton on the counter.
5. In music class we (set, sit) in small groups.
6. Margie (set, sat) the vase on the piano.
7. My dog will (set, sit) by my side.
8. Don't (set, sit) the ice cream on the stove.
9. Anne will (set, sit) under the hairdryer.
10. Did the old man (set, sit) his hat down?

Write the correct verb from the two given in parentheses. Check your answer by reading the sentence to yourself.

1. (May, Can) whales live underwater?
2. We will (let, leave) the campgrounds tomorrow.
3. (Set, Sit) your cards in front of you.
4. Beth has (taught, learned) me the words to the song.
5. (May, Can) we please open the gifts now?
6. Don't (let, leave) the water run.
7. Tall people should have (set, sat) in back.
8. Nobody (teaches, learns) babies to talk.
9. Sarah (may, can) stand on her head without help.
10. The coach will (let, leave) us rest now.
11. (May, Can) I see your new bike?
12. You should never have (let, left) your bird out of its cage.
13. Henry (taught, learned) us the rules for basketball.
14. The movers will (set, sit) the furniture in place.
15. (Teach, Learn) me that card trick, Raoul.

Part 4   Using Contractions

Sometimes a verb is combined with another word to make one word. These shortened forms are called **contractions.** Here are some examples:

isn't = is not	that's = that is, that has
weren't = were not	won't = will not
I've = I have	where's = where is, where has
She'd = she would	can't = can not

Remember when you write a contraction to use an **apostrophe** (') to show where letters are left out.

Exercises **Make contractions correctly.**

A. Copy each contraction below. Place the apostrophe where it belongs.

1. Ive	5. theres	9. thats
2. well	6. arent	10. Im
3. theyve	7. dont	11. heres
4. cant	8. hes	12. isnt

B. Copy the following sentences. Make a contraction of the underlined words in each sentence.

1. You are the first to arrive.
2. Francis has not eaten lunch yet.
3. They are all ready to go to the beach.
4. We are on Debra's softball team.
5. I will help you carry these books.
6. What has happened here?
7. I think she would like to go.
8. Beth will not go near snakes.
9. Where is the bike pump?
10. It is Bill's football.

Part 5 Using Negatives Correctly

Some contractions are made by joining *not* with certain verbs, like this: *is + not = isn't.*

The **apostrophe (')** takes the place of the *o* in *not*. Words made in this way are called *not*-words.

have + not = haven't	is + not = isn't
were + not = weren't	do + not = don't
would + not = wouldn't	could + not = couldn't

The *no*-words are different. You can see *no* in all but one:

no   nobody   none   never
no one   nothing   nowhere

Together, the *not*-words and the *no*-words are called **negatives.** Two negatives used together make what is called a **double negative.** Do not ever use double negatives. They are always incorrect.

Wrong: Melvin does**n't** do **nothing.**
Correct: Melvin does**n't** do anything.
    or
Correct: Melvin does **nothing.**

The sentences below show the right way to use negatives. Read the sentences aloud until they sound correct and natural to you:

There is**n't** any flour left.
There is **no** flour left.

Do**n't** ever do that again!
Never do that again!

We have**n't** gone anywhere this week.
We have gone **nowhere** this week.

Have**n't** you ever ridden in a plane?
Have you **never** ridden in a plane?

Exercises   Use negatives correctly.

A.   Copy these sentences. Choose the correct word from the two given in parentheses. Then read the completed sentence to yourself.

1. Doesn't (nobody, anybody) want to play tennis?
2. Don't those boys have (anything, nothing) to do?
3. Haven't you (never, ever) been to the ocean?

4. There isn't (none, any) of the pie left for us.
5. Adam doesn't go (nowhere, anywhere).
6. Isn't there (no one, anyone) we could ask?
7. There weren't (any, no) prizes left for Jason and her.
8. I guess no one (is, isn't) coming.
9. (Does, Doesn't) nobody want to sing along?
10. (Weren't, Were) none of you at the picnic?

B. Write the correct word from the two given in parentheses. Check your answer by reading the sentence to yourself.

1. There won't be (anything, nothing) left for lunch.
2. Those girls don't do (nothing, anything) wrong.
3. Nothing was (never, ever) said about the broken window.
4. We didn't hear (anybody, nobody) crying.
5. Doesn't (nothing, anything) ever go wrong at camp?
6. We don't want (any, no) trouble.
7. I couldn't see (nothing, anything) on the stage.
8. Isn't there (any, no) milk left in the carton?
9. The bus didn't have (no, any) empty seats.
10. Manuel's glasses (were, weren't) nowhere to be found.

REVIEW Using Troublesome Verbs Correctly

The Right Verb After *There, Here,* and *Where* Write the correct form of *be* from the two given in parentheses.

1. There (is, are) two reasons for our delay.
2. Here (is, are) the best map of the area.
3. Where (was, were) the children hiding?
4. There (was, were) no commercials during that program.
5. Here (is, are) the scripts for the show.

Confusing Pairs of Verbs Write the correct verb.

6. Will you (learn, teach) me the school song?
7. Barb (let, left) her gym shoes in her locker.
8. (May, Can) we please take the subway downtown?
9. Bev and Gloria (set, sat) together on the bus.
10. Ms. Barnes (let, left) us choose our project topics.

Contractions Make a contraction of the underlined words.

11. We are writing a news article.
12. Roberto has not watered that plant for days.
13. I will never trust Freddie again.
14. What has been discussed in student council?
15. Dad said he would take us bowling.

Negatives Write the correct word.

16. The curtain hasn't (never, ever) gone up on time.
17. I have (any, no) money left.
18. (Does, Doesn't) anyone recycle cans?
19. Report cards show (nothing, anything) but grades.
20. Didn't anyone (never, ever) submit the homework?

Using Pronouns

Part 1 Substituting Pronouns for Nouns

Read the two paragraphs below. Which paragraph sounds more natural?

> *Ned* and *Carla* wanted to earn money to go to the movie. *Ned* and *Carla* asked *Ned* and *Carla's* mother for a job. *Ned* and *Carla's* mother told *Ned* and *Carla* that *Ned* and *Carla* could polish the living room furniture. *Ned* and *Carla* worked hard. *Ned* and *Carla* earned enough money for the movie.

> *Ned* and *Carla* wanted to earn money to go to the movie. *They* asked their mother for a job. *She* told *them* that *they* could polish the living room furniture. *Ned* and *Carla* worked hard. *They* earned enough money for the movie.

Did you decide that the second paragraph sounds more natural? How did the second paragraph avoid using the names *Ned* and *Carla* too often? Try to find the places where the following words were used instead of those names: *They, their, them.* Can you find where *she* was used instead of *Ned and Carla's mother?*

The words *they, their, them,* and *she* are **pronouns.** Use of the pronouns in the second paragraph did not change the meaning of the paragraph, but it did improve the sound.

A pronoun is a word used in place of a noun.

You use pronouns to do three things.

1. To refer to yourself:

     I asked *my* mother to give *me* a ride.

2. To refer to the person you are talking to:

     Did *you* bring *your* camera?

3. To refer to other persons, places, or things:

     The people ran from the lion. *They* were afraid of *it.*

Like nouns, pronouns can be singular or plural. Usually, the whole word changes to make different forms. Study this chart of all the forms of pronouns.

Singular Pronouns

Person Speaking:	I	me	my, mine
Person Spoken To:	you	you	your, yours
Other Persons, Places and Things:	he	him	his
	she	her	her, hers
	it	it	its

Plural Pronouns

Persons Speaking:	we	us	our, ours
Persons Spoken To:	you	you	you, yours
Other Persons, Places and Things:	they	them	their, theirs

Exercises   Find pronouns.

A.   Number your paper from 1 to 10. List the pronouns used in each sentence.

> Example: He gave me a new watch.
>   He, me

1. I wore my new boots today.
2. Katy displayed her model ships in our classroom.
3. Steve, do you read comic books?
4. Dad brought me to the roller rink.
5. The horse tugged at its reins.
6. Roger told us a secret.
7. She took the rock and skipped it across the water.
8. The waitress asked them for their order.
9. Carrie threw snowballs at him and me.
10. We rubbed our fingers to keep them warm.

B.   Copy the sentences below. Use pronouns instead of nouns where they will make the sentences sound better.

> Example: Geno was riding Geno's bike.
>   Geno was riding his bike.

1. Ted ran in the 50-yard dash. Ted was the winner.
2. Maria likes baseball, and Maria plays every Saturday.
3. The building is closed. The building is very old.
4. The men saw Jim walking down the road. The men waited for Jim.
5. Betty brought Betty's new book to school.
6. Tom and I are neighbors. Tom and I walk to school together.
7. The boys wore the boys' best suits for the school program.
8. Sam is Lisa's brother. Sam is two years older than Lisa is.
9. We ate the fruit. The fruit was cold and sweet.
10. Toni, would Toni lend me Toni's pencil, please?

Part 2   Using Pronouns as Subjects

You remember that the subject of a sentence tells who or what does something. Find the subject of each of these sentences:

I visited my uncle.   He has a motorcycle.
We drove along River Road.

Did you find that the subjects were the pronouns *I*, *He*, and *We*? These are three of the pronouns we use often as subjects. Four others are *you*, *she*, *it*, and *they*.

Usually we have no trouble using these pronouns as subjects. However, when there are two parts in a subject, we sometimes get confused.

Which of these sentences is correct?

Rita and *she* played together.
            or
Rita and *her* played together.

To figure out which pronoun to use in a subject with two parts, try each pronoun separately with the verb.

She played.   Her played.

You can hear that *She* is the correct pronoun. So the correct sentence is *Rita and she played together*.

Follow the same plan when there are two pronouns in the subject.

Example: (She, her) and (I, me) took piano lessons.
Try: *She* took piano lessons.   *Her* took piano lessons.
Try: *I* took piano lessons.   *Me* took piano lessons.
Now you know the correct pronouns:
She and *I* took piano lessons.

Here are two important rules for you to study about using pronouns as the subject of a sentence.

1. Only these pronouns may be used as the subject:

Subject Pronouns	
I	we
you	you
he, she, it	they

2. If the pronoun *I* is used with one or more nouns or pronouns as the subject of a sentence, put *I* last.

Robert and I were in Boston.　　*He and I* saw the marathon.

Exercises　Use pronouns as subjects.

A.　Choose the correct words from those in parentheses.

1. Frances and (I, me) are going to a party.
2. Jane and (her, she) will be there.
3. Donald and (them, they) visit me often.
4. Philip and (he, him) went to the circus.
5. (Juan and I, I and Juan) ate the cookies.
6. (I and Donna, Donna and I) watched the parade.
7. Ms. Coburn and (we, us) saw a movie yesterday.
8. Eva and (me, I) will finish the work.
9. (He, Him) and his mother painted his room.
10. You and (I, me) make a good team.

B.　Follow the directions for Exercise A.

1. Lydia and (I, me) started arguing.
2. Rusty and (them, they) don't play fairly.
3. Elena and (she, her) demonstrated a cartwheel.
4. Someday you and (me, I) will play first string.
5. (I and Joanne, Joanne and I) apologized to Kim.
6. My parents, my teachers, and (I, me) had a conference.
7. Uncle Jerry and (we, us) ate dinner at Pizza Hut.
8. Alex and (he, him) are best friends.
9. Julie and (they, them) raced for the front seat.
10. (She, Her) and Carl caught two trout.

Part 3 Using Pronouns After Linking Verbs

Read these two sentences:

The doctor is *she*.   *She* is the doctor.

These sentences mean the same thing. As you can see, the pronoun following the linking verb *is* can be made the subject without changing the meaning of the sentence.

Pronouns used after linking verbs are called predicate pronouns. Predicate pronouns are the same as pronouns used as subjects. You can see the same thing happening in the following pairs of sentences.

The best player was he.
He was the best player.

The semifinalists were Dan and I.
Dan and I were the semifinalists.

The teams in the playoffs will be the Cubs and we.
The Cubs and we will be the teams in the playoffs.

Remember to use these pronouns after linking verbs:

I	we
you	you
he, she, it	they

Exercises   Use pronouns after linking verbs.

A.   Number your paper from 1 to 10. Write the correct pronoun from the two given in parentheses.

1. The new library aides are Darla and (he, him).
2. Tim's closest neighbors are Lee and (I, me).
3. The family's biggest eaters are Dad and (her, she).
4. The only shoppers left were (them, they).

5. Your biggest fans are Deena and (me, I).

6. The lifeguards are Melissa and (I, me).

7. The first people in line were Roseann's brother and (her, she).

8. The co-captains are Stewart and (I, me).

9. The cooks for the banquet are Candy and (him, he).

10. My dad's bosses are Mr. Jones and (she, her).

B. Follow the directions for Exercise A.

1. Kim's ski instructors were Tim and (her, she).

2. The newest teachers are Mr. Reynolds and (she, her).

3. The last group of swimmers was (us, we).

4. The newspaper's editor is (her, she).

5. The crossing guards are Vanessa and (he, him).

6. One of the disc jockeys is (her, she).

7. Our biggest rivals are (they, them).

8. Judith's lab partners are Jon and (he, him).

9. My favorite comedians are (she, her) and Bill Cosby.

10. The most reliable bus drivers are Curt and (her, she).

Part 4 Using Pronouns as Objects

Which pronoun should be used in each of these sentences?

1. The cat scratched (they, them).

2. Eddie asked Rachel and (she, her) a question.

3. Divide the candy among (we, us) now.

If you are not sure which pronoun to use in a sentence, first decide if the missing pronoun is in the subject or follows a state-of-being, or linking, verb. You know that if the pronoun is in the subject, or follows a linking verb, you use *I, you, he, she, it, we, you,* and *they.*

If a pronoun is not used as the subject or as a predicate pronoun, use *me, you, him, her, it, us, you,* and *them.* These pronouns are called the **object pronouns.** (You can see that the pronouns *you* and *it* stay the same as subject or object pronouns.)

Object Pronouns	
me	us
you	you
him, her, it	them

In Example 1, the subject is *cat.* Since the missing pronoun is not in the subject, we cannot use *they.* The correct sentence is: *The cat scratched* **them.**

In Example 2, what is the subject? Is the missing pronoun in the subject? Since the missing pronoun is not in the subject, we cannot use *she.* The correct sentence is: *Eddie asked Rachel and* **her** *a question.*

In Example 3, *you* is the understood subject. The missing pronoun is not in that subject. Which pronoun did you choose? The correct sentence is *Divide the candy among* **us** *now.*

Exercises Use pronouns as objects.

A. Write the correct pronoun from the two given in parentheses. Then read the sentence to yourself.

1. Eduardo's mother called (him, he) and his brother.
2. The speeding car almost hit Bill and (I, me).
3. Would you like to visit Pete and (we, us)?
4. Sue chose Brian and (she, her) for the team.
5. Mort made dinner for Hal and (she, her).
6. Louella finally found Marion and (they, them).
7. Telephone Mike and (I, me) after the game.
8. Jan saw Mary Lou and (me, I) at the store.

9. Did you see Ann and (I, me) at the track meet?

10. Can you give Arlene and (she, her) your address?

B. Follow the directions for Exercise A.

1. The letter surprised Joan and (us, we).
2. Jody's father sent (he, him) a postcard from Kansas City.
3. My sister helped Ellen and (she, her) with the work.
4. Did you meet Valerie and (she, her) at the park?
5. I made chocolate sundaes for (them, they) and me.
6. A loud crash frightened Angelo and (we, us).
7. The officer handcuffed Mills and (he, him).
8. Hit some fly balls to Emily and (me, I).
9. Mrs. Johnson settled the argument between Jason and (I, me).
10. Show Roberto and (she, her) to their seats.

Part 5   Using *We* and *Us*

Read each pair of sentences. In each pair, which sentence is correct?

1. We boys are going hiking.
        or
   Us boys are going hiking.

2. Have you ever seen us girls in a hockey game?
        or
   Have you ever seen we girls in a hockey game?

Read the sentences without the word *boys* or the word *girls*. You will see that in the first example the pronoun is in the subject. *We* is the correct pronoun. The correct sentence is: *We* boys are going hiking.

In the second example, the pronoun is in the object. *Us* is the correct choice. The sentence is: Have you ever seen *us* girls in a hockey game?

Whenever you have trouble choosing pronouns, try each pronoun alone in the sentence.

Exercises **Use *we* and *us* correctly.**

A. Number your paper from 1 to 10. Write the correct pronoun for each sentence. Check by reading each sentence to yourself.

1. (We, Us) boys went to the gym.
2. Mother sent (we, us) girls to the grocery store.
3. (We, Us) cyclists took our lunch with us.
4. In the woods (we, us) hikers saw a deer.
5. The new band costumes are for (we, us) two.
6. After lunch, (we, us) gardeners rested for a long time.
7. The coach praised (we, us) girls for our victory.
8. Terence told (we, us) Scouts about his climb.
9. The food was divided among (we, us) four.
10. Mr. Scott, this present is from (we, us) students.

B. Follow the directions for Exercise A.

1. (We, Us) girls took the bus downtown.
2. The gentle pony nuzzled (we, us) visitors.
3. (We, Us) boys had a tug-of-war.
4. Finally, Jamie spotted (we, us) wanderers.
5. (We, Us) six planned a farewell party.
6. A net fell on top of (we, us) girls.
7. The child asked (we, us) bystanders for help.
8. The girls challenged (we, us) boys.
9. Together (we, us) swimmers pulled the boat to shore.
10. An acrobat performed for (we, us) boys.

Part 6 Possessive Pronouns

To make the possessive form of a noun, you add an apostrophe or an apostrophe and *s* to the noun. Pronouns have special possessive forms. These do not use apostrophes at all.

Here are the possessive pronouns for you to study.

Possessive Pronouns	
my, mine	our, ours
your, yours	your, yours
his, her, hers, its	their, theirs

Now read these sentences that use possessive pronouns:

This is *my* coat.	We have *our* tickets.
The coat is *mine*.	These tickets are *ours*.
Is that *your* hat?	Are those *your* books?
Is that *yours*?	Are those *yours*?
Here is *his* dog.	Do you like *their* pets?
The dog is *his*.	The pets are *theirs*.
Where is *her* cat?	
This cat is *hers*.	

Its and *It's*

The major problem most people have with possessive pronouns is confusing the possessive *its* with the contraction *it's*.

Its (without the apostrophe) is the possessive form of *it*.

> Example: That book is missing *its* cover.
>
> (The cover belongs to the book)

It's (with the apostrophe) means *it is* or *it has*.

> Example: *It's* a library book.
>
> (*It is* a library book.)

Exercises   Use possessive pronouns and *it's*.

A.   Copy each of the following sentences. Where there is a blank, write a possessive pronoun according to the information in the parentheses.

> Example: I found _____ notebook. (The notebook
>   belongs to you.)
>
>   I found your notebook.

1. _____ handwriting can be read easily. (The handwriting belongs to you.)
2. Did you see _____ faces? (The faces belong to them.)
3. Those keys are _____. (The keys belong to you.)
4. Next comes _____ turn. (The turn belongs to him.)
5. The error is _____. (The error was made by her.)
6. The reward is _____. (The reward belongs to us.)
7. This is _____ chance. (The chance belongs to us.)
8. That was _____ mistake. (The mistake was made by me.)
9. The fingerprints are _____. (The fingerprints belong to him.)
10. The pictures are _____. (The pictures belong to them.)

B.   Copy the following sentences. Insert apostrophes where they are needed.

1. Its a home run!
2. Its raining outside.
3. The leopard chased its prey.
4. What is its title?
5. The puppy dropped its dish.
6. My mother makes candy, and its delicious.
7. The railroad stopped its service to Clinton.
8. Our school has its own hockey team.
9. Grandpa has a beard. Its white and thick.
10. Its too early to buy tickets for the game.

REVIEW Using Pronouns

Subject Pronouns Write the correct pronouns.

1. Cora and (I, me) babysat for triplets.
2. (Him, He) and his brother traded rooms.
3. (Her, She) and her sister work as cashiers.
4. The other team and (we, us) lined up for the kickoff.
5. Suzanne and (me, I) agreed on a plan.

Pronouns After Linking Verbs Write the correct pronouns.

6. The men in uniform were (him, he) and Dad.
7. Our school's nurse is (her, she).
8. The best dancers were George and (she, her).
9. The co-pilots are Jackie Miller and (he, him).
10. The only people in the audience were (us, we).

Object Pronouns Write the correct pronouns.

11. Geraldo gave directions to (they, them).
12. Francie invited (we, us) to her party.
13. Cathy split a candy bar with (me, I).
14. Brooke showed Mark and (her, she) the ballet steps.
15. A taxi took Diane and (he, him) to the airport.

Possessive Pronouns Copy the following sentences. Where there is a blank, write the appropriate possessive pronoun.

16. Bill injured _____ ankle. (The ankle belongs to him.)
17. The company hires _____ own guards. (The guards belong to it.)
18. The sketches are _____. (The sketches belong to her.)
19. The car has kept _____ shine. (The shine belongs to it.)
20. All of the ideas were _____. (The ideas belong to them.)

Using Adjectives

Part 1   What Are Adjectives?

What do you see in your mind when you read this sentence?

I saw dogs.

Although the sentence expresses a complete idea, it does not make the idea clear. It needs words to describe *dogs* more exactly. Here are a few ways the sentence could be clearer. What do you see when you read these sentences?

I saw huge, furry dogs.   I saw vicious, wild dogs.
I saw small, playful dogs.   I saw four lovable dogs.

The words *huge, furry, small, playful, vicious, wild, four,* and *lovable* tell you more about *dogs*. They make the meaning of the word more exact. These words are called **adjectives.**

Adjectives are used with nouns and pronouns. They may come before the noun or pronoun they describe.

I saw *brown* and *black* dogs.

They may also come after the word they describe. Sometimes adjectives follow a linking verb and describe the subject.

The dogs were *friendly*.   They were *restless*.

You can notice a big difference between these two sentences:

I saw small, playful dogs.
I saw vicious, wild dogs.

You can see how different adjectives change, or *modify*, the meaning of the word they describe. For this reason, adjectives are called **modifiers.**

An adjective is a word that modifies a noun or pronoun.

Usually, when we use two or more adjectives together, we separate them with commas. Adjectives telling numbers do not have to follow this rule.

The *four lovable* dogs belonged to *two young* children.
Several dangerous alligators lived in the *warm, murky* pond.

Exercise   Find adjectives.

In each of the following pairs of sentences, only the adjectives have been changed. Number your paper from 1 to 5. For each pair of sentences, list the nouns that are modified. After the noun, write the adjectives that modify it.

Example: a. The short *man* lifted the heavy *box*.

b. The strong *man* lifted the huge *box*.
man—short, strong   *box*—heavy, huge

1. a. The small girl ran through the grassy field.
    b. The careless girl ran through the muddy field.

2. a. Twenty clowns wore new costumes.

   b. Wacky clowns wore silly costumes.

3. a. Many children won different prizes.

   b. Lucky children won valuable prizes.

4. a. Soft music played on an old radio.

   b. Classical music played on a nearby radio.

5. a. A blue purse lay in the dusty hallway.

   b. A full purse lay in the busy hallway.

Some Adjectives Tell *What Kind*

Most of the adjectives used so far in this section describe what someone is talking about. Adjectives of this type tell *what kind*. Here are some adjectives used so far to tell *what kind*:

huge	brown	furry	vicious	playful
small	black	friendly	dangerous	lovable
wild	eager	murky		restless
young		slimy		

In the last three columns, you can see these five endings often found on adjectives: *-y, -ous, -ful, -able,* and *-less.*

Exercises   Use adjectives that tell *what kind.*

A. Read each sentence. Write each adjective that tells *what kind.*

1. There were joyful shouts from the stands.
2. Mr. Chalmers is a capable carpenter.
3. Jed wore his warm, red parka.
4. We sang funny songs on the long trip.
5. Marguerite threw out the old, dirty sneakers.
6. Cecilia put a large poster on the blank wall.

7. The spare room is a hopeless mess.
8. Max drew furry, monstrous creatures.
9. Long, colorful streamers hung from the ceiling.
10. A beautiful sunset lit the rosy sky.

B. In this exercise, you will write your own sentences using adjectives that tell *what kind*. The following list gives ten nouns with an adjective modifying each noun. Write at least five sentences. Use two of the adjective-noun combinations in each of your sentences. You may add some adjective-noun combinations of your own in any of your sentences.

fearless captain	piercing scream
spicy pizza	exhausted doctor
dark room	silky shirt
rocky ground	poisonous air
freckled face	thoughtful friend

Some Adjectives Tell *How Many*

Some adjectives tell *how many* of the thing someone is talking about. Here are examples of adjectives that tell *how many*:

six animals	*many* birds	*several* people
three stores	*few* lions	*more* insects

Exercises **Find adjectives that tell *how many*.**

A. Read each sentence. List the adjectives that tell *how many*.

1. Two jets power the plane.
2. Eight children raced past our house.
3. A trainer groomed four horses.

4. We waited at the bus stop for forty minutes.
5. Curt read several books this month.
6. Lucinda put nine roses in one vase.
7. The question has many answers.
8. Those girls threw a dozen snowballs.
9. Jupiter has fourteen moons.
10. Countless stars fill the sky.

B. Number your paper from 1 to 10. For each sentence below, list the adjectives that tell *how many*.

1. Both eggs hatched.
2. This program lasts thirty minutes.
3. We picked three bushels of apples.
4. Mother bought a dozen glazed doughnuts.
5. Ken did twenty push-ups.
6. Seven cars were damaged in the accident.
7. Few boys were at the movie.
8. I have six dollars in my wallet.
9. Dee had one scoop of strawberry ice cream.
10. There are thirty children and only twenty-five desks.

Some Adjectives Tell *Which Ones*

Some adjectives tell *which one* or *which ones* someone is talking about. Here are four adjectives in this group that we use often:

this team	*these* mitts
that field	*those* players

Adjectives that point to persons, places, and things always come before the word they point to.

Exercise **Find adjectives.**

Number your paper from 1 to 10. Make two columns. Head one column *Which Ones,* and head the other *How Many.* Find the adjectives in these sentences, and write them in the correct column.

Example: This bush has seven roses.

Which Ones	How Many
this	seven

1. These four stones are quartz.
2. Those three colors are my favorites.
3. This house has nine rooms.
4. Will this pie serve six people?
5. This book has many torn pages.
6. Several sandwiches are in that bag.
7. This record player has three speeds.
8. That octopus in the picture has only seven arms.
9. We bought a dozen cookies at that bakery.
10. Some swans swam on that pond.

You have learned that adjectives modify nouns and pronouns. You have also learned that adjectives tell three different things about the nouns and pronouns they modify. Study this chart. It will help you to recognize adjectives and to use them correctly.

An adjective tells

* **what kind**
* **how many**
* **which one**

about the noun or pronoun it modifies.

A. Write each adjective and the noun each modifies.

1. Put these three blue boxes on that empty shelf.
2. We had several sheets of green paper.
3. Many young people crowded into one tiny room.
4. Look at that silver tray of delicious chocolate cookies.

B. Follow the directions for Exercise A.

1. Does that noisy dog herd this flock of sheep?
2. This tall lighthouse warns stray ships of dangerous rocks.
3. Hand me that old purple sweatshirt with long sleeves.
4. Two stocky men with dark beards robbed several banks.

Part 2   Articles

The words *a, an,* and *the* are called **articles.** Since they always modify nouns, they are also adjectives.

You may use the word *the* before singular or plural nouns beginning with any letter.

> *the* alphabet   *the* sentences   *the* onion   *the* record

You may use the words *a* and *an* before singular nouns only. Follow these rules in choosing the correct article:

1. Use *a* before words beginning with consonant sounds:

> *a* person   *a* fresh egg   *a* story   *a* black olive

2. Use *an* before words beginning with vowel sounds:

> *an* average person   *an* egg   *an* impossible story

Some words begin with a silent *h.* In these words, you do not say the *h* sound. Instead, you begin the word with a vowel sound after the *h.* Therefore, you follow the second rule, and use *an.*

> *an* hour   *an* honor   *an* honest child

Exercises   Use articles.

A.   Copy the following sentences. Fill in the blanks with *a* or *an*.

1. Do you keep _____ diary?
2. Roger Jones is _____ honorable judge.
3. Sarah held _____ brush and _____ comb.
4. Gordon got _____ haircut.
5. The train left _____ hour ago.
6. _____ dachshund has _____ long body.
7. Diana tossed _____ horseshoe.
8. _____ old woman opened _____ umbrella.
9. I had _____ nightmare last night.
10. The forester carried _____ ax and _____ saw.

B.   There are eight nouns below. Write four sentences, using one noun in each sentence. Place an article (*a*, *an*, or *the*) and another adjective before each noun.

1. wolf	3. movie	5. book	7. idea
2. lunch	4. team	6. sister	8. friend

Part 3   Predicate Adjectives

When an adjective follows a linking verb like *is* or *seemed*, it is part of the predicate. But it often modifies a noun or pronoun in the subject. Look at these examples:

The slopes were *icy*.

Jill is *right*.

The patient seems *frightened*.

They were *rude*.

When an adjective following a linking verb modifies the subject, it is called a **predicate adjective.**

Exercises   Use predicate adjectives.

A.   Copy these sentences, putting a predicate adjective in the blank. Draw an arrow from the predicate adjective to the word it modifies.

1. Joel seemed _____ yesterday.
2. The buzzer on my alarm clock is too _____.
3. Our gym is _____ and spacious.
4. The strings on this tennis racket are _____.
5. Billy Joel's singing is _____.
6. This country road is very _____.
7. A swan dive looks _____.
8. The sky was _____ and gray.
9. The price of those skis is too _____.
10. The berries of that tree are _____.

B.   Number your paper from 1 to 10. Write the predicate adjective in each sentence.

1. Unless we hurry, we will be late.
2. Alfred Hitchcock's films are quite scary.
3. I will be nervous on stage.
4. CB radios are popular with truckers.
5. The food in the cafeteria tastes spicy.
6. The fruit on the tree looked almost ripe.
7. Megan felt full after the banana split.
8. Several of the records seem unbeatable.
9. The new fashions look weird.
10. The TV picture looks awfully hazy.

Part 4 Proper Adjectives

In this section, you have already used many adjectives formed from common nouns, for example, *furry, playful, lovable.* **Proper adjectives** are adjectives formed from proper nouns.

You know that a proper noun names a particular person, place, or thing. By adding adjective endings to some proper nouns, we change them into proper adjectives. Here are some examples:

Proper Noun	Proper Adjective + Noun Modified
Spain	Spanish music
China	Chinese food
Mexico	Mexican jewelry
Bible	Biblical verse

Very often a proper name is used as an adjective without the addition of an adjective ending. Here are some examples of the second kind of proper adjective:

Ford engine   Cinderella story
Hitchcock thriller   Beethoven symphony

A proper adjective is an adjective that has been made from a proper noun. (A proper adjective begins with a capital letter.)

Exercises Use proper adjectives.

A. Number your paper from 1 to 10. Write each proper adjective in these sentences. Capitalize correctly.

1. Ms. Ames wears french perfume.
2. Jonathan asked for swiss cheese on rye.
3. Grandpa sent a bushel of florida oranges.
4. Who won the emmy award for best comedy actress?
5. Scientists studied the martian soil.

6. Paula wears adidas shoes.
7. A yankee batter was hit by the ball.
8. Sue prefers dannon yogurt.
9. Nadia's bother has a dodge truck.
10. Two british ships docked in the harbor.

B. Follow the directions for Exercise A.

1. The play is similar to the cinderella story.
2. The french soldiers marched in long lines.
3. The arab countries export oil.
4. Are there guards at the canadian border?
5. Have you ever eaten german chocolate cake?
6. Most indian jewelry is made from turquoise and silver.
7. Drew is training for the olympic fencing team.
8. Many hollywood actors make commercials.
9. Craig's brother has a honda motorcycle.
10. People at the convention picked the republican candidate.

Part 5 Using Adjectives Correctly

Four adjectives that tell which one, or which ones, are *this*, *that*, *these*, and *those*. When they modify nouns and pronouns, they point out specific things.

> *This* book is more interesting than *that* one.
> *These* pencils are sharper than *those* pencils.

Using *Them* and *Those*

Look at these sentences carefully.

> I saw *those* men on the airplane.
> Jeanie saw *them*, too.

The word *those* is an adjective. It tells which men. The word *them* is not an adjective. It is never used to point to a noun. *Them* is a pronoun. It is used *in place of a noun.*

We found *those books* in the pack.
Someone left *them* there.

Using *This Kind* and *That Kind*

The word *kind* sometimes causes problems. It means just *one kind*. If you want to speak of more than one kind, say *kinds*.

When you use an adjective to point to *kind*, use *this* or *that*. Never say "those kind" or "them kind."

When you use an adjective to point to *kinds*, use *these* or *those*.

Study the sentences below to see how these words are used.

I like *this kind* of ice cream.
I wore *that kind* of hat last year.
Those kinds of doughnuts are the best.
I like *those kinds* of books.

Exercises   Choose the right word.

A.   Write the right word for each sentence. Check by reading the sentence to yourself.

1. We like (them, those) butterscotch candies best.
2. Do you have any of (those, them) magazines?
3. (This, Them, These) kind of tire is safest.
4. (Them, These) kinds of problems are very hard.
5. I use (that, those, them) kind of pen at school.
6. We read (those, them) books last summer.
7. (This, Them, These) kind of story appeals to me.
8. Will you take (those, them) packages to the office?
9. Where can I see (them, those) kinds of monkeys?
10. (Them, Those) clothes must be washed.

B. Follow the directions for Exercise A.

1. (Those, Them) firecrackers exploded.
2. (That, Those) kind of cookie is chewy.
3. Do (them, those) gloves keep you warm?
4. Audrey always makes (this, these) kind of shot from midcourt.
5. I am allergic to (that, them, those) kind of fruit.
6. (Those, Them) reins control the horse.
7. Queen Elizabeth wore (them, those) jewels.
8. Terry likes (this, these) kinds of projects.
9. Many farmers in the U.S. grow (them, those) grains.
10. Marietta builds (that, those) kind of model airplane.

Part 6 Making Comparisons with Adjectives

You often use adjectives to compare people, places, and things. The adjectives used to describe must be changed slightly when they are used to compare.

For example, you could describe two students with these sentences:

Marilyn is *tall*.   Frank is *tall*.

What if you want to compare the two, and to say that they are not the same size? You would use one of these sentences:

Marilyn is *taller* than Frank.   Frank is *taller* than Marilyn.

Now, suppose you want to compare a third student with Frank and Marilyn. Charles is taller than Frank, and taller than Marilyn. What would you say?

You probably gave this sentence:

Charles is the *tallest*.

Here are the rules for using short adjectives in comparisons:

1. When you compare two people, places, or things, you usually add -er to the adjective.

tall + er = taller   happy + er = happier
large + er = larger   funny + er = funnier

(Notice that if the adjective ends in *e*, you drop the *e* before adding *-er*. If the adjective ends in *y*, change the *y* to *i* before adding *-er*.)

2. When you compare three or more people, places, or things, you usually add -est to the adjective.

tall + est = tallest   happy + est = happiest
large + est = largest   funny + est = funniest

If the adjective ends in *e*, drop the *e* before adding *-est*. If the adjective ends in *y*, change the *y* to *i* before adding *-est*.

Using *More* and *Most* in Comparisons

You do not always add *-er* or *-est* to make comparisons. If the adjective is a long one, use *more* and *most* instead of adding *-er* and *-est*.

Ted has been *more careful* since the accident.
Barbara was the *most careful* of the three girls.

My puzzle is *more difficult* than yours.
This is the *most difficult* dive of all.

Here are the rules for using long adjectives in comparisons:

1. Use *more* when comparing two persons, places or things.

more difficult   more terrible   more dangerous

2. Use *most* when comparing three persons, places, or things.

most difficult   most terrible   most dangerous

Use only one form of comparison at a time. If you use *-er* or *-est,* do not use *more* or *most* in the same comparison. You should not say, "my brother is *more bigger* than I am." Instead, you should say, "My brother is *bigger* than I am." What about this sentence: "Our dog is the *most smartest* dog on the block." This sentence is incorrect. It should be "Our dog is the *smartest* dog on the block."

The Forms of *Good* and *Bad*

A few adjectives change to completely new words when they are used in comparisons. Here are two important adjectives of this kind:

good   better   best
bad   worse   worst

Read these examples:

My father is a *good* bowler.
Doug is a *better* pitcher than Dan.
Is Patty the *best* swimmer in the class?

The weather is *bad* today.
Will tomorrow's storm be *worse* than this?
The blizzard in Chicago was the *worst* storm this year.

Exercises   Make comparisons with adjectives.

A.   Some of the following adjectives add *-er* and *-est* when they are used in comparisons. Others are used with *more* and *most.* Number your paper from 1 to 10. Copy each adjective. Then write the two forms it uses in comparisons.

Examples: slow
           slow, slower, slowest

           colorful
           colorful, more colorful, most colorful

1. helpful   6. intelligent
2. dark   7. wonderful
3. dangerous   8. silly
4. pretty   9. curious
5. hard   10. great

B. Number your paper from 1 to 10. Write the correct adjective form for each sentence. Check by reading each sentence to yourself.

1. The cheetah is the (most fastest, fastest) animal of all.
2. A whale is (larger, more large) than an elephant.
3. Laura is the (most happy, happiest) baby I've seen.
4. This map is (more useful, usefuller) than the globe.
5. Pat is (carefuller, more careful) than Tom.
6. Darren is the (fastest, most fast) runner of all.
7. The lake is (more deep, deeper) than it was last year.
8. Your house is (more large, larger) than ours.
9. The last math problem was also the (most hard, hardest).
10. This is the (most delicious, deliciousest) pie I have ever eaten.

C. Follow the directions for Exercise B.

1. Which of the two pails is (larger, largest)?
2. I picked the (thinner, thinnest) of the four books.
3. This piece of cloth is the (biggest, bigger) of the two.
4. In our dance class, who is the (more graceful, most graceful)?
5. Was Harry's the (worse, worst) injury of the race?
6. I read the (longer, longest) of the three books.
7. Of the thirty flavors, which is (better, best)?
8. The (bigger, biggest) of the two packages was mine.
9. Which of the two ponies is (gentler, gentlest)?
10. In Jane's family, her mother is the (better, best) athlete.

REVIEW Using Adjectives

Recognizing Adjectives Write the adjectives in each sentence. Beside each adjective, write the noun it modifies. Put the noun in parentheses. Ignore *a, an,* and *the.*

> Example: The talented skater   won two medals.
>   talented (skater)   two (medals)

1. The teacher speaks in a quiet voice.
2. Jessica paints with vivid colors.
3. Those four magazines are for young people.
4. A large, muddy dog bounded into the full classroom.
5. We play pool with two special cues.
6. The new committee had several foolish plans.
7. That dentist uses a noisy old drill.
8. Many tall buildings line those elegant streets.
9. That boy has curly black hair.
10. Jean wore one bracelet and four rings.

Predicate Adjectives Write the predicate adjective in each sentence.

11. That style of jacket is popular.
12. Our victory over the Wildcats was lucky.
13. The mob in the street seems orderly.
14. These award winners are grateful.
15. Everyone in class looked sleepy.

Adjectives in Comparisons Choose the correct form of the adjective from the two given.

16. Of the four questions, this one is (harder, hardest).
17. The sun is (brighter, more bright) today.
18. That measurement is (accuratest, most accurate).
19. This licorice is the (chewier, chewiest) I've ever had.
20. Is Sally (younger, youngest) than Ray?

Using Adverbs

Part 1   What Are Adverbs?

In **Section 8,** you learned that adjectives are modifiers that tell *what kind, how many,* or *which ones* about nouns and pronouns.

There is another kind of modifier called an **adverb.** Study the examples below.

> The students worked **quietly.**
> The pigeons flew **away.**
> My train leaves **soon.**
> The clerk was **very** helpful.

Adverbs tell *how, where, when,* or *to what extent.* Adverbs can modify verbs, adjectives, or other adverbs.

Adverbs Modify Verbs

The baby crawled.

How? The baby crawled *quickly.*

Where? The baby crawled *everywhere.*

When? The baby *sometimes* crawled.

Adverbs Modify Adjectives

That box is heavy.

How heavy? That box is *terribly* heavy.

This is an interesting book.

How interesting? This is an *extremely* interesting book.

Adverbs Modify Other Adverbs

Dale goes to McDonald's often.

How often? Dale goes to McDonald's *very* often.

He always orders cheeseburgers.

To what extent? He *almost* always orders cheeseburgers.

An adverb modifies a verb, an adjective, or another adverb. It tells *how, where, when,* or *to what extent.*

Many adverbs are formed by adding *-ly* to an adjective, as in these examples:

quick—quickly	happy—happily	powerful—powerfully
slow—slowly	sad—sadly	careless—carelessly

Here are some other examples of words often used as adverbs:

How? well, hard, fast, much

Where? here, there, everywhere

When? now, never, always, often

To what extent? very, too, quite, almost

If you are not sure whether a word is an adverb, ask yourself two questions. Does the word modify a verb, an adjective, or another adverb? Does it tell *how, where, when* or *to what extent?* If you can answer *yes* to these questions, the word is an adverb.

Study this chart to help you recognize adverbs and to use them correctly.

An adverb tells
✳ **how** ✳ **when** ✳ **where** ✳ **to what extent**
about the verb, adjective, or other adverb.

Exercises Use adverbs.

A. In these sentences the words in *italics* are adverbs. Find the verb that each adverb tells more about.

1. Trigger whined *sadly*, but Luke left him behind.
2. Luke started *slowly* up the mountain.
3. He *carefully* watched where to put his feet.
4. One of the rocks slipped *suddenly*.
5. Luke scrambled *wildly* for a footing.
6. Then blackness surrounded him *completely*.
7. When he awoke, his head throbbed *painfully*.
8. He moved *slowly* in the darkness.
9. A cold nose touched his cheek *lightly*. It was Trigger!
10. Trigger barked *joyously*.

B. Write every adverb used in each sentence.

1. The bikers were hopelessly lost.
2. The hunters never found the deer.
3. This watch is always wrong.

4. Yesterday the trains were late.

5. The driver instantly stopped the car.

6. Debbie tugged quite hard on the rope.

7. Leroy outgrew his clothes very quickly.

8. My canteen is almost empty.

9. The bus nearly hit the sign.

10. Merle peered timidly around the corner.

Part 2 Making Comparisons with Adverbs

Adverbs, like adjectives, can be used in comparisons.

> John Henry worked *harder* than the steam engine.
> He worked the *hardest* of all the drillers.

There are three ways adverbs are changed to show comparisons.

1. Some short adverbs add *-er* when two persons or things are being compared. They add *-est* when three or more are compared.

hard	harder	hardest
fast	faster	fastest

2. Most adverbs that end in *-ly* use the word *more* in comparing two persons or things. They use *most* in comparing three or more.

carelessly	more carelessly	most carelessly
quickly	more quickly	most quickly

3. Some adverbs change their forms completely when they are used in comparisons.

well	better	best
badly	worse	worst
much	more	most
little	less	least

Exercises   Make comparisons with adverbs.

A. The following adverbs are examples of all three groups discussed in this chapter part. Copy each adverb. Then write the two forms it uses in comparisons.

> Example: much
>
> much, more, most

1. rapidly
2. little
3. happily
4. naturally
5. fast
6. carefully
7. brightly
8. badly
9. loudly
10. well

B. Number your paper from 1 to 10. Choose the correct adverb form from the parentheses. Write it on your paper.

1. Please wake me (earlier, more early) tomorrow.
2. Louise pushed (hardest, harder) than Dan.
3. The squirrel came (more near, nearer) to us.
4. The new toaster works (more well, better) than the old one.
5. Of the two girls, Anna jumped (higher, highest).
6. Colin runs (faster, more fast) than I can.
7. Jess swam (more evenly, evenlier) today.
8. The team played (best, bestest) in the finals.
9. Of the three cereals, I like Wheaties (least, littlest).
10. The black fish ate (most greedily, more greedily) of all.

C. Follow the directions for Exercise B.

1. Anna writes (neatlier, more neatly) than I do.
2. This sailboat finished the race (sooner, soonest) than that one.
3. Sequoias grow (taller, more tall) than other trees.
4. The swift flies (fastest, most fast) of all birds.
5. The fog spread (lower, more low) over the city.

6. This train rides (more smoothly, smoother) than any other.

7. Which of the two movies ends (most happily, more happily)?

8. Of the two girls, Donna was dressed (more warmly, most warmly).

9. Trish draws (better, best) of all the artists.

10. Train travel costs (less, least) than air travel.

Part 3   Adjective or Adverb?

Adjectives tell about nouns. Adverbs tell about verbs. Sometimes it is hard to tell which modifier to use. This confusion happens because many adverbs and adjectives look alike.

Many adverbs are made by adding *-ly* to an adjective. See how this works:

Adjective:	The *loud* music bothered me.
Adverb:	We sang *loudly*.
Adjective:	Traffic was *slow* tonight.
Adverb:	Traffic moved *slowly* tonight.

Now look at this sentence:

My brother Jim drives (*careful, carefully*).

Would you use *careful* or *carefully* in the sentence?

To find the answer, ask what you are trying to say. Are you triyng to say:

how many Jim drives?
which one Jim drives?
what kind Jim drives?

Or are you trying to say:

how Jim drives?

You are trying to say *how*. The kind of word that tells how something happened or how something was done is an adverb. This adverb modifies the verb *drives*. You would use the adverb *carefully* in this sentence.

My brother Jim drives *carefully*.

When you are choosing the correct modifier, ask yourself:

1. Which word does the modifier tell about?
2. What does the modifier tell?

The chart below will help you to answer these questions.

An adverb tells	An adjective tells
* **how**	* **what kind**
* **when**	* **how many**
* **where**	* **which one**
* **to what extent**	
about a verb, adjective, or adverb.	about a noun or pronoun.

Exercises **Choose the right modifier.**

A. Number your paper from 1 to 10. Copy each sentence, putting in the correct modifier. Underline the modifier. Draw an arrow from the modifier to the word it modifies. Then write *Adjective* or *Adverb* to show how the modifier is used.

Examples: The batter hit the ball (solid, solidly).

The batter hit the ball *solidly*. Adverb

Carol was (hopeful, hopefully) about the test.

Carol was *hopeful* about the test. Adjective

1. I see (perfect, perfectly) without glasses.
2. Ramon ran (quick, quickly) to the corner.

3. Janet was (eager, eagerly) for the play to begin.

4. My father handles his tools (careful, carefully).

5. Harriet won the game (fair, fairly).

6. The sky was (clear, clearly).

7. Faith decorated the room (colorful, colorfully).

8. The old turtle moved (slow, slowly) through the grass.

9. The sun shone (bright, brightly).

10. A group of students talked (quiet, quietly) in class.

B. Follow the directions for Exercise A.

1. The younger children ran (noisy, noisily) to the gym.

2. The cake smells (deliciously, delicious)!

3. The tractor moved (slowly, slow) across the field.

4. Dale spoke (soft, softly) on the phone.

5. The racer turned the corner (sharp, sharply).

6. The prospector made a (careful, carefully) search of the area.

7. Your serve is (near, nearly) perfect.

8. To their trainer, the animals seemed (hungry, hungrily).

9. Paul was (shy, shyly) with the strangers.

10. Lance stitched the seam (perfect, perfectly).

Using *Good* and *Bad,* and *Well* and *Badly*

You will have no trouble with the words *good* and *bad* if you follow this rule:

Use *good* and *bad* to describe nouns or pronouns. These words are adjectives.

> Examples: Jane has a *good* clarinet.   (what kind)
>
> Jim has a *bad* cold.   (what kind)

Follow this rule for using *well* and *badly*:

Use *well* and *badly* with verbs to tell how something is done. These words are adverbs.

Examples: Jane plays the clarinet *well*.   (*how* she plays)

Jim behaved *badly*.   (*how* he behaved)

Exercises   **Use *good* and *bad*, and *well* and *badly*.**

A.   Number your paper from 1 to 10. Copy each sentence. Draw an arrow from each underlined modifier to the word it modifies. Then write *Adjective* or *Adverb* to tell how each modifier is used.

Example: You are good at spelling.

You are good at spelling.   Adjective

1. Dark clouds are a bad sign.
2. Tina has good news.
3. Hank draws very well.
4. The ferris wheel is a good ride.
5. Rosalie skates better than anyone else in the class.
6. That bike is in bad shape.
7. The fashion model dresses well.
8. Jane sings better than I do.
9. Last spring Matt had the worst cold ever.
10. Of all my friends, Gabe keeps a secret best.

B.   Follow the directions for Exercise A.

1. The other team played badly.
2. Did you eat a good breakfast?
3. We planned the party well.
4. Tony has a bad temper.
5. My friend writes good letters.
6. The old car rattles badly.
7. The worst storm of the year hit Boston.
8. Tracy sees better with her glasses than without them.
9. This radio works best during the day.
10. Mona's cold is worse today.

REVIEW Using Adverbs

Recognizing Adverbs Copy each sentence. Circle the adverb. Draw an arrow from the adverb to the word it modifies.

Example: Paint spilled everywhere.

Paint spilled (everywhere)

1. The cards were hidden somewhere.
2. The fly ball landed far in the outfield.
3. A new movie opened yesterday.
4. A snow plow slowly cleared the streets.
5. Grease from the frying pan splattered everywhere.
6. Our friends called later.
7. This comic book is very rare.
8. Janice almost forgot her club dues.
9. Brian practices the piano often.
10. Marla completed the puzzle quickly.

Adverbs in Comparisons Write the correct form of the adverb.

11. One actor spoke (more softly, most softly) than the other.
12. Jake walks the dog (more often, most often) than Beth does.
13. School is dismissed (earlier, more early) on Tuesday.
14. Of the three shirts, this one fits (better, best).
15. The helicopter flies (lower, lowest) than the jet.

Adjective or Adverb? Write the correct modifier for each.

16. The police followed the suspect (close, closely).
17. Todd read that mystery (quick, quickly).
18. The accident happened quite (sudden, suddenly).
19. Last night's snowfall seems (light, lightly).
20. The downhill slope looked (dangerous, dangerously).

Using Prepositions and Conjunctions

In this section you will learn about prepositions and conjunctions. These are two groups of words that do not have meaning in themselves. They are used only to connect and relate other words in a sentence to each other. However, prepositions and conjunctions are very important. They serve to show relationships and to combine ideas.

Part 1　What Are Prepositions?

Prepositions are words that show relationships. Read these sentences and notice the relationships expressed.

> Your album is *on the table.*
> Your album is *beside the table.*
> Your album is *under the table.*
>
> Sarah studied *before the game.*
> Sarah studied *during the game.*
> Sarah studied *after the game.*
>
> I took the photo *of my parents.*
> I took the photo *without my parents.*
> I took the photo *for my parents.*

In the first group of sentences, you can see that the words *on, beside,* and *under* show the relationship of the album to the table. The words show location.

In the second group of sentences, *before, during,* and *after* show the relationship of Sarah's studying to the game. The words show time.

In the third group of sentences, *of, without,* and *for* show the relationship of the photo to parents. The words show other different relationships.

All these words that show relationship are prepositions.

You can also see that prepositions do not show relationships by themselves. They begin a **phrase,** a group of words that belong together but have no subject or verb. *On the table, before the game,* and *of my parents* are examples of prepositional phrases in the sentences you've just read. What are the other prepositional phrases?

A preposition is a word used with a noun or pronoun, called its *object,* to show the relationship between the noun or pronoun and some other word in the sentence.

A prepositional phrase consists of a preposition, its object, and any modifiers of the object.

Here is a list of words often used as prepositions. Most of these prepositions show location. Others show a relationship of time. Still others show people and things in special relationships. Study these prepositions and see the relationships that each of them expresses.

Words Often Used as Prepositions

about	before	down	of	through
above	behind	during	off	to
across	below	for	on	toward
after	beneath	from	onto	under
against	beside	in	out	until
along	between	inside	outside	up
among	beyond	into	over	upon
around	but (*except*)	like	past	with
at	by	near	since	without

Exercises Find prepositional phrases.

A. Number your paper from 1 to 10. Write the prepositional phrase in each of the following sentences.

1. There is gum on my shoe.
2. Jeff opened his book to the index.
3. Under the new rules, our team can't compete.
4. This portrait of George Washington is two hundred years old.
5. Louisa May Alcott wrote about her own times.
6. All the cans on this shelf are dented.
7. We went bowling with my cousins.
8. The Plains Indians depended primarily upon the buffalo.
9. The pinch hitter rifled the ball into left field.
10. Everybody in my family has blue eyes.

B. Read each sentence. How many different prepositions can you find that fit each blank space? (You may want to refer to the list on page 335.) Write at least two prepositions to make phrases for each sentence.

Example: Pick up the ball _____ the table.

on, under, beside, behind

1. B. J.'s dog was playing _____ the house.
2. Cornelia heard a strange noise _____ the hall.
3. A flock of birds flew _____ the river.
4. Who put the butter _____ the oven?
5. An American flag flew _____ the house.
6. We found these coins _____ the bookcase.
7. The pen _____ the desk is mine.
8. The winners of the contest will travel _____ Alaska.
9. You'll find the sugar bowl on the shelf _____ the salt shaker.
10. The clown jumped _____ the platform.

Using Prepositional Phrases

The group of words that includes a preposition and its object is a **prepositional phrase.** All the words that modify the object are also part of the phrase.

Example: We rode *in the bus.*
We rode *in an old, broken-down bus.*

Gail was waiting *for dessert.*
Gail was waiting *for the special chocolate dessert.*

If a preposition has more than one object, all the parts of the object are included in the prepositional phrase.

Example: Weeds grew *in the lawn, the flower garden, and the vegetable garden.*

Exercises   Find the prepositional phrases.

A.   Number your paper from 1 to 10. Write all the prepositional phrases in each of the following sentences.

> Example: The yarn was stuck to the paper with glue.
>
> to the paper
> with glue

1. Everybody in the classroom saw the accident.
2. The doll beside the teddy bear has eyes made of black buttons.
3. Draw a line under the word that begins with a vowel.
4. Maureen and her little brother played on the swings for hours.
5. Donald plays clarinet in the orchestra at school.
6. The acrobat balanced on the tightrope stretched between two buildings.
7. Mary Ann waited near the school until four o'clock.
8. Alone in the room, Shawn hid the key to his locker.
9. The apartment across the hall has been empty for a month.
10. Mother hung a clock with a flower design above the door.

B.   Follow the directions for Exercise A.

1. During its journey, the space probe will travel past Venus.
2. Rosa tied a ribbon around the present for her cousin.
3. The puppy slept on a rug in the corner.
4. Janet finished her painting of the willow trees along the river.
5. Tell me about the characters in that story.
6. After the hurricane, the river spilled over its banks.
7. The squirrel ran up the maple tree outside my window.
8. You may choose among the last three dinners on the menu.

9. Dave shopped at the drugstore beside the new restaurant.

10. The team from El Paso plays against us before Thanksgiving.

Part 2 Objects of Prepositions

Using Nouns as Objects of Prepositions

You have seen that nouns may be used as subjects or objects of verbs. You will now study nouns used as objects of prepositions. Here are some examples of objects of prepositions:

> The Indians pitched their tents *near the* **river.**
> Mickey left his gym shoes *in his* **locker.**
> The winning run was scored *by* **Bonita.**
> The movie was *about the* **arrival** *of* **aliens** *on* **earth.**

Exercise   Find nouns used as objects of prepositions.

Number your paper from 1 to 10. For each sentence, write the prepositional phrase and underline the object of the preposition.

1. Kathy cleared the dishes from the table.
2. These Civil War photographs are by Matthew Brady.
3. Nobody in that movie is well known.
4. Elizabeth Blackwell began the study of medicine here.
5. The new couch will be delivered before Friday.
6. The temperature went below the freezing point last night.
7. The lid on this jar won't budge.
8. During that year, gold was discovered in California.
9. Around the Christmas tree were piled numerous presents.
10. The football sailed over the goal posts and into the stands.

Using Pronouns as Objects of Prepositions

When a pronoun is used as the object of a preposition, its object form must be used.

The object forms are these:

me	us
you	you
him, her, it	them

Examples: The prize was awarded *to us.*
Was there a message *for me?*
Laura's mother was looking *for her.*

Using Pronouns in Compound Objects of Prepositions

Usually you make few mistakes in using the object form of pronouns in the object of a preposition. However, you may become confused when the object of a preposition is compound. Read these examples to yourself.

Simple Object	Compound Object
I talked *with* **her.**	I talked *with* **Darren** *and* **her.**
We stood *near* **him.**	We stood *near* **Jackie** *and* **him.**
Give that *to* **me.**	Give that *to* **her** *and* **me.**

If you are not sure which form to use, say the sentence with the pronoun alone following the preposition. Then say the complete sentence.

Example: We're waiting for James and (she, her).
We're waiting *for her.*
We're waiting *for James and her.*

Using *Between* and *Among*

Often people use the prepositions *between* and *among* as if there were no difference between them. There is a difference that you should know, so that you can use them correctly.

Use *between* to speak of two persons or things.

> Choose **between** *these two programs.*
> The next game is **between** *the Jefferson High team and us.*

Use *among* to speak of three or more. Here are examples:

> We will divide the jobs **among** *Nancy, you, and me.*
> There was a three-way tie **among** *the Yankees, the Red Sox, and the Indians.*

Exercises   Use pronouns as objects of prepositions.

A.   Choose the correct pronoun from the two given in parentheses. Write the complete prepositional phrase.

> Example: The villain shot at Superman and (he, him).
>
> at Superman and him

1. The coach called on Leo and (I, me).
2. The roof over Marcia and (them, they) started to leak.
3. The ladder shook underneath Juan and (she, her).
4. Will you sit beside your mother and (me, I)?
5. The car traveling behind Beverly and (us, we) broke down.
6. A firecracker exploded near Timothy and (we, us).
7. My advice to Norita and (him, he) was ignored.
8. The wolves howled at Thompson and (they, them).
9. The album by James Taylor and (her, she) went on sale today.
10. The rivalry between Ohio State and (them, they) started years ago.

B.   Follow the directions for Exercise A.

1. On your cue, turn towards Ms. Bennett and (she, her).

2. As Paula hurried past Brian and (him, he), she tripped.

3. Mr. Washington was looking at Jason and (I, me).

4. The puppy's high-pitched whine went right through Ginny and (we, us).

5. Terrence's kite flew above the other boys and (he, him).

6. That car almost bumped into Gayle and (they, them).

7. I ordered a cheese and mushroom pizza for Susan and (her, she).

8. Everyone but Peter and (us, we) has had a turn already.

9. The paper carried an article about the marching band and (they, them).

10. My pet duck likes to waddle after my friends and (I, me).

Part 3   Preposition or Adverb?

Several words that are used as prepositions are also used as adverbs.

> Example: We looked *up*.   (adverb)
>
>   We looked *up the chimney*.   (preposition)

If you aren't sure whether a word is an adverb or a preposition, study the way it is used. If it begins a phrase, it is probably a preposition. If it is used alone, it is probably an adverb.

Exercises   Find prepositions and adverbs.

A.   In each pair of sentences that follows, one word is used both as an adverb and as a preposition. Number your paper from 1 to 10. After each number, write *a.* and *b.* After each letter, write *Preposition* or *Adverb* depending on which you find in that sentence.

> Example: a. Look out!   b. Look out the window.
>
>   a. Adverb   b. Preposition

1. a. There was litter all around the store.   b. There was litter all around.
2. a. Don't come near!   b. Don't come near the cliff!
3. a. Can you get past the barrier?   b. Can that big Cadillac get past?
4. a. Those cans should be stored underneath the cabinet.   b. Those cans should be stored underneath.
5. a. Miguel will soon be coming along.   b. Miguel is coming along the path.
6. a. Please stand by.   b. Please stand by the window.
7. a. Above the fog, the lights glowed.   b. Above, the lights glowed.
8. a. Two skaters fell through.   b. Two skaters fell through the ice.
9. a. We've met before today.   b. We've met before.
10. a. Puffs of white smoke drifted up.   b. White smoke drifted up the chimney.

B. Follow the directions for Exercise A.

1. a. Agatha took her coat off.   b. Agatha took her coat off the hanger.
2. a. Many children walked behind the parade.   b. Many children walked behind.
3. a. Beyond, the sea stretched to the horizon.   b. Beyond the rocky shore, the sea stretched to the horizon.
4. a. Cut the cake into two layers and spread the filling between.   b. Spread the filling between the two layers.
5. a. My friends are waiting outside the house.   b. My friends are waiting outside.
6. a. A DC-10 flew over.   b. A DC-10 flew over the playground.
7. a. The stuntman fell down the chute.   b. The stuntman fell down.

8. a. Don't just stand around!   b. Don't just stand around the kitchen!
9. a. Abigail opened the freezer and put the meat inside.
    b. Abigail put the meat inside the freezer.
10. a. When the light changes, you can get across.   b. When the light changes, you can get across the intersection.

Part 4   Using Prepositional Phrases in the Right Places

Some prepositional phrases may be moved from one position in the sentence to another without changing the meaning of the sentence. Here is an example:

> We visited Meramec Cavern during our vacation.
> During our vacation we visited Meramec Cavern.

To give your writing variety, begin a sentence with a prepositional phrase now and then. However, too many prepositional phrases can become boring. Don't use them very frequently at the beginnings of sentences.

Some prepositional phrases do not move easily from one position in the sentence to another. The position of the phrase can make a great deal of difference in the meaning of the sentence.

> **Example:** Walter touched the flower with purple petals.
> With purple petals, Walter touched the flower.

The second sentence suggests that Walter has purple petals. This prepositional phrase should not be moved away from flower.

> **Example:** Gerri called the dog with a loud voice.
> With a loud voice, Gerri called the dog.

The second sentence puts the prepositional phrase where it belongs, next to *Gerri*. This position makes the meaning much clearer. A prepositional phrase should be placed either directly before or directly after the word it modifies.

Exercises   Use prepositional phrases correctly.

A.   The following sentences are confusing. By changing the position of one phrase in each sentence, you can make the meaning clear. Rewrite each sentence to make it clear.

1. Bill put the bowl on the table of potato chips.
2. The clock has Roman numerals over the mantel.
3. On the roof Marian spotted a squirrel.
4. Do you have the keys with you to the house?
5. Everybody signed Lisa's photo on the team.
6. With a torn cover, Gordon found an old math book.
7. On the clothesline, Thelma saw a chickadee.
8. The book isn't mine in my locker.
9. The pencils should be sharp on my desk.
10. From her aunt in Sacramento, Jennifer put away her hat.

B.   Follow the directions for Exercise A.

1. A painting hung on the wall of a sunset.
2. Under the car, Dorothy noticed the softball.
3. Penelope made a puzzle in her room of the United States.
4. Albert wrote a story for class about his cat.
5. With a curly red wig, Mr. Morgan watched the clown.
6. I have buttons on my dress of gold.
7. There is a beautiful carved mask in the museum of an Indian chief.
8. People for breakfast eat lots of eggs.
9. The special effects deserve a prize in that movie.
10. The crew in the distance sighted a whale.

Part 5 What Are Conjunctions?

You have learned that relationships between people and things are expressed by prepositions. Relationships are also expressed by another kind of word: a **conjunction**.

How is the word *and* used in each of these sentences?

> *Tracy* **and** *Deborah* went to the movie.
>
> The class *wrote* **and** *performed* the play.
>
> Allen's puppy *broke his leash* **and** *ran away*.
>
> Yastrzemski hit a *double* **and** two *singles* in the game.

Do you see that in each sentence, *and* connects words or groups of words of the same type? In the first example, *and* joins two subjects. In the second example, *and* joins two verbs. In the third example, *and* connects two predicates. In the last example, *and* connects two direct objects. The word *and* is a conjunction.

A conjunction is a word that connects words or groups of words.

Two other conjunctions we use often are *but* and *or*. Like *and*, they may be used to connect sentence parts.

> **Andrew** *or* **Ginny** will bring the potato chips.
> (compound subject)
>
> Our forward **shot** *but* **missed.**
> (compound verb)
>
> The class **could see a movie** *or* **study the science chapter.**
> (compound predicate)
>
> Please buy **bread** *or* **rolls.**
> (compound direct object)
>
> The package was **bulky** *but* **light.**
> (compound predicate adjective)
>
> The orchestra performed for the **faculty** *and* **parents.**
> (compound object of a preposition)

Exercises   Use conjunctions correctly.

A.   Number your paper from 1 to 10. In each sentence there is a compound subject, a compound verb, a compound predicate, or a compound object. Write which of the four you find. Write the compound words with their conjunction. Circle the conjunction.

> Example: The Mets survived that season but finished last.
>
> compound predicate
> survived that season (but) finished last

1. The snow and ice made the roads impassable.
2. For breakfast, Lorraine likes eggs or oatmeal.
3. The wind shook the windows and whistled down the chimney.
4. I glued the string and the toothpicks on the cardboard.
5. Our television and stereo were stolen last night.
6. Gerald takes piano lessons but doesn't practice.
7. The puppy yawned and stretched.
8. Football and soccer are Lennie's favorite sports.
9. Trudy accidentally splashed Doug and me with her paint.
10. Tecumseh and his brother led their forces against the U.S. Army.

B.   Write sentences with compound subjects, verbs, predicates, or objects as the directions ask for. Use *and, but,* or *or.*

> Example: Compound direct object. Use a noun and a pronoun.
>
> Please take Amy and me to the library.

1. Compound subject. Use two nouns.
2. Compound verb.
3. Compound direct object. Use two nouns.
4. Compound subject. Use a noun and a pronoun.
5. Compound predicate.

REVIEW Using Prepositions and Conjunctions

Prepositional Phrases Write all of the prepositional phrases.

1. The cash register on the counter is made of brass.
2. For hot-air balloons, races are tests of accuracy.
3. The jockey on Daredevil wiped mud from his eyes.
4. Behind the TV screen is a mass of wires.
5. The wagon drawn by horses plodded through the snow.

Objects of Prepositions Choose the correct pronoun from the two given. Write the complete prepositional phrase.

6. The taxi splashed water onto Joan and (I, me).
7. Two FBI agents explained their work to (us, we).
8. A tall man sat in front of Chris and (I, me).
9. The scenery was designed by Lee and (she, her).
10. The playoffs are between the Tigers and (us, we).

Preposition or Adverb? In each sentence, there is an adverb or a preposition. Write *Adverb* or *Preposition* to tell which you find in a sentence.

11. The runners jumped over the hurdles.
12. Below the deck the crew was working.
13. The Dodgers fell behind.
14. A light breeze rippled across the countryside.
15. We sang the national anthem and sat down.

Conjunctions and Compound Sentence Parts Write the compound sentence part with its conjunction.

16. This game requires skill and practice.
17. Cheryl or Denny will help me.
18. An omelette should be light and fluffy.
19. Carter read the paper but skipped the comics.
20. Ben dashed outside without a coat or gloves.

Using the Parts of Speech

Part 1   The Parts of Speech

You have studied verbs, nouns, pronouns, adjectives, adverbs, prepositions, and conjunctions. You have been learning to recognize these groups of words and to use them correctly in sentences. The name used for these groups of words is the **parts of speech.** In this section, you will review the parts of speech you have studied.

In this section, you will also learn about the eighth part of speech called **interjections.**

348

What Are Interjections?

In addition to the seven important groups of words you have studied, there is also a group of words called interjections.

An interjection is a word or short group of words used to express strong feeling. It may be a real word or merely a sound. It may express surprise, joy, anger, or sadness. An interjection is often followed by an exclamation mark (!).

Look at these examples of interjections:

No way! I'm not singing by myself.
Congratulations!
Ouch! That hurts.
Great!

Now you have learned about all eight parts of speech.

The Parts of Speech			
nouns	**verbs**	**adverbs**	**conjunctions**
pronouns	**adjectives**	**prepositions**	**interjections**

Words fit into these groups because of the way they are used in a sentence.

Exercises   Recognize the parts of speech.

A. Write each underlined word. Beside each word, write what part of speech it is.

1. Hamburgers were cooking on the <u>grill</u>.
2. Gail keeps her jewelry in a <u>blue</u> box.
3. <u>I</u> need a ride to town.
4. Luis smiled <u>warmly</u> at his friends.
5. <u>Never!</u> I wouldn't jump from here!
6. Tracy <u>and</u> Chuck can't keep secrets.
7. Vinnie peered at the sky <u>through</u> a telescope.

8. *The Farmer's Almanac* predicts the weather.
9. The tiger moved suddenly into sight.
10. Our group climbed sand dunes all morning.

B. Follow the directions for Exercise A.

1. Oh wow! This water is refreshing.
2. Do you remember your dreams?
3. Hans is worried about the math test.
4. Later we will have a sing-along.
5. Too many people crowded onto the bus.
6. These lights warn of approaching trains.
7. Lisa's birthday cake had twelve candles.
8. You can get candy or gum from the machine.
9. The arrow hit the bullseye.
10. A water snake skimmed across the pond.

Part 2 Using Words as Different Parts of Speech

You cannot tell what part of speech a word is, of course, until you see how the word is used in a sentence. Many words may be used in different ways.

In **Section 10,** you learned that the same word could be used as either an adverb or a preposition. For example, look at this pair of sentences:

> Climb up.
> (In this sentence, *up* is an adverb.)
> Climb up the ladder.
> (Here, *up* is a preposition.)

Other words may be used as several different parts of speech. Here are several more examples for you to study.

Please clear the table.
>(Here, *clear* is used as a verb.)

The day was clear and sunny.
>(And here, *clear* is used as an adjective.)

The farmer plants wheat in the spring.
>(In this sentence, *plants* is used as a verb.)

The plants grow best in light, sandy soil.
>(In this sentence, *plants* is used as a noun.)

My father is a plant foreman.
>(Here, *plant* is used as an adjective.)

I feel very well.
>(Here, *well* is used as an adjective.)

You skate very well.
>(In this sentence, *well* is an adverb.)

Notice that when a word is used as a certain part of speech, it follows the rules for that part of speech. For example, when you use *plant* as a noun, you form the plural by adding *s*: *plants*. When you use it as a verb, you would form the past tense by adding *ed*: *planted*.

There is only one sure way to decide what part of speech a word is. That way is to see how the word is used in the sentence.

Exercises   Tell the part of speech.

A.   In each pair of sentences that follows, one word is used as two different parts of speech. Number your paper from 1 to 10. After each number, write *a.* and *b.* After each letter, write the word in italics and tell how it is used. It may be a noun, verb, adjective, adverb, or preposition.

1. a. I *brush* my hair.   b. This *brush* is plastic.
2. a. *Name* your favorite foods.   b. What's your *name?*
3. a. The bus turned *around.*   b. Joggers run *around* the block.
4. a. The store is *open.*   b. *Open* this box.

5. a. *Place* the book on the desk.   b. Where is a quiet *place?*

6. a. She must take the *late* bus.   b. The speaker arrived *late.*

7. a. Carol fixed a *light* snack.   b. Turn on the *light.*

8. a. Hold your arms *high.*   b. *High* waves hit the ship.

9. a. A motorbike zoomed *past.*   b. I rode *past* your house.

10. a. *Flag* down that car.   b. Which *flag* is blue and green?

B.   Follow the directions for Exercise A.

1. a. We have a *color* TV.   b. What *color* is this?

2. a. The *last* act is best.   b. Which float comes *last?*

3. a. Rita has a new *watch.*   b. I *watch* the news every night.

4. a. Sunday was a *fine* day.   b. Does the judge *fine* people?

5. a. It's time for a *rest.*   b. Horses *rested* in the stable.

6. a. I asked for *more* milk.   b. Jody practices *more* often than Ed.

7. a. The young boys dashed *off.*   b. Randy fell *off* the wall.

8. a. The ship *sails* soon.   b. One *sail* was ripped.

9. a. We followed a *dirt* path.   b. *Dirt* covered the floors.

10. a. A small cart trailed *behind.*   b. The cat lay *behind* a bush.

REVIEW The Parts of Speech

Parts of Speech Read each sentence. Write the underlined word or words.   Then write what part of speech it is in each sentence.

1. Rena stuffed her notebook <u>into</u> a backpack.
2. Many people fly <u>kites</u> on the beach.
3. The movie was a <u>true</u> story.
4. The treasure was <u>hidden</u> underwater.
5. <u>Three</u> trees fell during the storm.
6. Allen <u>found</u> his friends at the baseball park.
7. Adam learned to type when <u>he</u> was ten.
8. We can reach the island by plane <u>or</u> ferry.
9. <u>Hooray</u>! It's vacation time.
10. <u>That</u> campground is closed.
11. <u>Help</u>! This boat is sinking!
12. <u>Jason</u> removed the horse's saddle.
13. Did anybody <u>bring</u> the hot dog buns?
14. The cowhand finally <u>roped</u> the steer.
15. A hot-air balloon floated <u>gently</u> with the breeze.
16. The boat sailed <u>away</u>.
17. The newsstand sells magazines <u>and</u> comic books.
18. What are the <u>key</u> issues in the campaign?
19. Finally, the storm blew <u>over</u>.
20. Jamie <u>tossed</u> a pillow at her brother.

Making Subjects and Verbs Agree

Do these sentences sound correct to you?

The ham sandwich are good.
One star shine in the sky.
My friends is coming with me.
Many families goes on vacations.

If you listen carefully, these four sentences probably sound incorrect to you. Each one of them puts together words that don't normally fit together. Each one of them breaks a basic rule in our language: the subject and verb in a sentence must agree.

Part 1 Rules for Making the Subject and Verb Agree

When a noun stands for one thing, it is **singular.**

    friend   bus   country

When a noun stands for more than one thing, it is **plural.**

    friends   buses   countries

Verbs, too, have singular and plural forms. In a sentence, the verb must always agree in number with its subject. The word *number* refers to singular and plural.

Notice these examples:

Singular	Plural
Jane **sings** in the church choir.	Some girls **sing** alto parts.
The baby **crawls** everywhere.	Most babies **crawl.**
Al **speaks** Spanish.	Those boys **speak** French.

When we talk about one girl, we say she *sings.* When we talk about more than one girl, we say the girls *sing.* One baby *crawls,* but many babies *crawl.* One boy *speaks,* but many boys *speak.*

The *s* at the end of verbs like *sings, crawls,* and *speaks* shows that the verbs are used with singular nouns. In the examples, the singular nouns *Jane, baby* and *Al* were the subjects. When the subject is plural, the *s* on the verb is dropped. Look again at the sentences above.

Remember these rules:

1. If the subject is **singular,** use the singular form of the verb.
2. If the subject is **plural,** use the plural form of the verb.

Prepositional Phrases After the Subject

Be careful with prepositional phrases that come after the subject and before the verb. Do not let yourself confuse the subject of the verb with the object of the preposition.

Examples: The members of the team (practices, practice)
every day.
The verb must agree with its subject.
Who practices? The *members* (subject)
of the team is a prepositional phrase describing
members.
The *members* of the team *practice* every day.

A pair of gloves (were, was) lost.
The verb must agree with its subject.
What was lost? A *pair* (subject)
of gloves is a prepositional phrase describing *pair.*
A *pair* of gloves *was* lost.

Exercises   Recognize singular and plural forms.

A.   On your paper, write the subjects listed below. After each
subject, write *Singular* or *Plural* to tell whether it will take the
singular or the plural form of the verb.

1. typewriter
2. trips
3. drawer
4. smile
5. fingers
6. lesson
7. menu
8. members
9. teachers
10. treehouse

B.   Write the subject and verb in each sentence. Tell whether
they are singular or plural.

1. The movie shows a strange creature.
2. This truck has four-wheel drive.
3. Today's newspaper contains a good editorial.
4. The books on the bookcase fell.
5. A box of apples sits in the corner.
6. The nurses in the hospital work hard.
7. One package of cookies lasts all week.
8. Monica's parents go camping frequently.
9. The girls on our block play basketball after school.
10. A string of firecrackers makes a loud noise.

Special Forms of Certain Verbs

A few verbs have special forms that you should keep in mind.

Is, Was, Are, Were. The verb forms *is* and *was* are singular. The forms *are* and *were* are plural.

> Singular: Carlos *is* nervous.   Carlos *was* nervous.
> Plural: Our buses *are* here.   Our buses *were* here.

Has, Have. The verb form *has* is singular. *Have* is plural.

> Singular: Paula *has* a plan.
> Plural: They *have* a plan.

Does, Do. The verb form *does* is singular. *Do* is plural.

> Singular: Joe *does* the cooking.
> Plural: They *do* the cooking.

Exercises   Use the correct verb.

A. Write the correct verb from the two given.

1. Which city (has, have) the largest population?
2. Every Sunday my family (have, has) a big breakfast.
3. The travelers (has, have) a lot of luggage.
4. Notre Dame (was, were) ahead at the half.
5. Franklin (does, do) his homework after school.
6. This ice-cream shop (has, have) twenty flavors.
7. Jan's left leg (is, are) in a cast.
8. These carpenters (does, do) a good job.
9. (Is, Are) calculators always right?
10. The winners of the tournament (is, are) very happy.

B. Follow the directions for Exercise A.

1. Runners usually (does, do) warm-up exercises.
2. (Does, Do) the gymnasts use the rings?

3. Jerry (does, do) a great Bill Cosby imitation.
4. The crate of oranges (is, are) heavy.
5. The waves in the Pacific (is, are) best for surfing.
6. This stack of letters (has, have) no address.
7. The bags by the door (has, have) gifts inside.
8. The dogs (is, are) in the kennel.
9. This batch of brownies (does, do) taste good.
10. Those pinball machines (was, were) fun to play.

Part 2 Special Problems with Subjects

Sometimes making subjects and verbs agree is more difficult. There are some subjects that are tricky to use. In this part you will be learning to use these tricky subjects with the correct verbs.

Certain Pronouns

The words listed below are singular. Each is used with a singular verb form.

each	either	everyone	anyone
one	neither	everybody	nobody

Read these sentences over until they sound correct and natural to you.

Each of my sisters *sings* well.
One of the gymnasts *is practicing.*
Is either of you *coming?*
Neither of the stories *is* long.
Everyone does homework.
Is anyone home?
Nobody leaves early.

Watch out especially for these words when they are used as subjects and followed by a prepositional phrase. If the object of the preposition is plural, don't make the mistake of using a plural verb form.

Example: Neither of the cars (is, are) new.
What is the complete subject? *Neither of the cars*
What is the prepositional phrase? *of the cars*
What is the subject? *Neither*
Neither is singular, so the verb must be singular.
Neither of the cars *is* new.

Exercises   Use the right verb form.

A.   Copy these sentences, leaving a space for the verb. Draw a circle around the prepositional phrase. Then, choose the right form of the verb and write it.

Example: Neither of the movies (were, was) good.

Neither (of the movies) was good.

1. Neither of the bikes (works, work) well.
2. One of the library books (are, is) overdue.
3. Either of those routes (is, are) fast.
4. Each of the pets (need, needs) special care.
5. Everyone in our class (like, likes) a good joke.
6. Nobody at the party (talk, talks) much.
7. Neither of the magazines (has, have) poetry.
8. One of the clues (leads, lead) to the treasure.
9. (Does, Do) either of the bunks feel comfortable?
10. Each of the players (try, tries) hard.

B.   Choose the right form of the verb for each sentence and write it.

1. Everybody on the bus (get, gets) off at Maple Avenue.
2. One of the phones (is, are) always busy.
3. Everyone in the cafeteria (eat, eats) with friends.

4. Each of the speed-skaters (deserve, deserves) to win.
5. Each of the boys (carve, carves) wood.
6. Either of the computers (prints, print) out responses.
7. Everybody in the art studio (studies, study) drawing.
8. Neither of the squad cars (patrol, patrols) this area.
9. Everybody in the stands (cheers, cheer) loudly.
10. Neither of the radios (have, has) a powerful sound.

There Is, Where Is, Here Is

Many of our sentences begin with *There*, *Where*, or *Here*. These words are never subjects. In sentences beginning with these words, the subject usually comes after the verb.

Before you can choose the right verb form, you have to know what the subject is. You have to know whether it is singular or plural.

There are your parents.   (*Parents* is the subject; the plural form *are* is correct.)

Here is the trail.   (*Trail* is the subject; the singular form *is* is correct.)

Where do the dishes belong?   (*Dishes* is the subject; the plural form *do belong* is correct.)

Exercises   Use the right verb form.

A.   Write the correct form of the verb from the two given.

1. There (is, are) no rules for this game.
2. Where (does, do) the ticket line start?
3. Here (is, are) the dugout for the players.
4. There (was, were) no boots in my size.
5. Here (is, are) my last dime.
6. Where (is, are) the nearest phone?
7. There (is, are) tears in Ted's eyes.
8. Here (is, are) the pizzas we ordered.
9. Where (is, are) the chess pieces?
10. Here (is, are) the girls' locker room.

B. Follow the directions for Exercise A.

1. Where (has, have) the salespeople gone?
2. Here (is, are) the relief pitcher.
3. There (is, are) poster paints for the project.
4. Where (does, do) your parents work?
5. Where (was, were) the President's bodyguards?
6. Where (is, are) the road to Springfield?
7. Here (is, are) the sandwiches you ordered.
8. Where (is, are) the batteries for the flashlight?
9. There (is, are) a club for model airplane buffs.
10. Here (is, are) the thief's fingerprints.

Compound Subjects

When two or more parts of a compound subject are joined by the conjunction *and*, use the plural form of the verb.

> The *judge* and the *lawyers* **were** in a meeting.
> **Are** my *hat* and *coat* upstairs?

When the parts are joined by *or*, *either—or*, or *neither—nor*, use the form of the verb that agrees with the nearer subject.

> Tom or *Dick* **is driving.**
> Neither Aunt Ginny nor my *cousins* **are** here.
> Either ten pencils or one *pen* **costs** a dollar.

Exercises Use the right verb form.

A. Choose the right form of the verb for each sentence and write it. If a conjunction with *or* or *nor* is used in the subject, also write the part of the compound subject nearer the verb.

> Example: Neither my cats nor my dog (have, has) fleas.
> dog, has

1. Neither Kelly nor Jason (plays, play) soccer.

2. Either the roast or the potatoes (is, are) burning.
3. Neither Lee nor her sisters (wants, want) that dress.
4. Martha and her brother (speaks, speak) Norwegian.
5. Both the costumes and sets (is, are) Ben's creations.
6. Either milk or fruit juice (is, are) nutritious.
7. Neither the stadium nor the park (holds, hold) the fans.
8. Either the books or the shelf (is, are) labeled wrong.
9. (Is, Are) Hal's bike and my scooter missing?
10. Neither his brothers nor he (likes, like) that program.

B. Follow the directions for Exercise A.

1. (Is, Are) the snow and ice melting?
2. Neither my dog nor my other pets (eats, eat) much.
3. Either the Scouts or another club (is, are) selling cookies.
4. Either the stereo or the records (sounds, sound) terrible.
5. Neither the park nor the back lot (has, have) a baseball diamond.
6. Chess and checkers (is, are) similar in some ways.
7. Either shouts or cheers (encourages, encourage) the team.
8. Either the head lifeguard or her assistant (sits, sit) here.
9. Neither our clothes nor our furniture (has, have) been packed.
10. (Is, Are) candy or flowers the usual Valentine's Day gift?

Using *I*

Although *I* stands for a single person, it does not usually take a singular verb form. The only singular verb forms used with it are *am* and *was*.

I **am** the shortstop.   I **was** in our garage.

Otherwise, the verb form used with *I* is the same as the plural form.

I **do** the dishes every day.   I **have** a friend in Mexico.

Using *You*

The word *you* can stand for one person or for several persons. It may be either singular or plural. Whether it is singular or plural, always use the plural verb form with the pronoun *you*.

> You **were** the only *person* with a bike.
> You **were** the only *students* in the hall.

Exercises   Use the right verb form.

A.   Write the correct verb form from the two given.

1. You (was, were) the biggest vote-getter.
2. I (is, are, am) watching a TV special on China.
3. I (makes, make) candles and paper flowers as a hobby.
4. (Was, Were) you riding a moped?
5. (Has, Have) you tried bagels and cream cheese?
6. After everyone left, I (was, were) lonely.
7. You (was, were) going to practice with us on Saturday.
8. You (has, have) a good stamp collection.
9. I (was, were) expecting a better report card.
10. I (draws, draw) cartoons for the school paper.

B.   Follow the directions for Exercise A.

1. Last week I (was, were) a crossing guard.
2. (Is, Are) you planning a surprise party?
3. You (makes, make) delicious fudge.
4. I (am, is) working on a paper drive.
5. (Has, Have) you read *Johnny Tremain?*
6. With that hat on, you (looks, look) silly.
7. Greg, you always (loses, lose) your ticket.
8. On Mondays I (takes, take) the garbage out.
9. I (am, is, are) using my new hockey stick.
10. During the last game, you (was, were) the dealer.

REVIEW Making Subjects and Verbs Agree

Making Subjects and Verbs Agree Write the correct form of the verb for each sentence. Check your answer by reading the completed sentence to yourself.

1. Our albums (contains, contain) many photos.
2. TV detectives always (solves, solve) the crime.
3. This sports story (quotes, quote) our coach.
4. The hand brakes on my bike (sticks, stick).
5. The bunch of wildflowers (comes, come) from the woods.
6. The booth for refreshments (stands, stand) behind the fence.
7. The lions at the zoo (is, are) fed at 2 P.M.
8. A swarm of ants (has, have) raided our food.
9. (Does, Do) this book of ghost stories scare you?
10. Each of my shirts (is, are) missing a button.
11. Neither of the skis (has, have) been waxed.
12. Everybody in the cast (likes, like) the director.
13. Where (does, do) the ski lift start?
14. There (is, are) several days of vacation this month.
15. Here (is, are) the deepest snowdrifts.
16. Coffee and colas (contains, contain) caffeine.
17. Neither the showers nor the pool (is, are) heated.
18. Either rain or high winds (has, have) delayed the flight.
19. I (believes, believe) there are flying saucers.
20. You (was, were) the strongest hitter on the team.

Using Compound Sentences

Part 1   A Review of the Sentence

Throughout this book you have been studying sentences. Let's review what you have learned.

The **sentence** has two basic parts, subject and predicate.

Subject	Predicate
Carpenters	build.
The girls	hike.
The four girls	hike every summer.
The girls from camp	hike in the forest.

The **subject** of a sentence names the person or thing about which something is said. The **predicate** tells something about the subject.

Compound Parts of the Sentence

You have also learned that all parts of the sentence may be **compound.** That is, all the parts of the sentence may have more than one part.

Compound Subject:
> *Charla* and *Dave* sit closest to the teacher.

Compound Verb:
> Lena *has read* and *studied* all morning.

Compound Predicate:
> The Earth *has one moon* and *revolves around the sun.*

A Definition of the Sentence

You can see that all of these sentences express one main idea. These sentences, like all of those you have been studying, are called **simple sentences.**

Now you are ready for a definition of the simple sentence:

A simple sentence is a sentence that contains only one subject and one predicate. The subject and the predicate, or any part of the subject or predicate, may be compound.

Exercises   Review simple sentences.

A.   Write each sentence. Draw a vertical line between the subject and the predicate.

1. "The Muppet Show" has many fans.
2. The roller rink rents skates.
3. The rings on a tree trunk tell its age.
4. Roberto and Ken are bowling this evening.
5. The dentist cleans teeth and fills cavities.
6. The mice escaped from the cage.
7. Donna builds great sand sculptures.
8. Lou and Gail drew pictures on their casts.
9. The door to the hallway slammed shut.
10. The church is much larger than the school.

B. Follow the directions for Exercise A.

1. The lumberjack chops trees for the sawmill.
2. Corn and tomatoes grow in our garden.
3. A blizzard stopped traffic and closed the airport.
4. One boy on the bus missed his stop.
5. Yesterday's game had two overtimes.
6. Bonnie was the leader of the band at practice.
7. The roads are slippery and dangerous.
8. The girls at the slumber party barely slept.
9. Ellen raked the leaves and bagged them.
10. The gymnast did flips and cartwheels on the mat.

Part 2 What Are Compound Sentences?

Sometimes two sentences are so closely related in thought that you join them together. Then you have a different kind of sentence. You have a sentence that has more than one subject and more than one predicate. You have a sentence with more than one main idea. This is called a **compound sentence.**

> Willie Mays was elected to the Baseball Hall of Fame, **and** he was thrilled.
>
> My family arrived at the airport on time, **but** the storm delayed our flight.
>
> Don will be a lifeguard this summer, **or** he will work at his uncle's store.

Now look at the parts of these compound sentences:

Subject	Verb	Conjunction	Subject	Verb
Willie Mays	was elected	and	he	was
family	arrived	but	storm	delayed
Don	will be	or	he	will work

A Definition of the Compound Sentence

A compound sentence consists of two or more simple sentences joined together.

Why would you want to write compound sentences. Why not use only simple sentences? You will know the answer as soon as you read this paragraph.

> I tried to water-ski last summer. I put on the water-skis. They fell off. Finally, I found the proper skis. The boat stalled. We had to get a different boat. I jumped into the water. I tried to get up on the skis. I tried at least twenty-five times. Each time I fell. At last, I succeeded. Skimming the water felt terrific. All the effort was worthwhile.

You can see that a long series of short sentences is boring and dull. Combined into compound sentences, they sound much better.

> I tried to water-ski last summer. I put on the water-skis, but they fell off. Finally, I found the proper skis, but then the boat stalled. We had to get a different boat. I jumped into the water, and I tried to get up on the skis. I tried at least twenty-five times, but each time I fell. At last, I succeeded. Skimming the water felt terrific, and all the effort was worthwhile.

Exercises Use compound sentences.

A. Label three columns **Subject/Verb, Conjunction,** and **Subject/Verb.** For each sentence, fill in the columns.

Example: Dana went to the movie, but I stayed home.

Subject / Verb	Conjunction	Subject / Verb
Dana went	but	I stayed

1. Lori got new shoes, but they hurt her.
2. Last summer Mom grew vegetables, and we picked them daily.
3. The forest is very dry, and everyone worries about fires.

4. Tracy pumped water, and we drank it immediately.
5. The food must be eaten, or it will spoil.
6. A dog barked loudly, and it scared us away.
7. Scott coughed all the time, but he wouldn't take medicine.
8. Jo Ellen used the liferaft, and Kate had the inner tube.
9. Connie went to the doctor, and she had allergy tests.
10. These tickets were expensive, but the seats are terrible.

B. Follow the directions for Exercise A.
1. Wendy made the team, but she is on the second string.
2. The game was tough, and the score ended in a tie.
3. Do you like hamburgers, or would you prefer a pizza?
4. Linda is very friendly, and she is always cheerful.
5. Two boats capsized, but the others reached the shore.
6. The defense is strong, but the offense is weak.
7. Katy had braces, and now her teeth are straight.
8. Keith is a good actor, but he didn't get the part.
9. Do you bring your lunch, or do you buy it at school?
10. Tom rolled the bowling ball, and he scored a strike.

Punctuating Compound Sentences

Since compound sentences are made up of two or more simple sentences, they may be long. To help the reader keep the thoughts clear, put a **comma** before the conjunction in a compound sentence. The comma alerts the reader to the end of the first idea, and it prepares the reader for the second idea.

> Jean took the sports page, *and* she read the scores.
> We could watch the game, *or* we could go downtown.
> I'd like to buy those pants, *but* I have no money.

You may leave out the comma only when the two sentences that you join are very short.

> Dinner was served and we ate.
> The sun shone and the birds sang.

Exercises Punctuate compound sentences.

A. Copy the following compound sentences. Add a comma wherever it is needed. Circle the conjunction that joins both parts of the sentence.

1. You must hold onto the lid or the popcorn will pop out.
2. The math test is tomorrow but I haven't studied yet.
3. The wind is strong and Noah is flying a kite.
4. Carol climbed the high snowbank and Julie followed her.
5. Down jackets are very warm and they are lightweight, too.
6. Pam met her friends at McDonald's and they ate together.
7. Sue finished the race but she lost her shoe.
8. Dan shot for the goal but he missed it by a foot.
9. Kim sawed and I hammered.
10. Did you make that skirt or did you buy it?

B. Follow the directions for Exercise A.

1. The sky was hazy but I got a sunburn anyway.
2. Doors slammed and windows shook.
3. Sarah shaped the clay and then she fired it in the kiln.
4. Mom selected the lumber and she made the bookcase.
5. The helicopter landed and three people got out.
6. Brad enjoys social studies but science is his favorite subject.
7. Is Gilda in the hospital or has she recovered?
8. Two outfielders ran for the ball but neither caught it.
9. Jeff walks the dog in the morning and Ramona walks it at night.
10. Candy learned some card tricks and she does them well.

C. Write three compound sentences. Underline the subject once and the verb twice in each part. Circle the conjunction that joins both parts of the sentence. (Be sure to use a comma. Also check capital letters and end punctuation.)

REVIEW Using Compound Sentences

Simple Sentences Write the subjects and verbs in these simple sentences.

1. Once again, Emily searched for the book.
2. Don and Liz made huge bubbles with their gum.
3. The baby squirmed and cried in the highchair.
4. Cathy played well at her recital.
5. Elliot slammed his locker and hurried to class.

Compound Sentences Copy each sentence. For both parts of the compound sentence, underline the subject once and the verb twice. Then add the punctuation needed to make the sentence correct.

6. Bill subscribed to *Tennis* and he reads every article.
7. Sandy lives in the city but she likes the country better.
8. One station plays jazz but the rest play rock music.
9. Are you hungry or have you eaten dinner?
10. The TV set is on but nobody is watching it.
11. Dad has a moustache and Uncle Joe has a beard.
12. First the swimmers warm up and then they race.
13. The house is empty but it makes eerie sounds.
14. Rain fell for days and the rivers overflowed.
15. Hal plays pool often but he always loses.
16. I start crossword puzzles and my sister finishes them.
17. Have you missed practice or was it canceled?
18. Rubber floats but metal sinks.
19. This horse is gentle but she moves very fast.
20. The pitcher threw a curve ball and the batter struck out.

Diagraming the Sentence

Part 1   What Is Diagraming?

A **diagram** of a sentence is a picture of the parts of a sentence. A diagram shows how the parts of a sentence work together and how they are related.

When you make diagrams, you follow patterns. It is important to follow the patterns exactly. You will need to be careful to put words in special places. You will need to be careful to make vertical lines, horizontal lines, straight lines, or slanted lines. Copy words exactly as they appear in a sentence, with capital letters or without them. Do not copy any punctuation marks except the apostrophes within a word.

In this section, you will be learning how to diagram parts of a sentence. Diagramming can help you understand sentences.

Part 2 Diagraming Verbs and Their Subjects

A sentence diagram always begins on a horizontal line. The subject is placed at the left side of the line. The verb is placed at the right side of the line. A vertical line cuts the line in two and separates the subject from the verb.

The Cubs won.

Dorothy Taylor sang.

Exercise Diagram verbs and their subjects.

Diagram the verb and its simple subject in each of the following sentences. (Ignore all other words.)

1. The jet climbed.
2. Rhonda hesitated.
3. The fireworks exploded.
4. Penguins waddle.
5. The candle drips.
6. A rainbow appeared.
7. The room darkened.
8. The bus swerved.
9. JoAnn went to the door.
10. My book dropped into the mud.

Part 3 Diagraming Subjects in Unusual Order

Unusual order does not change the positions of subjects and verbs on diagrams.

Down our street came the parade.

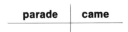

High above our heads flew the kites.

Exercise Diagram subjects in unusual order.

Diagram the subjects and verbs in the following sentences. (Ignore all other words.)

1. Around the curve came the cars.
2. Under the car hid the kitten.
3. In the field grazed some cows.
4. Onto the floor tumbled the eggs.
5. Over our heads hung buckets.
6. Into the pool dove Sandra.
7. From the woods came a deer.
8. Through the yard raced a rabbit.
9. Down the street zoomed a motorcycle.
10. Around in circles went the Tilt-a-Whirl.

Part 4 Diagraming Questions

When you diagram a question, put the subject and verb in normal order.

Have you heard the news?

Does Jim help with the cleaning?

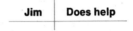

Exercise Diagram questions.

Diagram the subject and verb in each of the following questions. (Ignore all other words.)

1. Does the snake bite?
2. Should we feed the cat?
3. Did Mary lock the gate?
4. Did you solve the mystery?
5. When did the fire begin?
6. Have you ever seen a ghost?
7. Do you babysit at night?
8. Has the aquarium arrived?
9. Where are volcanos located?
10. Will the runner steal third base?

Part 5 Diagraming Imperative Sentences

When the subject of an imperative sentence is understood, show it on your diagram by writing (*you*).

Fold your paper in half.

Put this gift under the tree.

Exercise Diagram imperative sentences.

Diagram the subjects and verbs in the following imperative sentences. (Ignore all other words.)

1. Explain this paragraph.
2. Keep that smile on your face.
3. Find some more clues.
4. Read at your own pace.
5. Have a good time.
6. Open that old trunk.
7. Whisper in the library.
8. Ride your bike on the street.
9. Try a new approach.
10. Enter through the side door.

Part 6 Diagraming Sentences with *There*

There is usually just an "extra" word. It is placed on a separate line above the subject in a sentence diagram.

There are twenty students in this class.

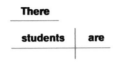

Were there many people at the dance?

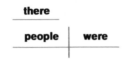

Exercise Diagram sentences with *There.*

Diagram the subjects and verbs in the following sentences with *There.*

1. Is there a chance of rain?
2. There are only seven cupcakes.
3. Are there new rules for this game?
4. There are two good programs on TV tonight.
5. There is a purpose for each lesson.
6. Were there footprints by the window?
7. There were several leaks in the ceiling.
8. There are people who live in caves.
9. Are there any books on that subject?
10. Is there time for another tennis match?

Part 7 Diagraming Compound Subjects and Verbs

To diagram the two or more parts of a compound subject, it is necessary to split the subject line. Put the conjunction on a connecting dotted line.

Jill and her father sailed the boat.

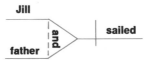

To diagram the two or more parts of a compound verb, split the predicate line. Put the conjunction on a connecting dotted line.

Sam swept, washed, and waxed the floor.

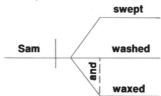

Exercise **Diagram compound subjects and verbs.**

Diagram the compound subjects and verbs.

1. Tara designed and built a small table.
2. Smoke and fumes pollute the air.
3. Chris waters, feeds, and prunes her plants.
4. The newscaster and sports reporter gave their reports.
5. Have Steve and Lisa visited the museum?
6. The wild animals gathered and drank at the stream.
7. There are sandwiches and fruit in the picnic basket.
8. We fished from the riverbank and caught three fish.
9. Toward the finish line dashed Judy and Carmen.
10. Forest rangers survey the forest and watch for danger.

Part 8 Diagraming Sentences Containing Direct Objects

When you diagram a sentence, place a direct object on the horizontal line following the verb. Separate it from the action verb by an upright line that does not cut through the subject-verb line.

My parents bought a new car.

For compound direct objects, continue the horizontal line a little way beyond the verb and then split it. Make as many parallel direct-object lines as you need. Put the upright line before the split, to show that all the words that follow are direct objects.

We met Laura, Dawn, and Billy at the bus stop.

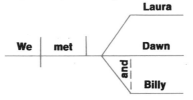

Exercise **Diagram sentences containing direct objects.**

Diagram the subjects, action verbs, and direct objects in the following sentences. (Some direct objects may be compound.)

1. The puppy took a nap.
2. He made a beautiful drawing.
3. We recycle bottles, cans, and newspapers.
4. Get a subscription to this magazine.

5. Ernest collects stamps and coins.
6. The hikers ate lunch on a hilltop.
7. Did the seventh-graders plan a party?
8. Beth and Rochelle played Scrabble.
9. We bought apples, plums, and strawberries.
10. Sergi hypnotized two people in the audience.

Part 9 Diagraming Sentences Containing Predicate Nouns

The diagram for a sentence containing a predicate noun is different from that for a sentence containing a direct object.

Dr. Sarah Powers is our dentist.

Notice that the predicate noun is on the horizontal line in the same position as the direct object. But the line that separates the predicate noun from the linking verb slants back toward the subject. This is to show its close relationship to the subject.

For sentences containing **compound predicate nouns,** use parallel lines. Put the slanting line before the main line is split.

Duke was a good pet but a poor watchdog.

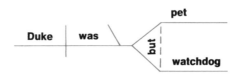

Exercise **Diagram sentences containing predicate nouns.**

Diagram the subjects, linking verbs, and predicate nouns in the following sentences.

1. The Pizza Palace is a new restaurant.
2. A tandem is a bicycle for two people.
3. Is Buddy the pitcher today?
4. Dolphins are mammals.
5. Are Sam and Dick best friends?
6. Spaghetti is an Italian dish.
7. Three string instruments are the violin, the cello, and the bass.
8. Two useful knots are the half-hitch and the butterfly.
9. Gwendolyn Brooks is a famous poet.
10. Ben Franklin was a writer, an inventor, and a statesman.

Part 10 Diagraming Sentences Containing Predicate Adjectives

You show predicate adjectives on diagrams just as you show predicate nouns. Place them on the horizontal line following the linking verb, and separate them from the verb by a line slanting back toward the subject.

That platform seems unsafe.

For sentences with compound predicate adjectives, use parallel lines. Put the slanting line before the main line is split.

The hikers were cold and tired.

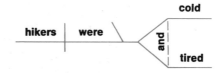

Exercise **Diagram sentences containing predicate adjectives.**

Diagram the subjects, linking verbs, and predicate adjectives in the following sentences.

1. The races were fun.
2. Diamonds are extremely hard.
3. Computers are quick and accurate.
4. Be careful.
5. My backpack is empty.
6. That watermelon is ripe, sweet, and juicy.
7. The moon is full tonight.
8. The bread and rolls from the bakery are delicious.
9. Soccer is very fast and rough.
10. Is Sherry happy in her new neighborhood?

Part 11 Diagraming Sentences Containing Adjectives

On a diagram, an adjective is shown on a line that slants down from the noun or pronoun it modifies. (Articles are shown the same way.)

The new cook made a thick, lumpy gravy.

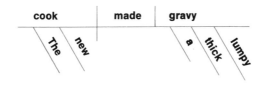

Mrs. Holmes is a patient, friendly teacher.

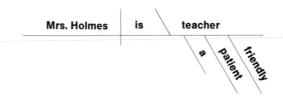

Exercise   Diagram sentences containing adjectives.

Diagram the subjects, verbs, and adjectives in the following sentences. Also diagram any direct objects, predicate nouns, or predicate adjectives.

1. Kirstin heard strange, squeaky noises.
2. The large, happy group sang lively songs.
3. That antique clock is beautiful and accurate.
4. Kathleen wrote those short, humorous poems.
5. The hefty weightlifter raised the heavy barbell.
6. Does this album contain old snapshots?
7. Ten acrobats walked the high tightrope.
8. The politician made an angry, forceful speech.
9. The lemon is a small, yellow, sour fruit.
10. An alert neighbor spotted the dangerous sparks.

Part 12 Diagraming Sentences Containing Possessive Nouns

In a diagram, possessive nouns are written on lines slanting down from the nouns with which they are used.

These are Ellen's books.

We heard the minister's sermon.

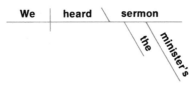

Exercise **Diagram sentences containing possessive nouns.**

Diagram the subjects, verbs, and possessive nouns in the following sentences. Also diagram any direct objects, predicate nouns or predicate adjectives, and adjectives.

1. The Riveras' black cat followed me.
2. Kendra's mother is an excellent pianist.
3. Bruce's serve is strong and fast.
4. Read Jack London's stories.
5. Cathy's dog found Dad's brown slippers.
6. The girls' chorus sang Beatles' songs.
7. Ms. Mason's class toured museums and historic places.
8. Did Douglas borrow Elena's new album?
9. The town's mayor proposed several laws.
10. The siren's shrill wail filled the air.

Part 13 Diagraming Sentences Containing Adverbs

Adverbs, like adjectives, are shown on diagrams on slanting lines attached to the words they modify. The following diagram shows an adverb modifying a verb.

Finally, the shy boy raised his hand.

The next diagram shows one adverb modifying an adjective and another modifying an adverb.

Some fairly young children play musical instruments very well.

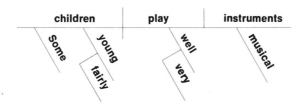

(Notice how *fairly* is attached to *young*. Notice how *very* is attached to *well*.)

Exercise   Diagram sentences containing adverbs.

Diagram the subjects, verbs, and adverbs in the following sentences. Also diagram adjectives, predicate adjectives or predicate nouns, and direct objects.

1. The climber moved upward quickly.
2. Finally, the police caught the suspect.

3. Fans wildly cheered the team's victory.
4. The butcher rapidly trimmed the steaks.
5. Tomorrow Al will referee the Bears game.
6. This train is too noisy.
7. This yellow is an extremely vivid color.
8. Did most students study hard?
9. They usually ride their bikes.
10. Very few stations play classical music.

Part 14 Diagraming Compound Sentences

It is not difficult to diagram compound sentences if you can already diagram simple sentences. A compound sentence is really two, or more, simple sentences joined together. Therefore, you draw the diagram for the first half of the sentence, draw a dotted-line "step" for the conjunction, and then draw the diagram for the second half.

Daniel slept soundly, but the other campers didn't close their eyes.

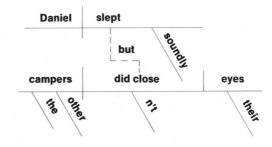

Sally is a strong swimmer, and she has won many races.

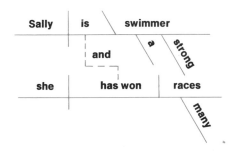

Exercise   Diagram compound sentences.

Diagram the following compound sentences. Diagram each part of the sentence. Then join the parts.

1. Winston hid Heather's mittens, but she found them.
2. The flowers are growing, but the weeds are growing faster.
3. Stacey arrived late, and she left early.
4. Did Dan walk, or did he ride his bike?
5. The door opened, but nobody entered.
6. Hop aboard, or you will miss the train.
7. Noah is a fair player, but he is tough.
8. Jan found a shiny silver ring, and he kept it.
9. Liz always takes out the garbage, but she never dries the dishes.
10. Badminton and volleyball are outdoor sports, but they are also played indoors.

REVIEW Diagraming the Sentence

Diagraming Sentences Diagram the following sentences.

1. Patty understands.
2. The runners ran quickly.
3. Can the baby walk?
4. Try harder.
5. Watch the screen.
6. There are some lovely shells.
7. Cars and trucks blocked the entrance.
8. The builders sawed and hammered.
9. Did the team win the final game?
10. Yolanda brought food, a blanket, and a radio.
11. Two popular evergreens are pine and spruce.
12. Does this book seem mysterious?
13. The wrestlers were breathless and weak.
14. Can the farmer's heavy tractor plow this rocky soil?
15. Randi washed and combed Evan's shaggy dog.
16. Very few people play this complex game correctly.
17. Drink that thick, creamy milkshake slowly.
18. Is that lovely fruit real, or is it wax?
19. Nancy Lopez is a golfer, and she has won many trophies.
20. We roasted the plump corn, and then we ate it greedily.

Capitalization

The use of capital letters is called **capitalization.** When you use a capital letter at the beginning of a word, you *capitalize* the word.

Capital letters are used to call attention to the beginnings of sentences and to certain special words. Using capital letters makes everything easier to read.

In this section you will be learning rules for capitalization. Study the rules and their examples. Refer to them whenever you need to check your work.

Proper Nouns and Adjectives

A **common noun** is the name of a whole group of persons, places, and things.

> hero   country   planet

A **proper noun** is the name of one particular person, place, or thing.

> Hercules   Switzerland   Mars

Begin every proper noun with a capital letter.

The words below are proper nouns. Some of them are made up of two words. Both words are parts of the name. Both begin with capital letters.

Independence Day	South America	February
Exton Mall	Lake Erie	Mary Shelley

A **proper adjective** is an adjective made from a proper noun.

> *Herculean* strength   *Swiss* cheese   *Martian* atmosphere
> (from *Hercules*)   (from *Switzerland*)   (from *Mars*)

Begin every proper adjective with a capital letter. Proper adjectives are usually used with common nouns. Do not capitalize the common noun.

Proper Noun	Proper Adjective	Adjective and Noun
England	English	English language
Rome	Roman	Roman numerals
Canada	Canadian	Canadian mountains
Indian	Indian	Indian corn

Most pronouns are treated like common nouns and are not capitalized. The pronoun *I*, however, is capitalized. Always capitalize the word *I*.

Number your paper from 1 to 15. Copy each word below, changing small letters to capitals where necessary. After each word, write the group that the word belongs to: *Common Noun, Proper Noun,* or *Proper Adjective.*

1. boston	9. park
2. city	10. actress
3. french	11. los angeles
4. mississippi river	12. woman
5. kentucky	13. disney world
6. elvis presley	14. donna summer
7. texan	15. school
8. singer	

Names and Initials

Capitalize the names of people and pets.

Carla   Michael   Snoopy

Begin every word in a person's name with a capital letter.

Billie **J**ean **K**ing   **J**immy **C**arter   **Q**uinn **C**ummings

An **initial** stands for a name. **Capitalize an initial and follow it with a period.**

Susan **B.** Anthony   **S. F. B.** Morse
P. T. Barnum   **O. J.** Simpson

Capitalize words for family relations when they are used as names of specific people.

Father	**M**other	**A**unt **E**m
Dad	**M**om	**U**ncle **H**enry
Pa	**M**a	**G**randma

However, if you use a possessive noun or pronoun before the word stating a relationship, that word is not capitalized.

Meet **A**unt **E**m.   *but* Meet Sally's aunt.

Today **F**ather fixed lunch.   *but* Today my father fixed lunch.

Titles and Their Abbreviations

You may have noticed that many people have special words before their names. Your dentist has the word *Doctor* before his or her name. So has your doctor. These special words are titles. Titles in names are capitalized.

Doctor Brown	**J**udge Clark	**M**ayor Ames
Governor Smith	**R**everend A. B. Hill	**S**enator Louis
Professor Jones	**P**resident **W**ilson	**S**ecretary Vance

There are also short forms for many titles. A shortened form of a word is an **abbreviation.** Abbreviations for titles are capitalized and followed by a period.

Doctor = **D**r.   Mister = **M**r.   Mistress = **M**rs.

The title *Ms.* has no long form. It is always capitalized and marked with a period. The title *Miss* has no short form. Do not place a period after the word *Miss* in a title.

Capitalize titles and their abbreviations when you use them with names. Follow an abbreviation with a period.

Exercises   **Use capital letters correctly.**

A.   Number your paper from 1 to 10. Copy the following sentences. Change small letters to capital letters wherever necessary.

    1. We live next door to dr. l. e. brown.

    2. My brother luis met superintendent julia f. jones.

    3. The mayor presented an award to miss allen.

4. My father knows judge mercedes blake and senator steven thomas.

5. Last Thursday senator phyllis r. grimes and professor a. e. ames visited our school.

6. The writer charles lutwidge dodgson used the pen name lewis carroll.

7. Perhaps i'll name my new puppies pepper and salt.

8. The best players on rhonda's team are rhonda and i.

9. Some famous indian leaders are chief joseph, sitting bull, and cochise.

10. At the convention, clara and her cousin b.j. met governor ridge.

B.   Follow the directions for Exercise A.

1. Katy moran's mom produces a television show.

2. Yes, aunt aretha and i met dr. cooley.

3. My neighbor, mrs. avellini, repairs cars.

4. A dog named benji adopted us.

5. My favorites are princess leia and luke skywalker.

6. One champion golfer is judy rankin.

7. The bill was introduced by senator s. i. hayakawa.

8. "Stamp out forest fires," smokey tells us.

9. Yesterday, grandma and my brother jeremy made fudge.

10. Timothy bottoms and joseph bottoms are brothers.

Months, Days, and Holidays

Capitalize the names of months, days, and holidays.
Do not capitalize names of seasons, such as spring and summer.

My birthday is **S**eptember 1.
We observe **L**incoln's **B**irthday on **F**ebruary 12.
Next **F**riday is the first day of summer.

Particular Places and Things

Capitalize the names of particular places and things.

Capitalize cities, states, and countries.

> Did you live in **K**ansas **C**ity, **K**ansas, or **K**ansas **C**ity, **M**issouri?
> The **U**nited **S**tates of **A**merica shares borders with **M**exico and **C**anada.

Capitalize both letters of the two-letter abbreviations for states, used in addresses on all mail.

> California = **CA**   Maine = **ME**   Wisconsin = **WI**

Capitalize streets, bridges, and buildings, such as schools.

> **C**hambers **E**lementary **S**chool is on **S**haw **A**venue.
> The **O**akland **B**ay **B**ridge was being repainted.

Capitalize all geographic names. Also capitalize such words as *north, south, east,* and *west* when they refer to a section of the country. Do not capitalize them when they are used as directions.

> The explorers traveled *south* along the **M**ississippi **R**iver.
> The **W**est is beautiful country.
> The storm is moving *east* over the **A**tlantic **O**cean.

Exercises   Use capital letters correctly.

A.   Copy the following sentences. Change small letters to capital letters wherever necessary.

1. Cactus grows in the southwest.
2. Vacation begins on tuesday.
3. The danube river flows into the black sea.
4. My friend miya osaka has relatives in japan.
5. On may 5, harper school will hold a carnival.
6. A time for picnics is independence day, july 4.
7. The international peace bridge connects canada and the united states.

8. Norman's little sister, linda, wrote to big bird at 123 sesame street, new york, new york.

9. Last saturday terry and i saw a ball game at comiskey park.

10. The aleutian islands are southwest of alaska.

B. Follow the directions for Exercise A.

1. The swedish ship passed through the panama canal.

2. Huge tortoises live on the galapagos islands.

3. The pentagon is the world's largest building.

4. The first monday in september is labor day.

5. Ms. e. e. stefano is the librarian at the carver public library.

6. I think elm street is made of bricks.

7. The first american in space was alan shepard, on may 5, 1961.

8. Last summer dad and i crossed the golden gate bridge.

9. The paddlewheel boat toured the missouri river.

10. Union troops were led by general u. s. grant of illinois.

Religions, Nationalities, and Languages

Capitalize the names of religions, nationalities, and languages.

> Three of the major faiths are Christianity, Judaism, and the Muslim religion.
>
> Many Mexicans speak both Spanish and English.

Clubs, Organizations, Businesses

Capitalize the names of clubs, organizations, and business firms.

> Mary Ann belongs to the Junior Photographers' Club.
>
> The Campfire Girls took a tour of the Bell Telephone Company offices downtown.

Exercises   Use capital letters correctly.

A.   Copy these sentences using correct capitalization.

1. Did o. j. simpson make commercials for avis?
2. Last december russian dancers performed here.
3. Juan valdéz speaks spanish at home and english at school.
4. The national geographic society has a good magazine.
5. Yes, aunt nancy, schwinn makes racers.
6. Did you see the beautiful indian cloth and jewelry?
7. The go fly a kite store at 1434 third avenue sells kites.
8. Many chinese people practice buddhism.
9. Jeb and i admired the israeli leader golda meir.
10. The sierra club holds nature outings each summer.

B.   Follow the directions for Exercise A.

1. My sister jeannine has posters of african kings.
2. The polish scientist madame curie discovered radium.
3. In october, logan school started the snowflake club.
4. Cathy stover has folk dolls from portugal and brazil.
5. The springfield bicycle league held a race on august 5.
6. The museum is open from october to june.
7. During the christmas season, f.a.o. schwarz is a busy store.
8. The spanish explorer balboa discovered the pacific ocean.
9. The white house is at 1600 pennsylvania avenue.
10. Last spring mom and i flew a delta jet to atlanta.

C.   Copy this paragraph using correct capitalization.

Our teacher, ms. abbott, told us about woodrow wilson the other day. At princeton university, professor wilson taught politics. He later became president of princeton university. Then he was known as doctor wilson. In 1912 the people elected him to the Presidency of the united states. After that he was called president wilson.

First Words

Any word is capitalized if it appears in certain places in written work.

Sentences

Capital letters are important sentence signals. They tell when a new sentence begins.

Begin every sentence with a capital letter.

> **M**y brother likes mushrooms on his pizza.
> **D**oes February have twenty-nine days this year?
> **L**ook out!

Direct Quotations

When you write the exact words somebody else said, you are **quoting** that person. The words are a **direct quotation.**

Capitalize the beginning of every direct quotation.

> "**T**oday we can expect two inches of snow," said the forecaster.

Usually, when you are writing what a person has said, you add words before or after the direct quotation to tell who said it. If these explaining words come at the beginning of a sentence, use a capital letter there. Use another capital letter at the beginning of the direct quotation.

> "**I**t's raining," my brother said.
> **M**y mother asked, "**I**s the cake still in the oven?"

Exercises   Use capital letters correctly.

A.   Copy these sentences using correct capitalization.

1. giant reptiles lived long ago.

2. "a robot has no brain," mr. rodriguez said.

3. maria asked, "may i use the microscope?"

4. "would you like to take a bike trip?" roosevelt asked.

5. wildflowers grow in the forest.

6. i explained, "a spaceship has gone to mars."

7. a kayak is similar to a canoe.

8. mother reminded me, "your fish must be fed."

9. mona asked, "have you seen my sweater?"

10. the teacher said, "admiral byrd was the first to fly over the south pole."

B. These sentences belong in one paragraph. Write them as a paragraph. Indent the first line. Begin each sentence with a capital letter.

many years ago lanterns were used to light the streets of big cities.

candles were used in the lanterns.

the people in each house had to hang out a lantern.

in paris, in 1666, nearly three thousand lanterns gleamed in the streets.

isn't it strange to think of a city street lighted with lanterns?

Poetry

Capitalize the first word in most lines of poetry.

Cats sleep fat and walk thin.
Cats, when they sleep, slump;
When they wake, pull in —
And where the plump's been
There's skin.
Cats walk thin.
—from "Catalog," ROSALIE MOORE

Sometimes, especially in modern poetry, the lines of a poem do not begin with capital letters.

Foghorns

The foghorns moaned
    in the bay last night
  so sad
  so deep
I thought I heard the city
    crying in its sleep.
        —LILIAN MOORE

Outlines

Capitalize the first word of each line of an outline.

The major ideas of an outline are marked with Roman numerals (I, II, III). The secondary ideas are marked with capital letters (A, B, C).

Systems of Measurement

  I. The British system
    A. Inch, foot, yard, mile
    B. Ounce, pound, ton
    C. Cup, pint, quart, gallon
 II. The metric system
    A. Meter
    B. Gram
    C. Liter

Letters

Capitalize the greeting and the closing of a letter.

Dear Sir: Dear Lucy,

Sincerely,   Your friend,

A. Copy the following poem, outline, and letter. Capitalize them correctly.

1. (poem)
   The Steam Shovel

   the steam digger
   is much bigger
   than the biggest beast i know.
   he snorts and roars
   like the dinosaurs
   that lived long years ago.
   —ROWENA BENNETT

2. (outline)
   The Lewis and Clark Expedition

   I. why it was needed
       a. the Louisiana Purchase of 1803
       b. lack of good maps

   II. why Lewis and Clark were chosen
       a. achievements of Meriwether Lewis
       b. achievements of William Clark

3. (letter)

   euclid park school
   cleveland, ohio
   march 17, 1982

   dear ms. lopez,
       we enjoyed your lesson about how to use a videotape camera. It was fun to see ourselves on television. in the future we will be able to videotape plays and other activities in our classroom.

   sincerely,

   william hodges

B. Follow the directions for Exercise A.

1. (poem)

   How To Tell the Top of a Hill

   the top of a hill
   is not until
   the bottom is below.
   and you have to stop
   when you reach the top
   for there's no more UP to go.
   —JOHN CIARDI

2. (outline)

   Planning a Vegetable Garden

      I. choose a good spot
        a. enough sunshine
        b. good soil
        c. proper drainage
     II. choose your crops
        a. tasty vegetables
        b. easily grown vegetables
    III. draw a garden plan

3. (letter)

   November 2, 1981

   dear sarah,

      i am sending you a photo I took of my newest pet. panda is a beagle and a very playful puppy. by next summer she should be ready to go on our long hikes. whatever we do at the lake, panda will do, too. I know you'll like her.

                 sincerely,

                 marie

Capitalizing Titles

Capitalize the first word and all important words in chapter titles, titles of magazine articles, titles of short stories or single poems, titles of television programs, and titles of songs.

Use quotation marks for these titles.

Chapter title:	Chapter 3, "Our Solar System"
Magazine article:	"Safety on Skateboards"
Short story:	"The Legend of Sleepy Hollow"
Poem:	"Catalog"
Television program:	"Nova"
Song:	"America the Beautiful"

Capitalize the first word and all important words in titles of books, newspapers, magazines, and movies.

Underline these titles. (When these titles are printed, they are *italicized.*)

Book title:	*Abe Lincoln Grows Up*
Newspaper:	*Chicago Tribune*
Magazine:	*National Geographic*
Movie:	*King Kong*

Do not capitalize a little word such as *the, in, for, from, by, at, a,* or *an,* unless it comes first or last in a title.

Exercises   Use capital letters correctly.

A.   Copy the following titles. Capitalize them correctly.

1. *rascal*   (book)
2. "east of the sun and west of the moon"   (story)
3. *little house on the prairie*   (book)
4. *and now miguel*   (book)
5. "the lady or the tiger?"   (short story)
6. "the life of the pioneers"   (chapter title)
7. "the top ten on television"   (magazine article)

8. *newsweek* (magazine)
9. "the horses of the sea" (poem)
10. *fantasia* (movie)

B. Follow the directions for Exercise A.

1. *m.c. higgins, the great* (book)
2. *wall street journal* (newspaper)
3. "a visit from st. nicholas" (poem)
4. *the lord of the rings* (book and movie)
5. "the highwayman" (poem)
6. "building better kites" (magazine article)
7. "soul train" (television show)
8. "the star-spangled banner" (song)
9. *freedom train* (book)
10. "casey at the bat" (poem)

REVIEW Capitalization

Using Capital Letters Correctly Copy each of the following sentences. Change small letters to capital letters wherever necessary.

1. wesley and craig phillips live on cherry street.
2. aunt rhoda has studied mexican art.
3. lloyd j. curtis sails on lake michigan.
4. last tuesday governor scott was re-elected.
5. my teacher, mr. olsen, rides a bike to school.
6. the first day of spring is march 21.
7. on wednesday, february 14, we celebrate valentine's day.
8. last may the mason family moved to georgia.
9. did french fries come from france?
10. the principal of skiles middle school is mrs. j. e. clark.
11. san francisco is west of the rocky mountains.
12. does the colorado river flow through arizona?
13. many chinese people are buddhists.
14. the reader bookstore on oak street sells spanish magazines.
15. the boys clubs of america sponsor service projects.
16. terry asked, "has the bell rung?"
17. "estes national park is terrific!" jenny said.
18. he has a heart of gold beneath
    but the lion just can't trust his teeth.
    —from "Why Nobody Pets the Lion at the Zoo"
    JOHN CIARDI
19. *the jungle book* is by rudyard kipling.
20. one very popular movie was *superman*.

Punctuation

Punctuation is the use of commas, periods, and other marks in writing. The marks used are called **punctuation marks.**

Good punctuation will help your readers understand what they read. It will show them where to pause or stop. It will tell them whether they are reading a statement, an exclamation, or a question.

In this section, you will be learning rules for punctuating correctly. Study the rules and their examples. Whenever you are writing, use this section to check your work.

Using the Period

The **period (.)** is used in several different positions for different purposes. This part discusses four of those positions.

The Period at the End of Sentences

A period is used at the end of a declarative sentence and at the end of an imperative sentence. The period is a signal that the sentence has ended. When you are reading aloud, the period tells you to drop your voice.

Declarative: Navaho Indians built homes called hogans.

Imperative: Help me find my sweater.

Use a period at the ends of declarative sentences and imperative sentences.

The Period After an Initial

An **initial** is the first letter of a name followed by a period. It is used to stand for that name. The letter is always capitalized.

Nancy L. Kassebaum   John F. Kennedy

Use a period after an initial in a name.

The Period After an Abbreviation

A short form for a word is an **abbreviation.** An abbreviation is usually followed by a period.

Here are abbreviations of the days of the week:

Sun.   Mon.   Tues.   Wed.   Thurs.   Fri.   Sat.

Here are abbreviations of months of the year:

Jan. Feb. Mar. Apr. Aug. Sept. Oct. Nov. Dec.

What three months are left out? Why? A word that is short in its regular form does not usually have an abbreviation.

Some abbreviations stand for more than one word and have more than one period.

D.C.   P.O.
District of Columbia   Post Office

A.M. (*ante meridiem*)   B.C.
means before noon   Before Christ

P.M. (*post meridiem*)   A.D. (*Anno Domini*)
means after noon   means in the year of the Lord

Below is a list of common abbreviations with the words that they stand for.

Titles

Mr.   Mrs.   Ms.
Mister   Mistress   (no long form)

Dr.   Rev.
Doctor   Reverend

Geographic Terms

Rd.   Ave.   St.
Road   Avenue   Street

Blvd.   U.S.A.
Boulevard   United States of America

English Measure

oz.   lb.   in.   doz.
ounce(s)   pound(s)   inch(es)   dozen

yd.   mi.   ft.
yard   mile   foot (or feet)

Not all abbreviations use periods. Here are some examples of this second type:

m	g	l
meter	gram	liter

mph	UN	ZIP
miles per hour	United Nations	Zone Improvement Plan

Note: A complete list of abbreviations used with ZIP codes is on page 447. All of the two-letter abbreviations are made and approved by the United States Postal Service. These special abbreviations are to be used only for the mail, on letters and packages. Here are a few examples of these special abbreviations.

HI	NM	VT	TX
Hawaii	New Mexico	Vermont	Texas

Using Abbreviations Correctly

You do need to recognize common abbreviations. But you also need to use abbreviations correctly.

Most abbreviations are used only in lists, addresses, arithmetic problems, or other special forms of writing. They should not be used in regular sentences. For example, on an application for a library card, or on an envelope, you may write your address in this way:

2176 So. Taylor Rd.

In a sentence, you should write this:

I live at 2176 South Taylor Road.

As a general rule, the only abbreviations you should use in sentences are titles with names (such as *Dr.* Perez), A.M. and P.M., and B.C. and A.D.

The Period After Each Numeral or Letter in an Outline

Use a period after each numeral or letter that shows a division of an outline.

How the Months Got Their Names

    I. Months named for real people

        A. July

        B. August

    II. Months named for gods

        A. January

        B. March

        C. May

        D. June

    III. Other months

Exercises   **Use periods correctly.**

A.   Copy these sentences, using periods where needed.

1. The Rev Jesse Jackson spoke at our school
2. Capt James Cook sailed across the ocean
3. Ms Sue Schneider refereed the game
4. J Fred Muggs was a famous chimpanzee
5. Ask Dr Jean Casey for an appointment
6. Be sure to bring warm mittens
7. Capt B J Hunnicutt talked to Gen Sherman Potter
8. Make yourself comfortable
9. Send your questions to Mr Thomas N Sane
10. Author P L Travers wrote about Mary Poppins

B. Copy the following, putting periods where necessary.

1. 1301 Ridge Ave
2. 260 B C
3. 4:15 P M
4. 4 Pond St, Winthrop, MA 02152
5. PO Box 253
6. Dec 15, 1980
7. 20 lb
8. Dr C G Opaskar
9. 5 ft 7 in
10. 55 mi

C. Copy this outline, putting periods where necessary.

Abraham Lincoln

I Before becoming president
  A Childhood
  B Early career
II As president
  A Civil War
  B Emancipation Proclamation
  C Death

Using the Question Mark

A **question mark (?)** is used at the end of every interrogative sentence. It is a signal that a question has been asked. When you are reading aloud, the question mark tells you to raise the pitch of your voice.

Are you ready to go?

What did you say?

Use a question mark at the end of every interrogative sentence.

Exercises   Use question marks correctly.

A.   Copy these sentences. Use either a period or a question mark at the end of each sentence.

1. I built a bookshelf in shop class
2. Does Jason collect stamps
3. Look at that printing press
4. What is batik
5. Can you grow a plant from orange seeds
6. How does this camera work
7. Mom made the costumes for our play
8. Do all of the problems on this page
9. When was the Battle of Gettysburg fought
10. Do you have this album

B.   Follow the directions for Exercise A.

1. Shari Lewis is a puppeteer
2. Are you babysitting for the Mayberrys
3. Measure the room in metrics
4. I make animals and flowers from paper scraps
5. Can you tie a half-hitch knot
6. Come and join our softball game
7. Have you ever made granola
8. Recycle glass bottles
9. What is that sound in the engine
10. The motor is racing

Using the Exclamation Point

An **exclamation point (!)** is used at the end of every exclamatory sentence and after words or phrases that show strong feeling.

It tells the reader that the sentence or words should be read with strong feeling. The exclamation point signals surprise, joy, fear, excitement, or shock.

> Don't open that door!
>
> Help! Fire!
>
> Good grief!

Use an exclamation point at the end of an exclamatory sentence or word.

Exercises   **Use the exclamation point correctly.**

A.   Copy these sentences. Use either a period, a question mark, or an exclamation point where it is needed.

1. Do you have a sweet tooth
2. Hooray We won
3. Oh, no The bus has gone
4. When does the dance begin
5. Where is your prize
6. We went to the new house
7. Let's play these records
8. May I use the shovel
9. Start with a simple project
10. Halt

B.   Number your paper from 1 to 5. Write an exclamation to express your feeling about five imaginary events.

> Example: *Event*—I received a 10-speed bicycle.
>
> *Exclamation*—This is just what I wanted!

Using the Comma

The **comma (,)** generally signals a pause in a sentence, or a separation between related ideas. When you are reading aloud, the comma tells you to pause briefly.

There are eight uses of the comma that you should know.

Use a comma to separate the day of the month from the year.

Thomas Jefferson died on July 4, 1826.

The stock market crashed on October 29, 1929.

If the date appears in the middle of the sentences, place a comma after the year, also.

Peace came on November 11, 1918, to the nations of Europe.

On August 9, 1974, President Nixon resigned.

Use a comma to separate the name of a city from the state or country in which it is located.

Toronto, Canada   Detroit, Michigan

Miami, Florida   Tokyo, Japan

If the name appears in the middle of a sentence, place a comma after the state or country.

We lived in Cherry Valley, Ohio, for several years.

Every year in Rutland, Vermont, there is a county fair.

Use a comma to set off the name of a person spoken to.

Will you close the door, Juan?

Miss Bristol, may I leave early today?

I think, Nancy, that I'll be late today.

Use a comma after introductory words such as *yes* and *no*.

No, planets are not stars.

Yes, an accident might happen.

Use a comma to set apart words or names in a series.

Two words or names are not a series. There are always three or more in a series.

> We had watermelon and sherbet for dessert. (no series)
>
> We had cake, ice cream, and chocolate milk for dessert. (series)

Read and punctuate a series carefully.
How many girls are named in each sentence below?

> I invited Mary, Louise, Sue, Ann, and Jean.
>
> I invited Mary Louise, Sue Ann, and Jean.

You see that changing the number of commas changed the number of girls from five to three.

Use a comma before or after a direct quotation.

> The crowd shouted, "Run to third base!"
>
> "I like swimming best," Ted replied.

Use a comma after the greeting of a friendly letter and the closing of any letter.

> Dear Joseph,   Yours truly,

Use a comma in a compound sentence. Place the comma at the end of the first complete thought.

> Casey struck out, and the game was over.
>
> The cookies burned, but we ate them anyway.

Exercises   Use commas correctly.

A.   Copy the following sentences. Put in commas where they are needed. Be ready to explain the reason for each comma you put in.

1. Dad where did you find my gloves?

2. Julie answer this riddle.

3. The Declaration of Independence was signed on July 4 1776.

4. Amelia Earhart was born in Atchison Kansas on July 24 1898.

5. Yes you may have another piece of cake.

6. A Kentucky Derby winner must be bold fast and strong.

7. Do you always stop look and listen at crossings?

8. "You'll feel better after a rest" the nurse said.

9. The birdcage fell and my parakeet screeched.

10. Courtney said "Pick a card."

B. Follow the directions for Exercise A.

1. No I'd rather have soup.

2. Stacey said "Try this trick."

3. The Astrodome is in Houston Texas.

4. This lake is cool deep and clear.

5. The guide arrived and the tour began.

6. Debbie did you see the seahorse?

7. "I'll be outside" Larry said.

8. The baby cried and Mom picked her up.

9. The fielder caught dropped and recovered the ball.

10. Sputnik was launched on October 4 1957.

C. Copy the following note, using necessary commas.

Dear Kate

Yes my parents said that I may visit you and your family in Little Rock on the weekend of July 4. I am so excited! I cannot wait to see you Kate. I will be arriving by bus on July 2 at 2:30 P.M. Be sure to give my best to Jodie Sara Maggie and your parents. See you soon.

Your friend
Ginny

Using the Apostrophe

The **apostrophe** (') is used for two different purposes. When you are reading aloud, it has no effect on how you say the word in which it appears.

The Apostrophe To Show Possession

A **possessive** is a word that shows that someone or something owns something else.

To form the possessive of a singular noun, add an apostrophe and an s.

The tent that belongs to James is James's tent.

The car that belongs to his mother is his mother's car.

To form the possessive of a plural noun that does not end in s, add an apostrophe and an s.

The hats that belong to men are men's hats.

The antlers of deer are deer's antlers.

To form the possessive of a plural noun that ends in s, add only an apostrophe.

The costumes of the actresses are the actresses' costumes.

The cages of the tigers are the tigers' cages.

Exercises   Use apostrophes to show possession.

A.   Make these words show possession. Write the possessive form.

1. Sarah	5. boss	9. the Smiths
2. our class	6. woman	10. tribe
3. people	7. workers	11. ranchers
4. puppies	8. Chris	12. hostess

B. Copy the groups of words below. Make the underlined word in each group show possession.

1. the kittens mother
2. the catcher mitt
3. bus drivers uniforms
4. Ann cousin
5. the children library

6. your grandparents house
7. the captain orders
8. the woman office
9. Geraldo uncle
10. the canary cage

The Apostrophe in Contractions

Do you often use the word *don't?* You use it as a short way of saying *do not.* The apostrophe shows that a letter has been left out.

A word made up of two words combined into one by leaving out a letter or letters is called a **contraction.** Here are some contractions used frequently:

isn't	=	is not		it's	=	it is
doesn't	=	does not		I'll	=	I will
don't	=	do not		I'm	=	I am
can't	=	cannot		they're	=	they are
won't	=	will not		we're	=	we are
haven't	=	have not		you've	=	you have
wouldn't	=	would not		she'd	=	she would or she had

Use an apostrophe in a contraction, to show where a letter or letters have been omitted.

Be especially careful with *it's* and *its.* Remember:

It's (with an apostrophe) always means *it is* or *it has.*
It's time for lunch.

Its (without the apostrophe) is the possessive of *it.*
The kitten played with *its* rubber mouse.

417

Remember that no apostrophe is used with the possessive pronouns *hers, yours, ours,* and *theirs.*

This piece of cake is *hers.*   *Ours* is the best team.
That one is *yours.*   *Theirs* is losing now.

Here are some contractions and other words that are often confused.

Who's means *who is* or *who has.*
Who's been eating my porridge?

Whose is the possessive of *who.*
Whose coat is this?

You're means *you are.*
You're the first person to give the right answer.

Your is the possessive of *you.*
I'll put *your* paper on the bulletin board.

They're means *they are.*
They're on the plane to Oregon now.

Their is the possessive form of *they.*
The band members played *their* instruments well.

There means a place, or it is used to begin sentences.
I am going *there* later.   *There* is someone at the door.

Exercises   Use apostrophes to show contractions.

A.   Below is a list of words you often say as contractions. Write each pair of words. Beside it write the contraction, using an apostrophe.

1. have not	5. would not	9. are not
2. does not	6. were not	10. had not
3. it is	7. I am	11. you are
4. was not	8. did not	12. she would

B. Copy the sentences below. Put in apostrophes where they are needed to show possession or to identify contractions.

1. Isnt that racket yours?
2. Whos building the fire?
3. I cant play chess.
4. Doesnt your city have a childrens museum?
5. Youll enjoy the Bee Gees records.
6. Vics room is full of pets.
7. Its a picture of a lions den.
8. The kittens are Mandys and hers.
9. Theyre in Mr. Baxters guitar class.
10. The box wont fit on this shelf.

Using the Hyphen

Often when you are writing you run out of space at the end of a line and cannot fit in all of the next word. When this happens, you write part of the word, followed by a **hyphen (-)**, on that line. You write the rest of the word at the beginning of the next line.

Use a hyphen after the first part of a word divided into two parts at the end of a line.

In prehistoric times, the dino-
saur roamed the earth.

Only words of two or more syllables can be divided at the end of a line. Never divide words of one syllable, such as *pound* or *might*. If you are in doubt about dividing a word, look it up in a dictionary.

A single letter must not be left at the end of a line. For example, this division would be wrong: *a-part*. A single letter must not appear at the beginning of a line either. It would be wrong to divide *dictionary* like this: *dictionar-y*.

A. Decide whether you can divide each of these words into two parts, with each part having more than one letter. Check the word in a dictionary to be sure. If you can, divide the word as you would at the end of a line. Add the necessary hyphen. If the word cannot be divided, just copy it.

Examples: a. arithmetic   b. able
              arith- or *arithme-*   *able*
                 metic   *tic*

1. bury   5. owl   9. live
2. adventure   6. copy   10. honest
3. sail   7. groceries   11. together
4. music   8. marbles   12. hungry

B. Follow the directions for Exercise A.

1. banner   5. equal   9. body
2. collection   6. history   10. measure
3. strange   7. sketch   11. neighborhood
4. pony   8. amazing   12. crafts

Using Quotation Marks

When you write exactly what someone says, you are **quoting** that person. If you write the person's exact words, you write a **direct quotation. Quotation marks (" ")** are the sign that someone is being quoted exactly.

Use quotation marks before and after the words of every direct quotation.

Read this sentence carefully:

Molly called, "The game starts in ten minutes."

Notice these things about the sentence above:

1. There is a comma (,) before the quotation.

2. Only the speaker's exact words are placed inside the quotation marks.

3. The quotation begins with a capital letter.

4. The punctuation at the end of the sentence is placed *inside* the quotation marks.

Study each of these sentences. See how each one follows the four rules.

Kenneth yelled, "There is a fire in the kitchen!"

Della asked, "Did anybody find a red glove?"

The director insisted, "Speak slowly and clearly."

A Quotation at the Beginning of a Sentence

Sometimes the quotation is placed at the beginning of a sentence.

"This plant needs water," Mr. Crockett said.

Notice that the comma ending the quotation is placed inside the quotation marks. Notice that the punctuation ending each of the following quotations is also placed inside the quotation marks. Notice, too, that there is also punctuation at the end of the sentence.

"There is a fire in the kitchen!" yelled Kenneth.

"Did anybody find a red glove?" Della asked.

"Speak slowly and clearly," the director insisted.

Exercises   Punctuate quotations correctly.

A.   Copy these sentences. Punctuate correctly.

1. Make up your mind Dennis urged.
2. I finished the puzzle he announced.
3. JoAnn asked Is that a sparrow?
4. The zookeeper warned Don't disturb the panda.
5. Where is the North Star she asked.
6. What causes a storm Lauren asked.
7. Mom raises bees said Jeff.
8. A chameleon changes color Terri noted.
9. Dad asked Where are your gloves?
10. Mr. Owens said Sing that verse again.

B.   Follow the directions for Exercise A.

1. What happened to my room Caroline asked.
2. The doctor called I need a bandage!
3. Put your feet in the stirrups she said.
4. Here's the entrance Kyle yelled.
5. Charlene asked What's your favorite color?
6. The monarch is a butterfly Alonzo explained.
7. Steve shouted My kite string broke!
8. Emily said I have a Venus flytrap.
9. I asked Have you read the comic strips?
10. Where is the Nancy Drew book Alison asked.

C.   Each of these five sentences has one mistake in it. Write the sentences correctly.

1. "Mary said, I will be home soon."
2. "Do you deliver the newspaper" Ms. Conklin asked?
3. Jeff yelled, "look out for the car!"
4. Lydia said, "You may use my skateboard".
5. "My watch broke, Spencer" complained.

Divided Quotations

Sometimes a quotation is divided. Words that tell who is talking, like *she said* or *he asked*, sometimes come in the middle of the sentence.

"After three hamburgers," Vic admitted, "dessert will be too much."

Divided quotations follow the capitalization and punctuation guidelines presented already. In addition, these rules apply:

1. Two sets of quotation marks are used.
2. The words that tell who is talking are followed by a comma or a period. Use a comma if the second part of the quotation does not begin a new sentence. Use a period if the second part of the quotation is a new sentence.

"Did you know," Katherine asked, "that mammoths once lived here?"

"Turn off the TV," Larry suggested. "Nothing good comes on now."

3. The second part of the quotation begins with a capital if it is the start of a new sentence, as in the second example above. Otherwise, the second part begins with a small letter.

Exercises   Punctuate divided quotations correctly.

A. Copy these sentences. Add punctuation and capital letters where they are needed.

1. Some people Josh noted don't laugh much.
2. I'm tired Suzanne said let's rest.
3. Will you write to me Jeff asked after you move?
4. During the summer Amy said we make ice cream.
5. What's cooking I asked it smells good.

6. We're late Mom said the show has started.
7. When does camp start Sonia asked I'm ready.
8. I have a layout Bill said for a model railroad.
9. I made sculptures Tom said out of soap.
10. We've looked at stars Lynn said we used a telescope.

B. Follow the directions for Exercise A.

1. My favorite ballplayer Kelly said is Pete Rose.
2. Drop the anchor Sandra called we'll fish here.
3. The space shuttle *Enterprise* Marilyn reported has been seen many times.
4. Chants and drumbeats the teacher noted were early music.
5. Thread the needle Dad said then make a knot.
6. Eric made a film I explained with clay figures.
7. Try this sauce my sister said it's very good.
8. Throw the boomerang Judith said it will return.
9. What's a tangram Joe asked is it a puzle?
10. What do fossils tell us Elena asked about history?

Using Quotation Marks for Titles

Use quotation marks to enclose chapter titles, titles of magazine articles, titles of short stories or single poems, titles of television programs, and titles of songs.

Chapter title:	Chapter 7, "The Civil War"
Magazine article:	"Finding Summer Jobs"
Short story:	"The Tell-Tale Heart"
Poem:	"How To Eat a Poem"
Television program:	"Little House on the Prairie"
Song:	"Happy Birthday"

Underlining

Underline the titles of books, newspapers, magazines and movies.

When you are writing or when you are typing, underline these titles, like this: <u>The Incredible Journey</u>.

When these titles are printed, they are printed in *italics*, rather than underlined.

Book title:	*The Incredible Journey*
Newspaper:	*Kansas City Star*
Magazine:	*Sports Illustrated*
Movie:	*Rocky*

Exercise Punctuate titles correctly.

Copy the following titles. Use quotation marks or underlining to make each title correct.

1. Babe, the Blue Ox   (short story)
2. The Moonspinners   (movie)
3. How To Train Your Dog   (magazine article)
4. Hot Rod   (magazine)
5. Karen   (book)
6. Seattle Times   (newspaper)
7. Women in America   (chapter title)
8. You Are My Sunshine   (song)
9. Family   (TV program)
10. Annabel Lee   (poem)
11. It's Like This, Cat   (book)
12. A Healthier You   (magazine article)
13. 60 Minutes   (TV program)
14. Sea Fever   (poem)
15. Baseball Talk   (book)

REVIEW Punctuation

The Period Write the following sentences, adding periods where they are needed.

1. E B White wrote several famous children's books
2. The bus will leave Washington, D C, at 4 P M
3. Write me at P O Box 640, Ada, Ohio, after June 1
4. Mrs K L Waverly visited the UN Building
5. The Battle of Hastings was fought in A D 1066

The Comma Write the following sentences, adding commas where they are needed.

6. On June 28 1919 the treaty was signed in Versailles.
7. No Sharla I've never been to Boston Massachusetts.
8. The interviewer asked "Mr. Cassidy what are your plans?"
9. Yes they sell oatmeal chocolate and sandwich cookies.
10. Dad made apple pancakes and they were terrific.

The Apostrophe Write each sentence, adding apostrophes where they are needed.

11. Jamess brother made a motorbike.
12. This theaters prices have increased again.
13. Arent the boys lockers just like ours?
14. Whos the womens diving champion?
15. Im surprised that youre here.

Quotation Marks Write each sentence, adding quotation marks where they are needed.

16. Jessica asked, How are pickles made?
17. The next holiday is Halloween, Maria said.
18. We had a picnic, Olivia said, beside a lake.
19. That tunnel goes through the mountains, Steven said.
20. Eve Merriam wrote the poem called Cheers.

Spelling

When you speak, you never have to think about how a word is spelled. When you write, however, correct spelling is absolutely necessary. Because you want your writing to make sense, you will want to be a good speller.

You can become a good speller by developing a few good habits and understanding a few basic rules. These habits and rules will help you to write clearly. In this section you will be learning the most important habits and rules of good spelling.

Plan Your Study of Spelling

There may always be a few words that will give you trouble. However, you will be able to master most words quickly if you work at developing the following habits.

Habits for Improving Your Spelling

1. Make a habit of looking at words carefully.

When you come to a new word, be sure you know its meaning. If you are not certain, look up the word in a dictionary.

Practice seeing every letter. Many people see a word again and again but don't really look at it. When you see a new word, or a tricky word, like *government*, look at all the letters. To help yourself remember them, write the word several times.

2. When you speak, pronounce words carefully.

Some words are spelled wrong just because they are not pronounced right. If you leave out the sound of certain letters, you will have a hard time spelling words correctly.

Here is a list of words that cause trouble because they are often pronounced wrong. The letters in dark print are the letters that are often left out in spelling because they are left out in pronouncing the words.

February	different	government
library	grocery	family
hundred	history	probably
several	funeral	everybody

3. Find out your own spelling enemies and attack them.

Look over your papers and make a list of the misspelled words. Also keep a list of new words that are difficult for you. Study these words until you can spell them correctly and easily.

4. Find memory devices to help with problem spellings.

Some words are difficult to remember. In these cases, a memory device may help you. A memory device is a trick, or a catchy sentence about the word, that you can remember easily. The device tells you how to spell the word. Here are two examples:

friend   *I* will be your friend to the *end*.
believe   There is a *lie* in be*lie*ve.

5. Proofread what you write.

To make sure that you have spelled all words correctly, reread your work. Examine it carefully, word for word. Don't let your eyes race over the page and miss misspellings.

6. Use a dictionary.

You don't have to know how to spell every word. No one spells everything correctly all the time. A good dictionary can help you to be a better speller. Use a dictionary whenever you need help with your spelling.

7. Study the few important spelling rules given in this section.

Steps for Mastering Specific Words

When you notice that you are having trouble with a certain word, take a few minutes to study it carefully. Give it all your attention. If you spend the time and energy to learn it correctly once, you will save yourself all the trouble of correcting it many times.

Follow these steps to master a specific word.

1. Look at the word and say it to yourself. Pronounce it carefully. If it has two or more syllables, say it again, one syllable at a time. Look at each syllable as you say it.

2. Look at the letters and say each one. If the word has two or more syllables, pause between syllables as you say the letters.

3. Without looking at the word, write it.

4. Now look at your book or list to see if you have spelled the word correctly. If you have, write it once more. Compare it with the correct spelling again. For best results, repeat the process once more.

5. If you have misspelled the word, notice where the error was. Then repeat steps 3 and 4 until you have spelled the word correctly three times in a row.

Exercises **Develop good habits.**

A. Here are some words that are often pronounced carelessly and then misspelled. Look at each letter of every word. Pronounce the words correctly to yourself. Write the words in alphabetical order.

1. regular	6. different
2. Saturday	7. diamond
3. general	8. poem
4. ruin	9. violet
5. police	10. finally

B. Write five of the words listed in Exercise A in good sentences. Check your spelling when you write the words.

C. Read through some of your recent papers to find words you have misspelled. Make a list of five to ten of your personal spelling enemies. Then study them, following the **Steps for Mastering Specific Words.**

Rules for Spelling

Many words in our language follow certain patterns. Studying the following rules should help you with these words.

Spelling Words with *ie* and *ei*

Many students and adults too, find it hard to tell whether *i* comes before or after *e* in spelling certain words. Your mother and father probably learned this old rhyme about the problem.

I before *e*
Except after *c,*
Or when sounded as *a*
As in n*ei*ghbor or w*ei*gh.

This rhyme does help. Look at the words below. Decide which lines of the rhyme work for each of these words.

believe	receive	weigh
niece	conceit	weight
relief	ceiling	eight

The rule will help you with most words. But you will have to study and remember these four words. They do not follow the rule. They are **exceptions** to the rule.

either   neither   seize   weird

Exercise   **Write words with *ie* and *ei*.**

Write sentences using at least ten words with *ie* or *ei*. (You may use more than one such word in each sentence.) Underline each of the *ie* or *ei* words you use.

Example: My *niece received eight* presents.

Adding Prefixes

A **prefix** is a syllable or group of syllables that is added to the beginning of a word to change its meaning. Here are some common prefixes and examples of their use:

Prefix	Base Word	New Word
re (again)	+ write	= rewrite (write again)
dis (not)	+ approve	= disapprove (not approve)
un (not)	+ able	= unable (not able)
in (not)	+ formal	= informal (not formal)
im (not)	+ possible	= impossible (not possible)
counter (against)	+ act	= counteract (act against)
pre (before)	+ view	= preview (see before)
mis (incorrectly)	+ spell	= misspell (spell incorrectly)

When a prefix is added to a word, the spelling of the word stays the same.

Adding the Suffixes -ly and -ness

A **suffix** is a letter or syllable added to the ending of a word to change its meaning. For example, the suffix -s is added to a singular noun to make it plural. The suffix -ed is added to a verb to change the action to the past. Adding a suffix sometimes adds a spelling problem to a word.

The suffix -ly added to an adjective changes it to an adverb.

Adjective	Adverb
The *total* price is ten dollars.	The car was *totally* ruined.
This puzzle is a *real* challenge.	This puzzle is *really* difficult.
My mother is a *careful* driver.	My mother drives *carefully*.

When the suffix -ly is added to a word ending with l, both l's are kept.

The suffix *-ness* added to an adjective changes it to a noun.

Adjective	Noun
Kirk is *open* and honest.	I admire Kirk's *openness*.
Meat with little fat is called *lean*.	Look for *leanness* when you buy bacon.

When the suffix *-ness* is added to a word ending with *n*, both *n*'s are kept.

Exercise **Add prefixes and suffixes.**

Find the misspelled word in each of these sentences and spell it correctly.

1. I liked the eveness of Tammy's haircut.
2. Spencer thoughtfuly brought a gift.
3. A dog is unnable to climb a tree.
4. Winding this watch is unecessary.
5. The thiness of this pencil makes it hard to hold.
6. Some people misstrust cats.
7. We admired the salesperson's openess.
8. Those hints were awfuly misleading.
9. Holmes uncovered a totaly new clue.
10. We usualy see movie previews.

Adding Suffixes to Words Ending in Silent *e*

Notice what happens when you add suffixes beginning with vowels to words that end in silent *e*.

hope + ing = hoping	fame + ous = famous
refuse + al = refusal	pale + er = paler
expense + ive = expensive	like + able = likable

When a suffix beginning with a vowel is added to a word ending in silent *e*, the *e* is usually dropped.

Now see what happens when you add suffixes beginning with consonants to words that end in silent *e*.

care + ful = careful   move + ment = movement
lone + ly = lonely   nine + ty = ninety
score + less = scoreless   bore + dom = boredom

When a suffix beginning with a consonant is added to a word ending in silent e, the e is usually kept.

The following words are **exceptions** to these two rules:

truly   argument   ninth   judgment   wholly

Exercise   **Add suffixes correctly.**

Add the suffix given for each word. Write each new word correctly.

1. place + ing   5. hope + ful   9. like + ly
2. use + able   6. come + ing   10. save + ing
3. sure + ly   7. make + er   11. desire + able
4. confuse + ion   8. safe + ty   12. remove + al

Adding Suffixes to Words Ending in y

See what happens when you add suffixes to words that end in *y* following a consonant.

baby + es = babies   lazy + ness = laziness
empty + er = emptier   carry + ed = carried
happy + ly = happily   story + es = stories

When a suffix is added to a word that ends with y following a consonant, the y is usually changed to i.

However, the y is not changed when the suffix -*ing* is added.

empty + ing = emptying   carry + ing = carrying
fly + ing = flying   apply + ing = applying

Notice, too, what happens when you add suffixes to words that end in *y* following a vowel.

> boy + s = boys   play + ed = played
> buy + er = buyer   stay + ing = staying

When a suffix is added to a word that ends with *y* following a vowel, the *y* usually is not changed.

The following words are **exceptions:** *paid, said.*

Exercise   **Add suffixes correctly.**

Add the suffix given for each word. Write each new word correctly.

1. hurry + ing	6. play + er	11. carry + ed
2. story + es	7. fly + ing	12. happy + ness
3. heavy + est	8. sky + es	13. early + est
4. fly + er	9. ready + ness	14. toy + s
5. enjoy + ed	10. easy + ly	15. cry + ing

Doubling the Final Consonant

What happens to these words when you add suffixes?

> spin + ing = spinning   fat + er = fatter
> hot + est = hottest   scrub + ed = scrubbed

You can see that the last letter is doubled when suffixes beginning with a vowel are added to these words.

In words of one syllable, ending with a consonant following one vowel, you double the final consonant before adding *-ing*, *-ed, -en, -er,* or *-est.*

The final consonant is **not** doubled when it follows two vowels.

> trail + er = trailer   shout + ed = shouted
> steam + ing = steaming   float + er = floater
> peel + ed = peeled   shoot + ing = shooting

Exercise   Double the final consonant.

Decide whether or not the final consonant should be doubled. Add the suffix as shown. Write the new word correctly.

1. fat + est
2. stop + ed
3. sad + er
4. hear + ing
5. pat + ed
6. bit + en
7. soon + est
8. get + ing
9. plan + ed
10. big + est
11. put + ing
12. hot + er
13. leak + ed
14. rot + en
15. hop + ed

Review Exercises   Use the spelling rules.

A. Find the misspelled words in these sentences and spell them correctly. (In some of the sentences, more than one word is misspelled.)

1. The surface of this desk is very iregular.
2. The wagons moved into the openess of the plains.
3. Beth recieved a carefuly wrapped gift.
4. Mom ordered a birthday cake specialy made.
5. I copied the poem on a clean peice of paper.
6. I beleive I hear a mysteryous sound.
7. The theif opened the safe easly.
8. Shopers spoted the bargains.
9. We're geting excited about the upcomeing play.
10. Hikeing and bikeing are two camp activities.

B. Add the suffix given for each word below and write the new word.

1. bite + ing
2. stay + ed
3. play + ing
4. try + ed
5. heat + er
6. shop + ed
7. make + ing
8. enjoy + s
9. waste + ing
10. fry + ed
11. hope + ing
12. tiny + est
13. sit + ing
14. big + er
15. hope + ful
16. fat + en
17. stumble + ing
18. live + able
19. worry + ing
20. run + ing

Homonyms and Other Words Often Confused

In writing, we are sometimes confused by two or three words that look almost the same. It is not always easy to know which word we should use.

Much of our confusion is caused by homonyms. Homonyms sound the same, or nearly the same, but are spelled differently and have different meanings. Here are some examples of homonyms:

by	The parade passed *by* my house.
buy	I want to *buy* that game.
meat	Pork, beef, and lamb are kinds of *meat*.
meet	Cara wants to *meet* her new neighbors.
threw	Bob *threw* the ball to the shortstop.
through	The laser burned a hole *through* the wood panel.

Homonyms are words that sound the same, or nearly the same. They are usually spelled differently, and have different meanings. Before you can use homonyms correctly, you must know what each one means. You cannot depend on spelling rules to help you. The best approach is to memorize which spelling goes with which meaning.

Following is a list of homonyms and other words that are frequently confused. Study the sets of words. Try to connect each word with its correct meaning. Refer to the list if you have further problems with these words.

accept means to agree to something or to receive something willingly.

> Ms. Daly will not *accept* excuses.

except means to leave out, or leaving out.

> Everyone *except* Carl won a prize.

all ready means completely prepared.

> The party decorations are *all ready*.

already means previously or before.

> The hikers have *already* returned.

capital means chief or important. It also means the city or town that is the official seat of government of a state or nation.

Begin every sentence with a *capital* letter.

Lincoln is the *capital* of Nebraska.

capitol is the building where a state legislature meets.

The *capitol* in Lincoln is a new building.

the Capitol is the building in Washington, D. C. in which the United States Congress meets.

The nation's lawmakers meet at the *Capitol*.

hear means to listen to.

I *hear* a drumbeat.

here means in this place.

Drop your fishing line *here*.

its shows ownership or possession.

We studied Mexico and *its* people.

it's is the contraction for *it is* or *it has*.

We visited Calico. *It's* a ghost town.

knew means understood or was familiar with.

Sherry *knew* many card tricks.

new is the opposite of old and means fresh or recent.

The horse has a *new* saddle.

know means to understand or to be familiar with.

The pilots *know* their flight patterns.

no is a negative word meaning *not* or *not any*.

This snowman has *no* hat.

lead (lĕd) is a heavy, gray metal.

The pipes were made of *lead*.

lead (lēd) means to go first, to guide.

The general will *lead* his army.

led (lĕd) is the past form of lead (lēd).

Pioneers *led* the way west.

438

loose means free or not tight.

My brother pulled his *loose* tooth.

lose means to mislay or suffer the loss of something.

If you leave, you will *lose* your place in line.

peace is calm or stillness or the absence of disagreement.

The rival tribes enjoyed a time of *peace*.

piece means a portion or part.

Liz molded the *piece* of clay.

plain means clear or simple. It also means an expanse of land.

Trish put a decal on the *plain* T-shirt.
Horses roamed across the *plain*.

plane refers to a flat surface or woodworking tool. It also is the short form of *airplane*.

A *plane* is useful in carpentry.
The small *plane* landed in a field.

principal means first or most important. It also refers to the head of a school.

The *principal* purpose of TV is to entertain.
Our school *principal* talked to parents.

principle is a rule, truth, or belief.

Superman's *principle* is justice for all.

quiet means free from noise or disturbance.

The rabbit is a *quiet* pet.

quite means truly or almost completely.

Those acrobats are *quite* daring.

right means proper or correct. It also means the opposite of left. It also refers to a fair claim.

Maria found the *right* key for the safe.
Hebrew is read from *right* to left.
The colonists felt freedom was their *right*.

write refers to forming words with a pen or pencil.

We must *write* a thank-you note.

their means belonging to them.

> The children took *their* rafts to the beach.

there means at that place.

> Plant the tomato seeds *there*.

they're is the contraction for *they are*.

> *They're* taking the train to Cleveland.

to means in the direction of.

> Snowflakes drifted *to* the ground.

too means also or very.

> My sister wants to come, *too*.

two is the whole number between one and three.

> The moose had *two* huge antlers.

weather is the state of the atmosphere, referring to wind, moisture, temperature, and other such conditions.

> Tornadoes usually occur during warm *weather*.

whether indicates a choice or alternative.

> Jon asked *whether* rubber sinks or floats.

who's is the contraction for *who is* or *who has*.

> *Who's* throwing those snowballs?

whose is the possessive form of *who*.

> *Whose* house is closest to school?

your is the possessive form of you.

> Did *your* wish come true?

you're is the contraction for *you are*.

> *You're* looking at a haunted house.

Exercises **Use homonyms and other confusing words correctly.**

A. Write the correct word from the two given in parentheses.

1. A dog can (hear, here) high-pitched sounds.
2. There are (know, no) lifeboats on this ship.
3. Did you (loose, lose) your library card?

4. (Their, There, They're) making stained glass.
5. Who knows the (right, write) answer?
6. This church is cool and (quiet, quite).
7. (Who's, Whose) banging those cymbals?
8. Penny has (all ready, already) finished her model glider.
9. No one (accept, except) Ramón had seen the bear.
10. Gravity is a (principal, principle) of science.

B. Follow the directions for Exercise A.

1. The bike trail begins (hear, here).
2. A giraffe nodded (its, it's) head.
3. The collectors (knew, new) about foreign stamps.
4. An elephant (lead, led) the circus parade.
5. Our cabin has (to, too, two) portholes.
6. The runners are (all ready, already) for the race.
7. I borrowed (your, your're) radio.
8. The artist started with a (plain, plane) white canvas.
9. Which city is the (capital, capitol, Capitol) of Texas?
10. Joe tied the rowboat with a (peace, piece) of rope.

C. Choose the correct homonym from the two or three in parentheses. (If you are not sure, look up each homonym in the dictionary.) Write the correct word.

1. What is the (some, sum) of five plus seven?
2. The dog followed the (heard, herd) of cattle.
3. May I borrow a (pair, pare, pear) of scissors?
4. The carnation is the state (flour, flower) of Ohio.
5. How do you control the (brakes, breaks) on the bike?
6. Rhea hates to (waist, waste) time waiting for people.
7. For this macramé project, I learned to tie a special (knot, not).
8. When Kenny fell, he complained of the (pain, pane).
9. The snowmobiles (road, rode) over the frozen marsh.
10. Gum is stuck to the (heal, heel) of my left shoe.

REVIEW Spelling

Spelling Look at each sentence carefully. Find the misspelled words. Write each word correctly.

1. Pat recieved many Valentines.
2. My neice is actualy older than I am.
3. It is immpossible to reeset this watch.
4. We noticed the eveness of Freda's writing.
5. This new ink is realy eraseable.
6. A furyous bull charged into the field.
7. Whistleing happyly, Carlos finished his project.
8. Jason hurryed to the nearrest phone.
9. Kelly's bating average is amazeing.
10. Jenny riped the letter and tosed it in the garbage.

Homonyms and Words Often Confused Write the correct word from the two words in parentheses.

11. Jody Turner (accepted, excepted) the nomination.
12. I (hear, here) a drumbeat.
13. The plant lost (its, it's) leaves.
14. This parade has (know, no) end!
15. How did you (loose, lose) your voice?
16. Please have a (peace, piece) of cake.
17. The horses tossed (their, they're) heads.
18. Lyle wondered (weather, whether) the team won or lost.
19. (Who's Whose) speech is next?
20. (Your, You're) garden is overgrown.

Guides for Good Handwriting

You write every day. You will always do some handwriting. You will write letters to friends. You will writes notes to yourself. You will fill out forms and sign receipts and documents. Your handwriting will be important all your life.

Your handwriting is also important for what it says to others about you. Some people may make judgments or decisions about you based on how you write, as well as on what you write. Sometimes people who affect your life may not meet you or talk with you. They may see only a form, an application, or a letter you write. So it will always be important that your handwriting speak clearly and neatly for you.

The Correct Forms for Writing

You know that there are two common ways of writing. One is called **manuscript writing.** It is very much like printing. Manuscript writing is useful in making labels and signs. Here are the alphabet and numbers in manuscript writing.

ABCDEFGHIJKLM
NOPQRSTUVWXYZ
abcdefghijklmnopqr
stuvwxyz 12345678910

The other style of writing is called **cursive writing.** This is the style that most people use.

Here are the alphabet and numbers in cursive writing.

ABCDEFGHIJKLM
NOPQRSTUVWXYZ
a b c d e f g h i j k l m
n o p q r s t u v w x y z
1 2 3 4 5 6 7 8 9 10

Guidelines for Good Handwriting

There are many different features to watch in order to have good handwriting. If you are careful about each of these features, your handwriting will be clear and attractive.

1. Slant your letters correctly. In cursive writing, slant all letters the same way. Which of these samples is easier to read?

Flying squirrels do not really fly.

Flying squirrels do not really fly.

2. Space your words and letters evenly. Crowded letters and words make writing difficult to read. Compare these two samples.

"If you mow the lawn," said Kate, "I'll paint the fence."

"If you mow the lawn," said Kate, "I'll paint the fence."

3. Form letters and numbers correctly. If letters and numbers are not formed correctly, they may be read incorrectly.

The first human walked on the moon on July 21, 1969.

The first human walked on the moon on July 21, 1969.

445

4. Join your letters carefully. The letters *u, v, w,* and *o* require particular care when joined to other words. The following samples show why.

Good	Poor		Good	Poor
young	*young*		*woman*	*waman*
level	*level*		*favor*	*fovar*
loan	*laan*		*hoed*	*haed*
awake	*avake*		*lawyer*	*lavyer*

5. Keep your letters even in height. This is easier to do if you keep your letters on the line. Make capital letters and tall letters about the same height. The samples below show you how much difference it makes. Be particularly careful with *e* and *l*.

About 70 million years ago, dinosaurs became extinct.

About 70 million years ago, dinosaurs became extinct.

ZIP Codes and State Abbreviations

In order to make sure that your letter reaches its destination, check the address, street, and ZIP code. The ZIP code is very important today. It enables the postal department to sort your letter for delivery as rapidly as possible. (If you don't know the ZIP code, call your local post office. Someone will give you the correct ZIP for any address in the United States and the territories.)

The United States Postal Service has published a list of approved abbreviations for states to be used on the envelopes. If you use these abbreviations, you *must* use the ZIP code with them.

ABBREVIATIONS OF STATE NAMES

Alabama	AL	Montana	MT
Alaska	AK	Nebraska	NE
Arizona	AZ	Nevada	NV
Arkansas	AR	New Hampshire	NH
American Samoa	AS	New Jersey	NJ
California	CA	New Mexico	NM
Canal Zone	CZ	New York	NY
Colorado	CO	North Carolina	NC
Connecticut	CT	North Dakota	ND
Delaware	DE	Ohio	OH
District of Columbia	DC	Oklahoma	OK
Florida	FL	Oregon	OR
Georgia	GA	Pennsylvania	PA
Guam	GU	Puerto Rico	PR
Hawaii	HI	Rhode Island	RI
Idaho	ID	South Carolina	SC
Illinois	IL	South Dakota	SD
Indiana	IN	Tennessee	TN
Iowa	IA	Trust Territories	TT
Kansas	KS	Texas	TX
Kentucky	KY	Utah	UT
Louisiana	LA	Vermont	VT
Maine	ME	Virginia	VA
Maryland	MD	Virgin Islands	VI
Massachusetts	MA	Washington	WA
Michigan	MI	West Virginia	WV
Minnesota	MN	Wisconsin	WI
Mississippi	MS	Wyoming	WY
Missouri	MO		

D

Declarative sentences
 defined, 201
 period with, 201-204, 219, 406,
  426
 subject in, 204-213
Definition, as context clue to
 meaning of word, 6-7
Definitions in dictionary, 168-172
Descriptive compositions, 104-
 105, 128-135
Descriptive paragraphs, 36-37,
 54-57, 76-83
Details
 in compositions, 102, 104, 110-
  111, 122-123, 128-133, 139,
  141
 in paragraphs, 34-35, 44-45,
  54-57, 63, 72-73, 76-77
Dewey Decimal System, 174-176
Diagraming the sentence and its
 parts, 372-388
Dictionary, 162-172
 abridged, 162
 alphabetical order in, 162-164
 definitions, 168, 170-172
 entries, information in, 167-172
  antonyms, 168
  colloquial meaning, 168
  definitions, 168, 170-172
  origin, or history, 167
  part of speech, 167
  pronunciation, 167
  special forms or endings, 167
  syllables, 167-169
  synonyms (*synonomy*), 168
 guide words, 165-166
 meaning, choosing right one,
  170-172
 unabridged, 162
Direct object of the verb
 compound, 345-346

defined, 246
diagraming, 379-380, 388
nouns as, 246-247, 250-251
predicate words or, distinguish-
 ing, 250-251
pronouns as, 299-301, 305
Double negatives, 290

E

either-or, neither-nor, or with
 compound subjects, 361-362,
 364
Empty sentences, 22-23
Encyclopedia, 180-182
 articles, 180, 182
 guide words, 180, 182
Ending in compositions. *See* Conclusion in compositions.
Ending sentence in "why" paragraph, 96-97
English language words. *See*
 Words.
Envelope, address, 149-150
Example(s)
 as context clue to meaning of
  word, 8-9
 used to develop paragraph,
  34-35, 44-45
Exclamation mark, or point, 412
 with exclamatory sentences,
  201-204, 219, 412
 with interjections, 349
 with quotation marks, 421-422
Exclamatory sentences
 defined, 201
 exclamation point with, 201-
  204, 219, 412
Explanatory compositions, 104-
 105, 138-143
 "how," 104-105, 138-143
 "why," 104-105
Explanatory paragraphs, 36-37,

86-89, 92-97, 104
"how," 36-37, 86-89
"why," 36-37, 92-97

F

Facts and figures, used to develop paragraphs, 34-35, 44-45, 54-55
Fiction books, 174-176
First-person point of view
   in compositions, 120-121
   in paragraphs, 50-51, 54-55, 72-73
Fly-on-the-wall viewpoint in paragraphs, 52-53
Fragments, sentence, 198-200, 220-222, 225
Friendly letters. *See* Letters.
Future tense of verbs, 251-253, 257, 259

G

good, bad, 320-322
good, bad, well, badly, 330-331
Guide words
   in dictionary, 165-166
   in encyclopedia, 180, 182

H

Handwriting, 443-446
   correct forms for, 444
   cursive, 444
   guidelines for, 445-446
   manuscript, 444
has, have, 357-358
Heading in letters, 146, 154-159
Helping verbs, 241-245, 257, 261
Homonyms, 437-442
"How" compositions, 104-105, 138-143
"How" paragraphs, 36-37, 86-89
Hyphen, at end of line, 419-420

I

and agreement with verb, 362-364
capitalization of, 390
with first-person point of view, 50-51, 72-73, 120-121
Idea book for writing, 108-109
ie, ei, 431
Imaginary narrative compositions (stories), 116-125
Imaginary subjects for paragraphs, 56-57
Imperative sentences
   defined, 201
   diagraming, 376, 388
   period with, 201-204, 219, 406, 426
   you as understood subject in, 213-214, 376
Importance of reasons, order of, in "why" paragraphs, 94-97
Indenting first line of paragraphs
   in letters, 146, 154
Initials
   capitalization of, 391-392, 404
   defined, 391, 406
   periods with, 391, 404, 406, 409-410, 426
Inside address of business letters, 154-156
Interjections, 348-350
Interrogative sentences
   defined, 201
   diagraming, 375, 388
   question mark with, 201-204, 219, 410-411, 421-422
Introduction in compositions, 102-103, 118-121, 128, 130-131, 140-141
Invitations. *See* Letters.
Irregular verbs, 260-288
is, was, are, were

453

Senses, as base for details in writing, 56-57, 76-77, 132-133
Sentence fragments, 198-200, 220-222, 225
Sentence patterns
 N LV Adj, 256
 N LV N, 255
 N V, 234
 N V N, 254
 Word order, 218
Sentences
 capitalization in, 397-398, 404
 complete, 20-21, 198-200
 complete predicate in, 204-207
 complete subject in, 204-207
 compound, 367-371
 compound predicate in, 216-217, 345-346, 366
 compound subject in, 214-216, 345-346, 361-362, 364, 366
 declarative, 201-204, 219, 406
 diagraming, 372-388
 empty, 22-23
 ending, in paragraphs, 46-47, 94-97
 end punctuation in, 201-204, 219, 406, 409-412, 426
 exclamatory, 201-204, 219, 412
 fragments of, 198-200, 220-222, 225
 imperative, 201-204, 213-214, 219, 376, 388, 406, 426
 interrogative, 201-204, 219, 410-411
 kinds of, 201-204, 219
 padded, 24-25
 in paragraphs, 28-37
 parts of, 204-206, 365
 run-on, 220, 223-225
 simple, 366-367, 371
 simple predicate (the verb) in, 207-211, 219

simple subject in, 209-214, 219
 topic, 32-35, 42-45, 68-69, 96-97, 102, 128-131, 134, 140-141
 writing, 20-25
Setting in stories, 116-117
set, sit, 287-288, 292
Signature in letters, 146, 153-157
Simple predicate (the verb), 207-211, 219
Simple sentences, defined, 366
Simple subject (subject of the verb), 209-214, 219
Singular forms
 of nouns, 299-230, 355-356
 of pronouns, 294, 358-359
 of verbs, 355-356
Social notes. *See* Letters.
Spatial order
 in descriptive compositions, 128-129, 132-133
 in descriptive paragraphs, 80-83
Specific verbs, 58-59
Spelling, 427-442
 habits for improving, 428-429
  memory devices, 429
 homonyms, 437-442
 rules for, 431-436
  adding prefixes, 14-15, 432-433
  adding suffixes, 12-13, 16-17, 432-436
  words with *ie* or *ei*, 431
 steps for mastering, 429-430
 words often confused, 437-442
State-of-being verbs (Linking verbs), 58, 238-239, 248-251, 257, 298-299, 305, 313-314, 380-382
Step-by-step order
 in "how" compositions, 138-143

in "how" paragraphs, 86-89
Stories, writing, 116-125
Subject card in card catalog, 177-179
Subject pronouns, 296-297, 305, 358-359
Subject of the sentence
    agreement with verb, 280-283, 292, 354-364
    complete, 204-207
    compound, 214-216, 345-346, 361-362, 364, 366
    defined, 204-205, 365
    diagraming, 373-378, 388
    in imperative sentences, 213-214, 376
    nouns as, 209-212, 345-346
    pronouns as, 213-214, 296-297, 305, 358-359
    simple, 209-214, 219
Suffixes, 16-17, 432-436
Syllables
    as shown in dictionary entries, 167-169
    dividing words into, 419-420
Synonyms, 10-11, 168-169
Synonymy in dictionary, 168

T

Tenses of verbs, 251-253, 257-263
Thank-you notes. *See* Letters.
them, those, 316-317, 322
there, here, where, introducing
    sentences, 282-283, 292, 360
Third-person point of view
    in compositions, 120-121
    in paragraphs, 52-55
this kind, that kind, 317-318
Time sequence
    in compositions, 112-113, 116, 122-123, 138-143
    in paragraphs, 68-71

Title card in card catalog, 177-179
Titles
    capitalization of, 392-393, 402-404
    of compositions, 124-125, 138-139
    of persons, 392-393, 396
    of written works, 402-404
        quotation marks with, 402, 424-425
        underlining for italics, 402, 425
Topic sentences
    in compositions, 102, 128-130, 134, 140-141
    in paragraphs, 32-35, 42-45, 68-69, 96-97
    writing lively, 42-43
Topic, narrowing the
    for compositions, 100-101, 108-109, 128-129
    for paragraphs, 40-41, 62
Transitions
    showing chronological order, 70-71, 112-113
    showing order of importance of reasons, 96-97
    showing spatial order, 82-83, 128-129
    showing step-by-step order, 88-89, 142-143

U

Underlining certain titles for italics, 402, 425
Understood subject (you), 213-214, 376
Unity in paragraphs, 30-31

V

Verb, the (simple predicate), 207-

211, 219

Verbs, 207-211, 219, 236-253, 257-292, 354-364

    action, 58-59, 236-239, 250-251, 257

    agreement with subjects, 280-283, 292, 354-364

    compound, 345-346, 366

    confusing pairs of, 283-288, 292

    in contractions, 288-289, 292

    defined, 207

    diagraming, 373, 388

    direct objects of, 246-247, 250-251, 299-301, 305, 345-346

    future tense, 251-253, 257, 259

    helping, 241-245, 257, 261

    irregular, 260-288

    linking, 248-251, 257, 298-299, 305

    main, 241-242, 244-245, 257

    in negative contractions, 289-292

    number, defined, 355

    object of, 246-247, 250-251, 299-301, 305, 345-346

    past participles, 259-264

    past tense, 251-253, 257, 259-263

    plural forms, 355-364

    present tense, 251-253, 257, 259-263

    principal parts of, 258-263

    regular, 259-260

    in sentence patterns, 234, 254-256

    separated parts of, 244-245, 257

    simple predicate (the verb), 207-211, 219

    singular forms of, 355-364

    specific, in writing, 58-59

    state-of-being, 248-251, 257, 298-299, 305

    subjects of, 209-214, 219

    tenses of, 251-253, 257-263

Vocabulary, developing, 2-17

W

we, us, 301-302, 305

well, badly, 330, 331

"Why" compositions, 104-105

"Why" paragraphs, 36-37, 92-97

Word endings, shown in dictionary entries, 167

Word parts, 12-17, 432-436

    base words, 12-13

    prefixes, 14-15, 432-433

    suffixes, 16-17, 432-436

Words, English language

    antonyms, 10-11, 168

    borrowed, 2-3

    compound, 2-3

    context clues to meanings of, 4-9

    from names, 2-3

    parts of, 12-17, 432-436

    synonyms, 10-11, 168-169

Writing

    compositions, 100-143

    letters, 146-159

    paragraphs, 28-97

    process of, 62-65

    sentences, 20-25

Y

you

    as understood subject, 213-214, 376

    and agreement with verb, 363-364

you're, your, 418, 440

Z

ZIP code, 149-150, 408, 447

Acknowledgments

William Collins + World Publishing Company: For entries appearing on pages 163, 165, 168, 170, 171, 230, and 263 from *Webster's New World Dictionary of the American Language,* Students Edition; copyright © 1976 by William Collins + World Publishing Company, Inc. For "Catalog" by Rosalie Moore; copyright © 1940, 1968, The New Yorker Magazine, Inc., reprinted by permission.

Photographs

James L. Ballard: 48

Woodfin Camp: Michal Heron, ii; Sepp Seitz, xiv; Ellen Pines, 90; Timothy Eagan, 126; Jim Anderson, 160, 182.

Magnum: Bob Adelman, 18; Arthur Tress, 26; Mark Godfrey, 38; Charles Gatewood, 60, 84, 172; Charles Harbutt, 66; Bob Honrigues, 74; René Burri, 98; Wayne Miller, 106; Paul Fusco, 114; Leonard Freed, 136; Dennis Stock, 144.

Illustrations

Publishers Newspaper Syndicate: For "B.C." cartoon on page 71; copyright © 1971, 1972 by Publishers Newspaper Syndicate; copyright © 1977 by Fawcett Publications, Inc. Jeanne Seabright: all handwritten letters. Ken Izzi: special mechanical art. Synthegraphics Corporation: diagrams. Montagu Design: special mechanical art. Marcia Vecchione: art production.